Paul O'Grady first came to fame in the guise of Lily Savage, and was nominated for a Perrier Award at the Edinburgh Festival in 1991. Lily took over the bed on *The Big Breakfast* and presented *Blankety Blank*, as well as having her own shows *The Lily Savage Show* and *Lily Live*, but has now retired (reportedly). Paul, of course, went on to further success presenting his chat shows on Channel 4 and ITV, *For the Love of Dogs* and *Animal Orphans* on ITV, *Blind Date* on Channel 5 and his weekly show on BBC Radio 2, inter alia. His four volumes of autobiography – *At My Mother's Knee, The Devil Rides Out, Still Standing* and *Open the Cage, Murphy* – were all *Sunday Times* bestsellers.

Also by Paul O'Grady

AT MY MOTHER'S KNEE ...
AND OTHER LOW JOINTS

THE DEVIL RIDES OUT

STILL STANDING

OPEN THE CAGE, MURPHY

PAUL O'GRADY'S COUNTRY LIFE

One man and his dogs – and other waifs and strays …

CORGI BOOKS

TRANSWORLD PUBLISHERS
61–63 Uxbridge Road, London W5 5SA
www.penguin.co.uk

Transworld is part of the Penguin Random House group of companies
whose addresses can be found at global.penguinrandomhouse.com

Penguin
Random House
UK

First published in Great Britain in 2017 by Bantam Press
an imprint of Transworld Publishers
Corgi edition published 2018

A CIP catalogue record for this book
is available from the British Library.

ISBN 9780552169653

Typeset in 10.5/14 pt Georgia Pro
by Integra Software Services Pvt. Ltd, Pondicherry

Printed and bound in Great Britain by Clays Ltd, Elcograf S.p.A.

Penguin Random House is committed to a sustainable
future for our business, our readers and our planet. This book
is made from Forest Stewardship Council® certified paper.

MIX
Paper from
responsible sources
FSC® C018179

1 3 5 7 9 10 8 6 4 2

*For all you townies who are considering
a move to a more rural idyll.
This book will either put you off or have you
rushing to an estate agent's.*

Introduction 1

Am I a Farmer? 55

Goats and Other Animals 59

Concerning Almost All Things
Feathered 75

Rural Idyll 97

Sheds and Apples 109

For the Love of Dogs 117

Pigs 149

Spring 155

The Geesestapo 171

May 179

Growing Your Own 191

Superstitions and Country Lore 217

High Tea 233

Halloween 255

Cows 265

Sheep 285

Cakes and Chaos 299

Conclusion 335

INTRODUCTION

Thanks to Enid Blyton, who nearly always accommodated her pixie and elf population in the colourful but highly toxic fly agaric, I fancied living in one of these red and white polka-dot toadstools when I was very little – a decent-sized one that could accommodate a five-year-old comfortably with all mod cons and enough bedrooms to put up the family when they came to stay.

When I grew out of Mrs Blyton's Enchanted Wood series I graduated towards a lifestyle akin to Pippi Longstocking's, who lived in a big old house with an assorted menagerie of animals, a trunk full of gold and no adult supervision, which apart from the gold (that's buried in the woods along with the Erica Von Savage Diamonds) is more or less how I'm living now.

Later on in life, after I'd read Tolkien's *The Hobbit*, I envied Bilbo Baggins and his smart hobbit hole with its round front door built into the side of a hill, although this fantasy clashed somewhat with my other dream of a stylish London apartment, all Eamesian chic à la Emma Peel of *The Avengers* or the colourful insanity of her successor Tara King, whose split-level flat boasted such inspired oddities as a Penny Farthing over the mantelpiece, an assortment of antique shop signs and a fireman's pole for making a quick descent from the upper floor when being pursued by the evil henchmen of a diabolical mastermind.

However, lurking in the background amongst all these whimsical dreams was a genuine desire to live somewhere in the countryside in a crumbling old farmhouse with lots of land, a pack of dogs and a cow or two. Sometimes the lure of the countryside grew too much and I'd play truant from school to walk around the country lanes of Heswall, a posh part of the Wirral, imagining what it would be like to live in some of the houses and to have so much open space all around you instead of a tiny backyard and a minuscule garden. I never believed for one minute that my desires would ever come to fruition so I put these fantastic notions to one side and contented myself with planning out my imaginary farm as I went off to sleep each night.

My love of the countryside stemmed from annual visits to my father's family in Ireland (when we weren't in the Isle of Man) who lived, and still do, on a farm in rural Glinsk, County Roscommon.

I can still remember my first encounter with a newly born calf. I was five years old and up till then the only animals I'd encountered were Joey our budgie, Aunty Annie's cat Jinksy, and our neighbour Mrs Long's dog, so the calf came as a bit of a shock.

'Give him a stroke,' my Uncle James said. 'He won't bite.'

He was having a laugh wasn't he? Stroke it? I was hanging off my mother's pencil skirt trying to crawl up her leg, desperate to put some distance between this behemoth and me.

'Don't be so nesh [delicate],' my ma laughed, pushing me towards the calf. 'He's lovely, give his little head a rub.'

And so I did, tentatively at first until I gained the confidence to run my fingers through his thick curly hair. The calf nuzzled my hand and then gave it a lick and at that moment, my fears now forgotten, the goddess Artemis, protector of young animals, cast a spell over me and a lifelong love of animals was born.

A corny if not slightly nauseating recollection but sadly one that's true, and if I close my eyes and have a think I can recall that moment clearly. I can also remember standing in a cowpat and covering my brand-new Ladybird sandals and white socks in sodden, stinking bovine effluence. My mother kicked off over that one and I imagine that in all probability I did the same.

Life on my Uncle James' and Aunty Bridget's farm was exciting for a young townie: there were haystacks to jump out of, eggs to collect, cows to milk and a decrepit but feisty donkey to ride. Kids could go into pubs, life was far more relaxed, and nobody minded if you ran around the farm barefoot or came home from the bog road after a day 'helping' to cut the turf filthier than a chimney sweep's apprentice. Yes, if I wasn't going to have Tara King's apartment then I was opting for a life in the country, the freedom of being outdoors, the excitement of having acres of land to explore and, above all, lots of animals from chickens to cows hanging around outside the house.

*

However, after saying goodbye to my home town of Birkenhead and emigrating to London I found myself living in a succession of dumps, each one worse than its predecessor and as far removed from hobbit holes or the elegant dwellings of secret agents as I could possibly get. My dreams of livestock and growing my own fruit and veg got as far as two moggies and a window box containing some ropey looking parsley in a tiny council flat on the South Lambeth Road that hadn't been renovated since the fifties.

I was in that flat for a number of years and as life went on I resigned myself to the fact that my bucolic vision would never come to fruition in a million years as slapping around the pubs and clubs doing 'The Act' I'd never earn enough to be able to afford it.

I love London, always have, from the moment I turned left out of Victoria coach station and found myself on the streets of Belgravia. I thought all of London was like the elegant, imposing houses of Eaton Place but was brought down to earth with a bang by the immediate reality of sharing a squalid little flat in Camden Town with two actresses and an occupational therapist and trying to get by on very little money.

I did make it to Eaton Place in the end, but sadly only to clean a ground-floor flat when I was working for London Domestics as a cleaner in the seventies. However, it was interesting to get to see inside one of these mansions that once required an army of servants to look after the single family that lived in them, even if it did mean swilling down the front steps.

My parents had always rented our house in Holly Grove and it seemed I was to follow in their footsteps until thanks to the success of a certain Lily Savage I was able, at the grand old age of forty, to buy a tiny little house near Tower Bridge out of my immoral earnings.

Central heating! Once I'd fathomed out how to set the timer on the boiler I discovered for the first time what it was like to wake up to a warm house in the winter and, unbelievably, a warm bathroom complete with shower. No more bending over the bath washing my hair with the aid of a pan or shivering in three inches of lukewarm water as I did back in Holly Grove; now I could luxuriate in a bath that I could actually stretch out in with hot water up to my neck, or stand underneath my newly installed power shower for as long as I wanted until I grew gills.

The house was small and narrow but it had a little garden and a garage. Convinced I'd be living there for quite a while I set about knocking down partition walls, replacing the staircase and flooring and transforming the minute bathroom, ripping out its beige and brown tiling and avocado-green bathroom suite and replacing it with marble and mirrors and art deco lighting and fittings salvaged from auctions. I lived in that bloody bathroom, forever polishing the marble walls until the novelty thankfully wore off and I reverted to my old ways of hanging towels on the floor and a mirror splattered in toothpaste and shaving foam.

(NB, when I say I set about knocking the walls in, what I actually mean is I employed my friend James and two builders to do the job. All I actually did was sign cheques.)

I was obsessed with wall sockets, coming from a home that only had one in the entire house until my parents had another one installed on the landing for my eighteenth birthday so I could play my record player in my bedroom. I made sure that my new house had more wall sockets than Robert Dyas. No more trailing wires or extension cords. At long last I felt like I was living in the civilized world.

It took nearly a year to renovate that house and to finance it I never stopped working, and when the time came for the builders to announce that the place was finished I hardly got to spend any time in it as I was permanently touring and living in hotels.

When I finally stopped touring and returned to civilian life I found that the house seemed bare and unlived-in, and just as nature abhors a vacuum so do I, so I set about 'filling' it up to make it feel more like home. Soon I couldn't move, and unless I stopped buying what Murphy, my partner and manager, described as 'junk' I wouldn't be able to get in or out.

Keeping it in some semblance of order was a nightmare, as was keeping it tidy, and on occasions my beautifully refurbished house looked as if a bunch of crackhead squatters had taken over. In my defence, even though I was no longer touring I was still hard at it and by the time I got home after a long day I had neither the time nor the inclination to get the hoover out and clear up.

'Get a cleaner,' everyone told me, but that was definitely something I didn't need in my life as I'd have to tidy up each week before they came. On rare days off I'd blitz the place, going through it like a tornado armed with the hoover, mop and bucket and a selection of interesting cleaning materials until it was gleaming, leaving Buster, my dog, wondering what he was doing in a strange house. It didn't stay immaculate for very long though as there was nowhere to put anything: the sofa was far too big for the front room, as was the coffee table and sideboard, and everywhere you looked there were CDs, VHS tapes and books, books, books, all of them with nowhere to live.

Like my mother I enjoyed 'going for a spin', which meant coercing some poor hapless sucker into taking you for an afternoon drive in their car. I couldn't drive at the time but luckily Murphy had recently bought himself a Jeep that he was obsessed with and was happy to go for long drives in the countryside on days when I found myself not working.

One afternoon we headed for rural Kent.

'I could live out here,' I said, drooling over the converted oasts and a particularly stunning fourteenth-century half-timbered house complete with the obligatory rambling rose growing around the door. 'I could definitely live in that. Pull over Murphy and see what that For Sale sign says.'

'It's not a For Sale sign, Savage,' Murphy replied as he drove on straight past my future home. 'The sign says that it's Ellen Terry's house and I doubt that the National Trust are ready to sell it yet.'

'Oh, that's a bugger,' I sighed. 'I could've swore that sign had an estate agent's name on it.'

'I keep telling you, get your bloody eyes tested. You need glasses.'

I stared out of the window at the passing scenery before trying to focus on a road sign up ahead. Even when I squinted I couldn't quite make out what it said until we got closer, but I wasn't going to tell Murphy that.

'I had no idea that Kent was so beautiful,' I said, changing the subject. 'Why have I never been down here before?'

I'd worked in Folkestone, Dartford, Chatham and Hastings (just over the Kent border in East Sussex) on one of my endless tours but on those occasions all I saw was the motorway, the town and the inside of whatever theatre I was playing. I never stayed the night as due to Kent's proximity to London it was silly not to drive back home – and as anyone who tours will tell you it's always preferable to sleep in your own bed whenever possible – so I really didn't know very much about 'The Garden of England'.

We stopped in a village that had an estate agent and as I eyed up the properties in the window for something I could afford I felt a growing excitement coursing through my veins.

'Look at that one, Murphy,' I sighed, pointing to a tiny cottage set on the edge of a wood. 'I wouldn't mind something like that.'

'Go in and ask if you can see it then,' Murphy said, egging me on. 'It's not a bad price for what it is.'

We went and viewed the property with its thatched roof, inglenook fireplaces and low ceilings with heavy oak beams.

'Look at the view,' the estate agent said, opening the leaded latticed window in the master bedroom for me. 'Imagine waking up to that.'

Leaning forward to take a look out of the tiny window I smashed my head on yet another low-slung beam for the fourth time since I'd crossed the threshold.

This place might be picturesque and reeking with history but it was totally unsuitable for someone of my height. The only person I could see living here without daily concussions was Jimmy Krankie.

We saw a few other properties before returning home, none of which, for various reasons, were suitable. However, I'd tasted blood by now and had become as obsessed with owning an affordable house as Mr Toad was with the motorcar when he first encountered one.

'What will you do with the flat in Saltaire?' Murphy asked on the drive home. 'I can't see you getting up there much if you bought a place in Kent.'

I'd bought a flat in that West Yorkshire village a couple of years earlier and I loved living there and certainly had no intentions of getting rid of it. Even so, I reasoned as I listened to Murphy, the journey up there from London took a lot longer than it did to get to Kent, and though Saltaire and the surrounding countryside is beautiful it wasn't quite as rural as I would've preferred. There was another important factor – the expense of running three homes.

'No point having three homes,' he went on as if reading my mind. 'You'll spend most of your time travelling. My advice would be to flog the flat in Saltaire and buy a house down here.' He cursed as a pheasant ran in front of the car.

'Bloody stupid bird must have a death wish. Look Savage, what's the point in working if you can't enjoy the rewards? You're always moaning about how you'd love to live in a house in the country, now here's your chance.'

'Won't you miss it?' I asked, meaning the Saltaire flat. 'Cos I know I will.'

'Of course I will, but we've done that now, and anyway, you can visit Yorkshire whenever the mood takes you. I think you should consider buying down here. It's nearer for London and work and you'll be able to afford it, especially if you sell the flat, you tight-fisted git. I mean, just look at that view,' he added, echoing the estate agent. 'It's beautiful.'

I was far from being tight-fisted as he well knew but old habits die hard and after years of being permanently skint I was always aware that the work might dry up and the wolf that I always suspected of lurking around the corner would get his chance to pounce and show me what big teeth he had.

Nevertheless Murphy was right. I was no Rothschild but with the proceeds of the sale of the flat and money I had sitting in the bank for a rainy day I'd be able to afford a reasonably priced house.

At least twice a week we scoured the estate agents of Kent for somewhere suitable. I saw former farm labourers' cottages, endless oast house and barn conversions, quaint cottages and even the odd mansion in need of renovation.

I always thought that one of the primary reasons for living in the country was having the advantage of not living close to your neighbours – an important selling point that all these properties lacked. I'm not antisocial, I just wanted to be able to play my music as loud as I liked and have my telly blaring if I chose to, something you can't or shouldn't do if you live with people above, below or next door to you.

I also had this fancy that I wanted to wake up to green fields, fresh air and birdsong and not the racket that comes with living in central London, and by now, passionate with the idea of living in the country and impatient to move, I considered buying a nine-bedroomed Gothic Victorian vicarage straight off the backlot of MGM. I swiftly changed my opinion after Murphy asked the eight-million-dollar question as we stood in the gloom on the vast upstairs landing.

'Can you honestly see yourself sleeping here on your own?' he said, looking out of the arched landing window at the cemetery behind the house.

On reflection I couldn't. Although the camp of living in the Addams Family's Kent mansion residence appealed to me the reality, if I was honest with myself, was something entirely different.

I put the idea of a Kentish home to one side and went back to touring the country with the musical *Annie*. It was during a Wednesday matinee in Manchester when I was sitting in my dressing room during the second half of the show (Miss Hannigan doesn't have a lot to do in the second half) that Murphy rang me.

He'd found the perfect property, he told me excitedly, with six bedrooms, the most sensational views, its own wood and, more importantly, totally private.

'How much?' I asked, cutting to the chase.

I was pleasantly surprised when he told me as I could afford it. It sounded like just what I was looking for.

'There's just one thing,' Murphy said, putting an instant dampener on the proceedings.

'What?' I asked, dreading the answer. Rats? Ghosts? It's in the middle of a motorway?

'If you want it then you have to trust me as apparently someone else is very keen and so ...' He paused so he could take another bite of his apple.

'Gerronwithit!' I shouted irritably as having to talk to anyone on the phone while they are eating drives me crackers and besides, I was eager to find out what the ominous 'so' was all about.

'All right Savage, keep your wig on,' he snapped back, taking another bite of his apple to rile me even further. 'You'll have to put an offer in by tomorrow if you want it,' he replied, mouth full, maddeningly casual. 'A couple of other cash buyers are very interested.'

'But I haven't seen it ...' I said, my voice trailing off. 'I can't buy a house sight unseen can I?' the voice of sensibility and reason in my head that rarely got a chance to exercise its vocal cords suddenly asked.

'That's why I said you have to trust me, Savage,' Murphy replied. 'It's wonderful, it really is. I've faxed the details to the theatre and I've put the estate agent's brochure in the post, you should get it in the morning. Have a look, see what you think. It looks like the kind of house you'd find in one of those Enid Blyton books.'

Enid Blyton. A childhood fancy was instantly awakened by those two magic words and at that moment I knew I was destined to live there.

Needless to say I bought it sight unseen, but thankfully I fell in love with it the moment I stepped out of the car. Now, nearly two decades later, I remind myself of my childhood dream when I open the bedroom curtains each morning and look out on to a vista of grey skies and rain-sodden fields – those I can actually see that is, thanks to the heavy blanket of fog that usually encircles the house. It rains a lot now. It never seemed to when I first moved in as then the summers were those of childhood, when days were long and permanently sunny. Now it just rains, and we continue to dismiss global warming when the evidence is staring us in the face.

Here's an early diary entry. I rarely keep a diary but occasionally I'll write something down. I must've had the proverbial hump the morning I wrote this …

> I stare absently out of the window as I swig my tea watching the morning fog slowly disperse to reveal the woods and the view of the fields below. The trees near the house are fascinating as the last knockings of a grey mist are trailing eerily through the branches of the trees like the widow's weeds of the banshee before they gradually fade away. The only birdsong I can hear is the racket that the jackdaws are making in the woods and I feel a bit like the character in *The Woman in Black*, trapped in Eel Marsh House …

Cheerful, isn't it? I'll admit that some days I most certainly have a love–hate relationship with living in the country. It's not all halcyon days of lying in the sun in a meadow full of poppies, and it's on the grim weather days like this that I indulge in a fantasy of mine, for the umpteenth time: the possibility of emigrating to the Venice Lido – not that I ever will as apart from property on the

Venice Lido being some of the most expensive real estate in Europe and the Lido not being quite what it used to be since they closed the old Hotel des Bains, the love I feel for my house and indeed my now adopted home of Kent far outweighs the occasional urge to sell up and move.

It's cold for the time of year and the temptation to get back in bed is irresistible but the dogs need to be let out for a run and to do their business before Eddie decides to do it under the piano.

I've got six dogs now: Louis, the eldest, followed by Olga, Bullseye, Eddie, Boycie and the latest addition, Conchita. My friends also have dogs and on those occasions when everyone has assembled here there can be as many as ten dogs in the house. The scent of Eau de Wet Dog permeates the place on these never-ending rainy days.

After I've seen to the dogs I feed the animals – the pigs, goats, chickens, ducks, barn owls and, if necessary, the sheep. Once, on a cold winter's morning, I fed the pigs wearing just a white towelling dressing gown and a pair of wellies that were a bit on the large side. I got stuck in the mud, which was unusually deep, and found myself tilting forward unable to stop myself as I made my slow descent into the waiting mud bath, ending up face down in it. Strangely enough, being immersed in mud on a cold winter's morning is quite a soothing experience and I lay there for a bit until Blanche, one of my pigs, wandered over to investigate which made me extract myself as quickly as I could in case she sat on me or, worse, used me as a lav, which has happened more than once before.

Once all my critters have been fed and watered I make myself breakfast. Now, at this point I should say that I sit down to a repast of freshly squeezed orange juice, accompanied by just-baked breakfast rolls straight from the Aga, homemade preserves and a newly laid egg courtesy of one of my hens.

Of course I do no such thing.

I can't stand eggs – there isn't enough cash in the banks to get me to eat a soft-boiled one, yuck! – and I haven't got the time to squeeze oranges and bake bread, so usually my country breakfast is a mug of tea and three Weetabix, which I eat in a hurry before they turn mushy in the milk.

I don't know what I'd do without Weetabix. When I go filming in the wilds of Africa or Borneo I always take a box with me just in case I can't get hold of any and the food on offer isn't to my taste.

There's a smell in the kitchen that is becoming unbearable. I recognize it from old and it signals that from somewhere underneath the floorboards a dead rat is slowly turning to jelly as it decomposes. I love all animals except for rats and mice. Sorry but I just can't stand them. I would rather be in a room with a couple of tigers than either a rat or a mouse.

There's a few rats that have taken up residence in the loft. I can hear them charging around and running the length of the house as I lie in bed at night. It sounds as if a gang of hefty lads in hobnail boots are having a kick-around with a concrete football. But I resign myself to the fact that this is all part and parcel of living in a rural area and make a note to ring the rat-catcher first thing.

When I was a teenager one of my many jobs was working behind the bar of Yates's Wine Lodge in Moorfields, Liverpool. The rat-catcher who came on a regular basis to dispose of the vermin that liked to sup on the 'Aussie White' down in the cellar was straight out of Dickens. He was a big man with a club foot and a crunched-up face like Popeye's who would tell me horror stories about the size of the rats he'd caught in and around the city. 'Bigger than a cat, sum of 'em,' he'd exclaim proudly, fixing me with his watery eye. 'And vicious with it.' Consequently I avoided the cellar at all costs. If a barrel needed changing then I always made sure I was busy doing something very important hoping one of the other barmen would deal with it.

There was nothing Dickensian about the pest control expert who turned up to solve my problem. He arrived in his van and after inspecting the house both inside and out as well as the surrounding outbuildings he discovered how the big buggers were getting into the house: it appeared mine had used the honeysuckle growing up the side to climb up and gained access via a missing tile in the roof.

'They can get in through the smallest space,' he explained as he examined the rat droppings in the loft, 'and I'm afraid to tell you that you have a serious infestation.'

That honeysuckle came down faster than Joan Crawford with an axe in a rose garden, and while humane traps were laid in the loft, traps containing poison were set in the outhouses. As this poison is Warfarin-based I had the pleasure of witnessing numerous large rats in their final death throes haemorrhaging blood from both ends and vowed there and then to never use such extreme measures to rid myself of vermin ever again.

A lot has happened over the years that I've lived in this house, both bad and good. There's been quite a few memorable parties and get-togethers, but apart from the social side I've also learned a lot – for instance I can now identify wild flowers and herbs whereas once upon a time a plant was just a plant. I'm more aware of the seasons than I ever was living in the city, and I've even surprised myself by making chutney, jams, butter and ice cream.

I used to worry that I was going to seed, churning out gallons of ice cream instead of 'clubbing it'. But once I discovered that I actually no longer want to go out every night, I came to terms with the fact that secretly I was beginning to prefer staying in and indulging myself by trying out new skills, wondering if the strawberry jam I was making would ever reach a rolling boil, or worrying if the orphaned lamb with bloat that I was sitting up with all night would see the sunrise.

Instead of attempting to get this new country lifestyle to adapt to my old one I went with the flow. It took a while but slowly I learned to relax and seriously embrace the joys of living in the countryside in all its diversity.

'Nothing ever happens in the countryside,' I've heard city dwellers say. 'It's just fields and sheep.' They couldn't be more wrong, but to discover what it's really like to live in the depths of the countryside you have to get stuck in, get involved and embrace all the wonders rural life has to offer.

I firmly believe that we have our own microclimate down here in my part of the world for if it's snowing in Liverpool then it'll be a sunny day down here and vice versa.

As I said, the weather's been lousy lately, grey skies and non-stop rain for weeks, but suddenly the weather turned overnight from grim to beyond glorious and changing me in the process from what my mother would call 'Misery on Poverty's back' into someone that a person who didn't know me might describe as having a 'sunny disposition'.

I'm sickeningly cheerful and happily indolent and apart from doing a bit of washing I spend the day lying pegged out in the sun. 'Like a lizard on a rock' as Murphy was wont to remark.

'Killer temperatures!' the front cover of a tabloid screams at me in the post office, and I couldn't be happier at the news.

It's so hot I sleep with all my bedroom windows open and the curtains pulled back – unusual behaviour for a nocturnal animal like me who normally prefers to sleep in the pitch dark and doesn't like to be woken at the crack of dawn by a face full of sunbeams.

As the windows are flung open to the elements a couple of bats, part of one of the many colonies that inhabit the roof, boiler room and the neighbouring woods, decide to pop in to see how we're all doing.

Naturally this sends the dogs berserk, Bullseye in particular, who leaps up and down, perfectly erect and poised, snapping at the air with his powerful jaws and putting me in mind of that crocodile perpetually trying to get a bite out of Captain Hook.

The commotion rouses me out of my doze with a start and in my confused state I start shouting to no one in particular.

'What the hell's going on?' I roar dramatically. 'I can't be woken up like this, I'm a very delicate mechanism – one tilt of the mantelpiece and this clock stops!' Which I thought quite a good analogy considering the hour and the circumstances.

This blinding piece of off-the-cuff dialogue was wasted on Olga who was sat on the bed intent on getting hold of whatever was hanging from the curtain. Olga, I hasten to remind you, is a cairn terrier and not a mysterious Russian lady spy (in case you were wondering).

A tiny bat crawls slowly up the curtain while the other one flies out of the bedroom door and vanishes down the landing.

I remove the little bat from the curtain before he/she crawls up into the folds of the pelmet and after releasing it out of the window I go in search of its companion who by now has disappeared quicker than Farage following the announcement that we were out of Europe. After a quick scout around there's no sign of the bat so I give up and go back to bed.

No doubt he'll turn up in the back bedroom hanging from the mantelpiece and demanding tea, toast and bluebottle jam in the morning.

There has been the ominous rumble of distant thunder since the early part of the evening and thankfully the hot night air, disgustingly heavy and oppressively still, has now stirred itself from its slumber and from my bed I can see that a light breeze is disturbing some papers on the desk under the window.

Unable to get back to sleep now I turn the radio on, hoping to catch the *Shipping Forecast*, but as I've missed it I tune into another station that turns out to be called France Bleu. Nevertheless they're playing Dvořák's 'Song to the Moon' which is apt as tonight the moon is full and in the clear night sky she is looking particularly beautiful.

I lie there dozing, feeling myself being lulled by Renée Fleming's beautiful voice when suddenly and without warning a clap of thunder as deafening as the boom of a cannon cracks overhead followed quickly by a flash of forked lightning so violent it lights up the fields and the garden allowing me to see them clearly from my bed for a full three seconds.

The breeze turns somewhat livelier and a gas bill and a letter on the desk from a woman who wants me to do something about the bile bears of China fly across the room in the sudden heavy gust of wind.

From a mild electrical storm the heavens suddenly pull all the stops out and produce the full orchestra. The house shakes underneath it and I rush around closing windows to keep the driving rain out.

Strangely the dogs don't bark but I can see that they are spooked by the maelstrom – as indeed, if I care to admit it, am I. I've been in some pretty violent tropical storms in the Far East in the past but they were nothing compared to this beauty that's raging now.

I remember how my mother would open both the front and back doors and take the phone off the hook 'to let the fireball escape' whenever there was a bit of thunder and lightning, but I don't know what she would've done if she'd found herself in the middle of this one.

'The gods are annoyed tonight,' I say to Eddie, my Jack Russell cross, and instantly regret it as the tale of Bert Savoy comes to mind.

Bert Savoy was a popular female impersonator on the American vaudeville stage in the early 1900s. He portrayed a sassy, brassy trollop who sailed extremely close to the wind with his outrageous double entendres – it's Bert who is credited with moulding the young Mae West into the slinky, wisecracking vamp (exactly like Bert's stage character) that she eventually became.

At the peak of his career Bert was out walking one day after a matinee with some friends on the beach at Long Island when an electrical storm started to whip up.

'Hmm, I see Miss God is throwing a hissy fit,' Bert was reported to have said, and in the next instant he was struck by lightning and killed.

I put all thoughts of poor Bert out of my mind and shove a shivering Eddie under the duvet to calm him as I wait for the power to go, which it inevitably does when we have even the mildest of storms. As I dwell on this possibility the bedside light and the radio predictably turn off.

The raging storm is sufficiently out of control now and if you saw it in a horror film you'd say it was laughably over the top. Eddie, normally as hard as nails, has turned into a complete wuss and I can feel him shaking against my leg underneath the duvet.

Even Olga, who is usually unfazed by such excessive displays of nature's antics, moves up the bed and gets close to me before changing her mind in case I think she's gone soft, independent beast that she is, and jumping off to hide underneath it. Plonking Eddie safely in the crossed paws of Bullseye, looking hangdog and pathetic on his cushion, I go downstairs in search of the torch, which should live under the sink but is never there. The lightning really is impressive and I open the back door to get a better look, standing on the step and watching the rain, which is coming down in sheets.

Seized by a fit of madness, I take myself off into the garden and stand in my sleeping attire (an old T-shirt and a pair of ancient pyjama bottoms) underneath the raging sky half expecting to hear a voice shouting from somewhere 'Get in you soft sod!'

I'm awestruck at the sheer power and magnificence of this unpredictable beast that has been unleashed in the heavens, and standing there in the garden battered by the wind and rain I really am aware of just how extremely unimportant I am in the wider scheme of things. I also feel defiant in the face of the storm, aware that like Bert Savoy a rogue fork of lightning just might pick me as a target. I can't resist a chorus of 'I'm a Lonesome Little Raindrop' and am grateful that nobody from Social Services is looking over the fence.

As soon as it had arrived the storm clears, leaving only a few minor grumbles and the occasional spiteful flash of lightning in its wake. The rain has dwindled into a light drizzle and the moon, released from her temporary imprisonment from behind the dark clouds, reappears as they gradually part, brushing herself down then, being the celestial pro that she is, smiling as brightly as Joan Collins at a premiere as if nothing had happened.

It's cool now and the air, perfumed by honeysuckle and nicotiana, smells clean and fresh. Before I return to the house I look in on the animals. The pigs are snoring contentedly in their shed – no battle of the gods is going to disturb them – and the goats, who have plenty of shelter and are more sensitive than their porcine neighbours to the weather, are prancing around their paddock as if their football team has just won the Premiership.

The chickens are sensible birds and not being fond of the rain are tucked away in their hen house while Minerva, my barn owl, sitting on the roof of the hen house, stares at me inquisitively through large unblinking eyes as if wondering what on earth I'm up to in the garden in the early hours of the morning soaked to the skin.

I return to the house totally exhilarated by this unusual nocturnal excursion and not in the least bit bothered that I'm wet through as it feels like I've just taken a peculiarly cleansing shower.

The electricity has returned, and as I climb the stairs I can hear the announcer on the radio proudly congratulating the royal couple, known as Kate and Wills by the tabloids, on the birth of their first child.

Had this've been medieval times then the future king of England's birth falling on the hottest day of the year when the moon was full and the wrath of the tempest shook the earth, it would either have been considered an omen of good fortune or a prophetic warning that dark times were just around the corner ...

Drying myself off, I imagine how they'll talk about the storm tomorrow in the supermarket.

'Did you hear that storm last night?' they'll ask each other excitedly, blocking up the aisle with their trollies as they stand and swap horror stories about how it affected them, each one trying to outdo the other with exaggerated tales of devastation and destruction.

I open the window again before I get into bed. The dogs have forgotten their fears and are asleep now, Louis snoring louder than a ward full of men with bronchial conditions. It's quiet outside again – the calm following the storm – and in no time at all I too fall into a deep sleep.

The air is cooler the morning following the storm but the sun continues to shine.

'At last,' I think as I watch a healthy mass of bees who have come out of hiding and are gorging on the heads of the lavender that is prolific around the garden, a glorious purple and as fragrant as an old lady's knicker drawer.

(I mean that in a good way you understand as my ma and all her cronies had little homemade twists of muslin containing lavender in their knicker drawers. Not that I make a habit of rooting around and sniffing old ladies' knicker drawers I can assure you of that.)

I've noticed the steady demise of the bee population since I've been here so it's good to see so many back again. I've become a bit obsessive about the absence of bees and find it very worrying that without them we'll probably starve. Bees are nature's fertilizers and yet nothing is done about the fact we have a major disaster on our hands. Pesticides that cause colony collapse disorder as well as a vampyric mite are all hastening the death knell for the bee.

Pity the same can't be said about the wasp which together with the mosquito have got to be the most irritating bugs ever invented.

What was Mother Nature thinking the day she gave life to these bloody things? Did she possibly have PMT? Did she suddenly snap one day and announce she was sick of making butterflies, robins, fluffy bunnies and puppies and out of sheer spite created a creature to match her mood and named it accordingly?

The Wasp.

All right, I know they have their uses as part of the food chain, but they ruin picnics, eat all my fruit on the trees in the orchard and then have the barefaced cheek to sting you. I hate them.

I was given the most wonderful instrument of execution called 'The Executioner Pro'. It looks like a tennis racket but with a push of the button on the handle the bluebottle you've just hit is given a killer zap of electricity resulting in instant death. Wasps take a little longer and a few more zaps than your average fly, and like a redneck radio DJ in the Deep South on the morning a prisoner on death row is going to the chair I hear myself saying as I go for the wasp hanging around the fruit bowl, 'You're gonna fry boy, you're gonna FRY!'

Of course there are other ways of dealing with our enemy The Wasp without turning into a psychopath. I've discovered that hanging brown paper bags in the fruit trees manages to keep the majority of them off the Victoria plums and apples as supposedly it makes them believe that a colony has already set up home there.

Wasps are attracted to bright colours, so if you are going on a picnic or intend to eat lunch in the garden then I'd advise against summery pastels and dig out your funeral coat instead. Funnily enough they dislike red – maybe they're Tories, I wouldn't be surprised.

Here's a tip.

If you are unfortunate enough to be stung by a wasp, or a bee, then rub the affected area with a raw onion. Honestly, try it, as you'll be amazed. I was stung by a wasp that had crept into my mug of tea in the garden and while taking a swig it bit me on my lower lip. Not wishing to look like I'd been up to Harley Street to have the gob pumped up with silicone I remembered my ma's words, ran into the house and rubbed the affected area with a chunk of raw onion for a good twenty minutes. The result was no pain or swelling and I remained as thin-lipped as ever. It was as if I hadn't been stung at all, even if I did stink a bit, which meant I couldn't kiss anyone, but as nobody wanted me to it didn't really matter. Garlic is just as effective only I didn't have any of that close to hand so I'll have to wait until the next time I get stung before I can test that one out.

Be warned, if you do kill a wasp by stunning it with a copy of your newspaper of choice and then crushing it satisfactorily with your heel as it lies on the floor you'll probably notice a sudden influx of the things. A dying wasp releases a pheromone that attracts others to the scene of the crime. All of a sudden there's hundreds of the little swines gathered for what I can only imagine is a sort of wasp wake, demanding sherry and whisky and a nice piece of that fruitcake please, and possibly a boiled ham and mustard sandwich.

I've planted lots of flowers in the garden that bees and butterflies love such as honeysuckle, buddleia and of course tons of lavender. Pick lavender first thing in the morning as the heat of the day causes the flowers to retain their oils – or so my ma advised, and as she was usually right about all things flora that's what I do, mixing the dried heads with some wormwood and rosemary and then tying them up in a bag cut from a yard of butter muslin just like the ones I was on about that old girls have in their knicker drawers.

I ignore the fact that this might be considered old ladyish behaviour because when they're hung in my wardrobe my clothes, sweaters in particular, survive uneaten. Moths loathe the smell and, like the rats before them, they do the decent thing and change lodgings.

I was given a sweater as a Christmas present once that obviously cost a ridiculous amount of money. It was woven from the softest cashmere with a jet-black sheen that the designer claimed 'reeked of elegant simplicity' and I thought it was the business. Hanging it up in the wardrobe on one of those padded coat hangers nicked from a hotel I gave it one final loving stroke before closing the door on it for the night.

In the morning I took it out of the wardrobe and, carefully pulling it on over my head before looking in the mirror to see if I reeked of elegant simplicity, my jaw hit the floor. My beautiful sweater that cost the same price as a terraced house in run-down areas of the north of England had been turned into what resembled lace overnight. A family of moths with very expensive tastes had obviously had a midnight feast, gorging themselves on my pride and joy. There were more holes in my sweater than a golf course.

That's why I couldn't give a monkey's what anyone thinks when I make moth-deterrent bags to hang amongst my clothes although unlike the ones you find in village fetes I don't embroider mine, nor do I tie them up with coloured ribbon; I keep it butch and tie them up with brown twine instead. I suppose highfalutin shops would call them shabby chic. Anyway, now everyone wants one as they've proved to be so effective and, as Valerie Singleton was often heard to say, 'Later on I'll be showing you how to make your very own.'

The garden, revived by its long drink last night, is blooming.

The bushes in my allotment are laden with gooseberries, raspberries and an abundance of black and redcurrants. I've got strawberries coming out of my ears and even the tiny *fraises des bois* that grow on the bank along the drive have come out in force this year. I love the taste of these delicate wild strawberries that I tell the grandkids are cultivated by the fairies.

Hang on. I can't believe I admitted that so cheerfully – the grandkids I'm talking about here and not the bit about fairy gardeners for on the contrary, I believe that it's common knowledge in out-of-the-way country betting offices that the odds on the existence of the little people being a hard fact are pretty high.

Does the gnarled old hawthorn tree in the fields house a community of fairy folk? If so, woe betide anyone who tries to chop it down or mutilate it in any way as they will be 'put under the fluence' by the irascible little folk who live amongst its roots and branches, and yet the one who cares and protects this tree is said to be blessed with good fortune.

There was once an ancient country practice of hanging ribbons on the branches of the hawthorn when it first blooms and pagans still hang multicoloured ribbons on the hawthorn tree to celebrate Beltane, a witches' bank holiday known as May Day to mortals. The hawthorn is part of a Sacred Trilogy of trees, the other two being the oak and the ash.

I'm extremely interested in all these old traditions and practices and it's a shame that the majority of them have vanished, thanks in no small part to the Church which outlawed them with the introduction of Christianity.

I have two ancient oaks at the bottom of my field. I was told that they're called Adam and Eve, and regardless of whether you're a spiritual person or not, sitting underneath them in the summer, the great branches almost touching the ground and forming a canopy of leaves all around you allowing shafts of sunlight to break through here and there, a profound sense of peace descends over you for this is a special place and you sense that you are witnessing the theatre of nature, an organic, living, breathing cathedral.

Fanciful? Not really, not when you've been there.

The oaks in their summer finery are a rare and special treat and another good example of why, if you go for it and embrace the great outdoors, warts and all, living in the countryside can be a life-enhancing experience.

I'm sounding like a self-help tape now, one of those that has over an irritating soundtrack of New Age music an American voice telling you in a tone not dissimilar to Liberace's to clear your mind and feel yourself slowly drift … off … to … another … space … slowly … slowly … slowly. Such twaddle isn't for me. I find the country life therapeutic without any help from a slow-talking Yank and his panpipes, and despite the expense and the trials and tribulations I'd like to see out my days here. I couldn't imagine any other life now.

But it was a shock when I first moved here, when the realization of the enormous step I'd taken had actually sunk in. I felt as if I were just renting the house in the beginning as I'd often rented flats and houses when I was on tour, and in fact I came downstairs one morning after I'd been here a week and announced that even though it was a lovely house I wouldn't want to live in it.

'Bit bloody late for that,' Murphy said, wiping a garlic clove on some toast. 'You've bought it.'

I couldn't quite get it to sink in that the house was mine. After all it wasn't that long ago I was living in a tiny council flat and now here I was with six bedrooms and acres of land in Kent.

On my first night in the house I couldn't sleep I was so excited. My furniture from the London house looked sparse in its new surroundings and I couldn't wait to get my things down from the flat in Saltaire that I'd bought in second-hand shops and at local auctions to make the place feel like home.

I spent the night roaming around the rooms like a cat getting accustomed to its new surroundings (although I didn't spray), lugging pieces of furniture from one room to another and then spending ages standing back to see if it looked right, which it inevitably didn't and so back to where it came from it went.

As day was breaking I made a cup of tea and went out on to the patio which stretches the length of the house, and whose old paving stones are said to have come from the East End during the Blitz and been laid by Italian prisoners of war. As I stood drinking my tea in the early-morning sun a big burly badger ambled across the field in front of the house. He wasn't one of those pristine critters you see on wildlife programmes, this fella's tuxedo of black and white fur was filthy, and he put me in mind of a nightclub bouncer who'd been scrapping all night and was anxious to get home.

Rabbits, who didn't seem the least nonplussed that a human was at large, never mind a small white dog called Buster who may have looked innocent but who was in fact a trained killer, nibbled at the grass apparently oblivious to us both. It was only when Buster finally launched his attack that they scattered, only to reappear again later and carry on, business as usual.

The azalea bush that had taken root amongst the paving slabs on the patio was alive with butterflies of every variety settling on the flower heads for an early-morning drink, fanning their wings in the warm sun. I was to learn that some of these gorgeous butterflies were actually moths, and there was one that really intrigued me. At first I thought it was a baby hummingbird, and it was only when I was talking about it to a woman in the garden centre that an old chap overhearing what I was saying explained what it was. It was a moth. A *Macroglossum stellatarum* to be exact, or the hummingbird hawk-moth to you and me.

When one of these extraordinary little creatures turned up I'd study it intently, fascinated as it hovered above a flower sipping nectar with its long proboscis exactly as a hummingbird would with its beak. Unfortunately I haven't seen another one for quite a number of years now.

The lavender and catmint (or catnip) were smothered with bumblebees, some 'the size of pigeons' to quote Arrietty from *The Borrowers*, and I couldn't wait to get started on this garden and fill it full of hollyhocks and foxgloves, delphiniums and roses, transforming it into one of those magnificent gardens you see in country house and garden mags. There was one major flaw in my scheme: I didn't know the first thing about gardening. My mother was the one who had been blessed with a green thumb; mine was obviously poisonous as I only had to rub a leaf and the poor plant it was attached to would be given the last rites within the week.

Never mind, I was willing to learn and desperate to get stuck in, and I mentally started to plan the layout. 'This bed full of roses, all red – no, white ... that's it, all white' my brain prattled on. 'Or maybe I should have a mixture ... And here I'm going to have beds of lavender, tons of the stuff, and poppies and lilies and those long things Dame Edna likes ... gladioli. Oh and irises and calla lilies, I like them ...' And so it went on.

I'd imagined that plants didn't cost very much but was I in for a shock when I saw my bill for the skip-sized trolley full of plants I'd bought in a frenzy in the local garden centre, and that's not counting all the paraphernalia that goes with it: tools, compost, fertilizer, bone meal, rooting powder, plant food … the list is endless, and bloody expensive.

Cilla Black had wisely tried to warn me that when buying a house, the bigger the property the bigger the expense. Six bedrooms meant six beds, six duvets and twenty-four pillows, not to mention the bed linen that's needed for that little lot.

Curtains, carpets, lighting, redecorating … it was frightening, as were the bills. I turned one of the bedrooms, the smallest one, into another bathroom, and paid out a small fortune on curtains for every room. The money seemed to be going out as fast as it came in and I was in a permanent state of panic in case I couldn't do what I wanted with this beautiful house or, even worse, lost it due to lack of funds.

The Delphic Cilla had proved to be right.

Thank God for charity shops, auctions and eBay, as the contents of my house will prove. A £65 Arts and Crafts period dressing table that only needs a bit of TLC is preferable any day to an expensive designer one. Auctions are brilliant places to find something you like at a good price. Every stick of furniture in the bedrooms apart from the beds came from various auction houses from all over the country and they didn't cost me an arm and a leg either. OK, some of the drawers on the dressing tables might not be as smooth-running as their modern counterparts and the wardrobe might wobble a bit when you open it, but they've got character and they suit the house, so if I'm looking for furniture then I won't be forking out a fortune for a couple of chairs from Heals and then have to wait two months for them to be delivered, I'll pop down to the charity shop instead, or cruise eBay.

The house is just over a hundred years old, and although it sits in an imposing position it is not what you'd call grand or elegant. It's just a comfortable if not slightly eccentric family house surrounded by fields and woods with spectacular views over the fields below. These fields are littered with the charred corpses of trees, the victims of lightning storms, and yet some, even though they've been split in half and have toppled over, have managed to stay alive and produce new growth.

The woods are as wild as you can get in England, the habitat of rabbits, owls, jackdaws, foxes, badgers, pheasant and even, so I've heard, the endangered Kentish dormouse. Every time I walk through them I get the impression that everything stops and waits until you've passed by and then, when they hear the click of the gate as I close it behind me, normal activity is safely resumed.

I find woods relaxing and therapeutic. A walk through a wood on one's own is the best way to clear the mind and mull over any problems that might be bothering me. They also have a calming effect, as I was to find out when I questioned the move to the country and if it had been a wise decision.

After the mixture of emotions – delight, incredulity, shock, to name but a few – had settled down following moving into the house, another one kicked in that I hadn't really experienced before, and that was a strange feeling of isolation.

It happened one Saturday morning a couple of months after I'd moved in. I'd woken up surprisingly early, fed

Buster and the goats, who were more than happy that breakfast was at seven a.m., and then suddenly, as I was standing looking out of the window drinking a mug of tea, aware that it wasn't even 8.30 yet, it hit me, this terrible sense of dread and fear that there was a long, long day ahead of me, and another one tomorrow, which I would be spending all on my own. Now as I mentioned, this house has seen some parties in its day, not just during my time but the previous owners down the years were no slouches at throwing a hoolie either, and I hadn't really been alone since I'd moved in – quite the opposite in fact as there'd been a steady stream of visitors. I'd moaned that it was getting more like a hotel than a home with me as chief cook and bottle washer, but this weekend I was alone, for a change, and I didn't like it.

The nagging voice of doubt that was hollering in my ear was working overtime and the view from the kitchen window of outstanding beauty that usually lifted my spirits resembled nothing more than desolation. By the time I'd finished my tea I'd convinced myself that by moving out here to the wilds of the country I'd sentenced myself to a life of solitude, to a place where I'd slowly rot, forgotten and only ever visited under duress. I could just hear them: 'Do we have to go and visit him? He's as mad as a hatter and the house stinks as it's full of all manner of animals and he never washes ...'

Nobody can wind me up better than myself and I stood transfixed as I stared out of the window in horror at the realization I was caught in a trap of my own making. All I could see were fields and woodland and the only sound I could hear was the muffled clunking the fridge made when it was producing ice. At that moment I desperately wanted to see people, hear traffic, pop over the road to the shop – in short, I wanted to be in the city not stuck in the middle of nowhere. I felt well and truly trapped. Slumping into a nearby chair, the sound of blood pounding in my ears, drowning out the noise of the fridge, I saw my idyllic view of living in the country as nothing more than a beautiful prison.

As I said, I hadn't learned to drive at that point so a trip into the nearest town meant an expensive taxi ride there and back, and even though I could afford it I objected to having to spend forty quid just to buy a pint of milk. I didn't want to be reliant on cabs anyway. We're very lucky in our village as we have two shops and a pub, but it still means a good walk to get to them: there's no 'popping round to the shop', it's a fifty-minute round trip on foot.

Why didn't I just order food online? Because I didn't possess a computer that's why for, Luddite that I was at the time, I foolishly believed that I could exist quite happily in the modern world without one. All this talk of hard drives, downloading and double-clicking on a mouse, whatever that was, bored me stiff and sounded far too complicated for someone like me to try and master. 'Pen and paper is good enough for me' became my stock answer whenever the subject of my getting a computer was brought up. 'If I want information then I can get it from a book' I'd add, refusing to listen to any reasonable argument. Consequently, and for quite some time, I stubbornly struggled on in that area known as 'behind the times'.

Time flies when you're in a hurry but quite the opposite occurs when you've seemingly nothing to do. The clock was telling me it was only nine o'clock and yet I felt like I'd been up for hours.

'What the hell are we going to do all day?' I asked Buster, who was watching me from where he lay stretched out on the floor wearing a 'well I did try to warn you' expression. Buster was a city dog at heart who loved nothing more than to go on tour with me or charge around telly studios, and even though he'd found things to amuse himself since we'd moved such as chasing rabbits and barking at the chickens, I could tell that he'd rather be on a train or mooching backstage in a theatre any day.

'Shall we go for a walk?' I suggested, with a not-very-convincing cheeriness that nevertheless had Buster on his feet and hopping around barking excitedly before charging out of the kitchen door.

He wasn't quite as enthusiastic when he saw that the promised walk was taking place in the woods, which meant him having to cross the equivalent of dangerous territory to get to it – The Field. Buster hated long grass and had a morbid fear of any plant that remotely looked like a thistle, coming to a complete stop and flatly refusing to move any further whenever he encountered anything suspiciously thistle-like. Rather than spend all day in the field trying to persuade him to move, sat as he would be in front of a thistle as if it were a landmine, I'd invariably give in and carry him until we'd reached the safety of the woods.

Once inside the gate he became a different dog and would shoot off in search of rabbits. Fortunately a little plump shih-tzu/bichon frise was no match for the woodland rabbits who would charge off, bouncing over fallen trees and into the safety of the brambles. Buster hated brambles nearly as much as thistles but to prove a point he'd stand outside this tangled mess of thorns and bark incessantly like a canine ARP warden from *Dad's*

Army shouting at a hapless householder to 'turn that ruddy light off'.

Woods are peaceful places – when your dog isn't barking his head off, that is – and I love them, the wilder the better. For me the smell of a wood is evocative of Bidston Hill, woodland with a windmill and an observatory which as a child I would visit on a regular basis with my ma.

Unlike me she was an expert gardener who swore by the beneficial properties of leaf mould for enriching the soil in her tiny garden, and on these trips she always took a couple of stout bags and a trowel with her. Waiting until the coast was clear she'd drop to her knees and start digging furiously as if she were burying the loot from a bank robbery, filling the bags with the precious leaf mould while shouting out instructions to me in what she considered to be a whisper but in all probability could be heard all over the woods to 'keep an eye out'. Once the bags were full she'd wrap a tea towel tidily over the top of them so if anyone asked she could pass it off as washing – although why we'd be carrying washing in the middle of a wood is anyone's guess, and why anyone would even care that she'd dug up a bit of soil is another.

She'd've enjoyed being let loose in my garden, tackling it armed with a pair of secateurs and her faithful trowel and transforming it into a thing of beauty.

However, I don't believe she'd've enjoyed country life on a permanent basis as she valued her independence and without a bus stop within easy reach she too would've felt trapped, just as I was currently feeling sat as I was on the trunk of a fallen tree in the middle of a wood at 9.30 on a Saturday morning.

It's easy to let your imagination run riot in the silence of a deserted wood. I once heard the radio critic Gillian Reynolds speaking about the importance of letting your mind wander into the realms of fantasy. She spoke of woods and how she imagined trees as dwelling places for the 'little people' with tiny doors and windows carved into the trunks, and as I listened to her on the radio it was a revelation as I knew exactly what she meant. It was a shock actually as I thought I was the only one who allowed myself such flights of fancy as a brief escape from 'real life', but after listening to Gillian apparently I'm not.

Woods feature heavily in fairy tales. The huntsman was ordered by the Wicked Queen to take Snow White far into the forest and kill her, only being on the soft side spared her life instead and told her to hide in the forest where she sought refuge with seven dwarves, as you do. Cinderella's first encounter with her Fairy Godmother, artfully disguised as an old lady collecting kindling, occurs in a wood. Red Riding Hood strayed off the path on her visit to her elderly bedridden granny who for some reason was living deep in the middle of a wood and was nearly eaten by a glib-tongued wolf.

(In the original version of the story the wolf sexually assaults Little Red before eating her and then escapes unharmed without the threat of the woodcutter who kills him in later versions of the tale, but that's another story.)

Hansel and Gretel were abandoned in the woods, as were the 'Babes in the Wood'. Robin Hood and his merry men evaded the Sheriff of Nottingham by hiding in Sherwood Forest. Kings have hidden in trees. The list goes on.

Forests and woods have always been places of mystery, enchantment and danger, and sitting quietly on my tree trunk listening to the stillness I felt, as I always have, that unseen eyes were watching me.

I'd read somewhere that a certain flower, small and star-shaped with white petals known as an anemone, would give you the power to see 'beyond the veil' if eaten.

'Beyond the what?' Murphy asked as we walked through the woods together one day.

'The veil,' I replied, not sure where I was going with this one. 'The wall that separates the human from the spirit world. Hermits and anchorites of old would eat these flowers to enable them to seek answers from the visions they experienced. They also reckoned there was another form of life, sprites, fairies, wood nymphs and suchlike, and eating these flowers would enable you to see them.'

I felt quite proud of this speech as it sounded feasible what with the historical twist concerning hermits, and even though I'd elaborated somewhat about the supposed power of these flowers I believed that even a dyed-in-the-wool cynic like Murphy would go for it.

'D'ye know what, Savage?'

'What?'

'You don't half talk some shit.'

He didn't go for it, but nevertheless he was happy to try a few with me – purely for experimental purposes you understand. The taste was disgusting, a cross between fish oil and black pepper, and while we didn't see anything otherworldly, colours were briefly but strangely enhanced.

Now if this was telly or radio I'd have to say 'Don't try this at home' but as it's a book you can do what you like, it's your life after all, but be warned: even though we claimed nothing had happened after eating the anemones we later discovered as we made our way home that I'd grown a small set of wings and Murphy was sprouting horns …

There's a wide variety of flowers growing in the woods during the late spring: the prolific and vibrant red campion, the celandine with its yellow flowers, a creeper with bursts of tiny white flowers known as enchanter's nightshade, anemones, daisies, cow parsley and the yellow archangel, a flowering plant with little bursts of bright yellow flowers that looks exactly like a nettle yet it has no sting. Further down in the wood where the ground is boggy due to the last trickle of an ancient spring grow a variety of ferns, and dotted all around are the scarlet berries of the lords-and-ladies. I love these woodland plants as they start life as a delicate, pale green sort of lily shaped like an arrowhead with tiny purple flowers inside that eventually become a scarlet cluster of berries.

I'm extremely lucky as around Easter time these flowers in my small woodland find themselves competing with a thick carpet of bluebells. These are the true blue British variety that is indigenous to our woods and not the Spanish invaders that have taken over a lot of the UK's woodland. To lie amongst a vast carpet of bluebells on a warm afternoon and inhale their aroma is a curious experience. I did it with my two grandchildren recently. They took a bit of persuading at first, only agreeing to do so if they could pull their anorak hoods up so that 'nothing could get in their hair or ears'. While we lay there the youngest asked me to tell her a story, and before I knew it a tale unfolded about a family of gnomes who'd lived in the basement of a block of council flats until redevelopment had forced them

to move out and by various means they'd found themselves living in a wood in rural Kent.

How would they cope, being City Gnomes? And would they get on with the neighbours? And what were these neighbours like? A story started to develop, and I wrote it all down later. Woods certainly do stir the imagination, encouraging it to wander freely without embarrassment into the realms of fantasy, and as I said, if you're looking for a place to have 'a good think' then I'd strongly recommend finding a wood and going for a stroll – although not through mine please, that's private and is already occupied by me, not to mention an army of little people as well as the Big Bad Wolf.

*

As Buster was growing restless and kept fixing me with the evil eye we left the wood and walked across the field, startling rabbits as we made our way down towards the two ancient oaks, which is another great place to 'sit and putt' – a phrase often used by my friend Reg meaning to simply sit and do nothing. It's a privilege to have such trees on the land, it really is, and even though it is my land I never consider the trees to be my property, I merely take care of them for future generations to enjoy.

I've been reliably informed that these trees are over six hundred years old and each time I sit there staring up at the branches I inevitably start to think about all the things these grand old oaks have lived through. They've survived two world wars, which is a miracle as during World War Two this part of Kent was known as Bomb Alley as it was here that the German bombers returning home would offload any bombs they hadn't dropped on London. It's also remarkable that my house survived, especially as mine, like most of the houses in the neighbourhood, was one of the ones requisitioned by the army and would've been considered a prime target.

So, the moral of this tale is if you want to sort yourself out then go for a good long walk, and if you do come across a tree that you find particularly special then have a sit and a think. Of course this does not apply if you're in a safari park or considering sitting and putting under a tree on a busy main road: the former will get you killed and the latter not only looks odd, there's the possibility of being nicked too. But you get my drift, and far from fighting solitude I learned to embrace it.

My mood lightened and I realized that the whole point of moving to the country was to be able to have quality time doing things that I wanted to do. This was an extremely rare luxury as I was usually always working, and the reason I was feeling blue was that I didn't know how to relax or what to do with time on my hands. To coin a phrase that I'm not keen on, I didn't know how to stop and smell the roses.

When I was very young my dad brought a retired sheepdog home with him from Ireland. Bran had been a working dog all his life, used to the outdoors herding sheep and using his skills, and now here he was in Birkenhead with nothing to do. He went a bit stir-crazy after a while and I'm not in the least surprised because with time on my hands that's how I feel.

Determined now to get the balance of work and play right and to embrace life in the country I headed off for the house with Buster under my arm as he'd seen a thistle and refused to walk.

That weekend was a lesson to me in learning to enjoy my own company and the sense of freedom that comes with it, and I'm happy to say that now I look forward to time on my own.

If you lead a busy and stressful life then those moments when you can sit on the sofa and read a book undisturbed for an hour or so or spend time indulging in a hobby is not time wasted, it's a time to recharge the batteries and relax for once.

I've long stopped feeling guilty if I do absolutely nothing or spend an afternoon absorbed in that week's favourite hobby – I have many varied projects on the go (all unfinished) – nor do I worry if I don't see anybody for a day or two. I haven't turned into a miserable old recluse I've just learned to cherish having time on my hands in a beautiful part of the world.

But if you can't drive then that can make life in the sticks just a tiny bit difficult. Basically, unless you've got a bike, a horse, or you're prepared to walk then you're well and truly stranded, mate.

I couldn't drive, it was a fair old walk into the village to the corner shop, and the nearest town was miles away. I could've bought a second-hand Bentley with what I was spending on taxis, and as I couldn't be bothered learning to drive, egged on by Murphy, I bought a bike.

I wanted a really old-fashioned one with a bell and a basket on the front, the type you frequently see in a Joan Hickson *Miss Marple* with the rider waving cheerily to passing friends as they pass through the village.

However, I left the shop with something far more advanced and slightly scary. It was a very modern racing bike with about two thousand gears and a seat as thin as a razor blade, and getting up hills on it in a driving wind was just sheer misery. I'd give in and stop, half dead and barely able to breathe, and end up pushing the bloody thing up the hill, cursing as the pedal invariably caught my anklebone. Bugger this, I thought as I sat in the kitchen with my thighs on fire following the exertions up the steep hill, and I gave the racing bike away replacing it with an electric one that had a battery you charged overnight.

It went quite fast, this bike. I didn't even have to pedal if I didn't fancy it, just open the throttle and let the battery do all the work, which was handy on the steep hills. I grew lazy, preferring to let the battery do the work rather than my legs, and although you could hardly call this exercise at least I was able to get to the shops in record time.

Going down hills on the bike was a different story. I didn't actually realize how fast I was going until I overtook Murphy driving the Saab. I was given a lecture on road safety and a helmet that looked like a turtle's shell.

'You've gone feral,' Murphy said. 'You've turned into some sort of hillbilly.'

'What do you mean?' I asked, removing Solly, my favourite bantam chicken, from the chair and sitting down.

'Riding that bike like a maniac, climbing trees, bloody chickens in the kitchen,' he ranted. 'And just look at yourself, you're filthy!' He pulled a face. 'When did you last have a shave, or a shower?'

I couldn't really argue with him on that score. I'd had a whore's wash (a cursory wipe with a flannel) that morning but I hadn't shaved in over ten days and my hair, which badly needed cutting, had twigs in it, added to which my shorts were torn and probably could've stood up and walked on their own had they chosen to, and my T-shirt was on inside out and beyond redemption.

'Look at your feet!' he went on. 'They're disgusting.'

'I've been gardening in my bare feet,' I protested, startling Solly who'd been sitting quietly on my knee up till now and setting her off clucking angrily, which I loosely interpreted as 'no need for insults, Murphy' in hen talk. 'They're bound to get a little bit dirty,' I continued. 'And anyway, I couldn't find my shoes.'

I couldn't remember the last time I'd worn shoes, apart from an ancient pair of tennis shoes to ride my bike in. My feet were indeed disgusting, ingrained as they were with soil and muck, and as I examined them I saw that the soles had turned as leathery as a hobbit's.

But that's another one of the joys of living in the countryside. Providing you've got nothing important to do, you can quite cheerfully let yourself go.

It's like being on permanent holiday when there's a run of good weather and I found myself doing all sorts of things I hadn't done since I was a youngster.

Climbing trees for instance. You're never too old to climb a tree.

*

One part of the garden had been sunk to make a croquet lawn and next to it, almost hidden amongst the trees, was a little house in a state of disrepair. When I say house I'm not talking about a three-bed semi, just a pleasant little room where one could escape from the afternoon sun and sip lemonade, exhausted after a game of croquet. I imagined it to have contained wicker Lloyd Loom chairs with tartan blankets and a selection of books should madame or one of her guests fancy indulging in a little prose as they sat and fanned themselves.

It was a shambles when I inherited it, a ghost of its former self. It had been used as a tack room and somewhere to store hay and animal food. One section of the roof was missing and the windows were hanging off. In short, it was seriously in need of demolition, suitable only for the rats, spiders and nest of wasps that had taken up refuge there; yet there was something magical about this little house nestling in this miniature wood that surrounded it and it cried out to be restored.

Sean, along with two other builders, set to work. They remade the old roof using reclaimed tiles that matched the originals perfectly, repaired the windows, laid a new floor and virtually replaced the walls. The pièce de résistance was the addition of a wood-burning stove and electricity.

The result was wonderful, and after a raid on local junk shops, not to mention the addition of suitable bits from the house, the shed was transformed. It became known as the Witch's House for it could easily pass as the dwelling place of a sorceress, and over the years various additions have been made to give it that touch of authenticity.

Recently I was making a documentary about the origins of fairy tales and the Witch's House was used as a location for Red Riding Hood's grandma's house. I'll confess that before filming I hadn't used it for over ten years and consequently the interior resembled Miss Havisham's wedding breakfast with cobwebs as thick as woollen scarves that clung to my face as I cleaned the beams sending angry spiders of an unnatural size scuttling away to find other lodgings. I also discovered a skeleton as I swept the floor that looked part rat/duck/human and which I've kept as a curio.

It was so dirty that it took me two days to clean it and I wished that I'd got on to Channel 4 to see if they had any of those obsessive compulsive cleaners available as they'd have loved this place. Anyway, it was very satisfying to see it spotlessly clean again and after a bit of 'set dressing' it was once again habitable.

I lived in the Witch's House for a couple of days during a particularly bad winter when the house was completely cut off from the rest of the world.

It had snowed heavily for days and as the roads had become impassable the oil man couldn't get through which meant I had no heating, and as the little Raeburn that I was cooking off was oil-fired I had no means of cooking either. The electricity was the next to go followed closely by the landline, as the sheer weight of the snow brought down the cables. I had no choice but to abandon ship and take up residence in the Witch's House as I could cook on the wood-burning stove and I was closer to the rest of the animals, which made feeding a damn sight easier.

I was hand-rearing two lambs at the time so I could use the stove to warm up the bottles. It was no hardship living like this, on the contrary it was a pleasant and interesting experience. The old sofa substituted as a comfortable bed and I passed the time reading and listening to the battery-operated radio as I lay wrapped in the duvet with two lambs and Buster asleep at my feet.

I made porridge, soup and a cooked breakfast on that wood burner and the kettle was permanently on the simmer for a pot of tea. The lambs along with Buster were very obliging about not peeing indoors, as indeed was I, and to make sure we didn't let ourselves down we made sure we regularly braved the elements outside for toilet duties.

I'd taken quite a few supplies with me when we moved in. The frozen stuff I'd salvaged from the freezer sat outside in a canvas bag and as I'd also brought a pack of bottles of mineral water, I not only had something to drink but I could have a wash by boiling the kettle, filling the big china bowl that had previously contained pine cones and having a good swill with the flannel.

I was sad to return to the house when it stopped snowing and the electricity went back on, as there's something to be said for living the simple life. I doubt very much if I could handle it for ever but once in a while it makes an interesting change.

As I've no interest in playing the game the croquet lawn in front of the Witch's House seemed the perfect location for a pond. The previous owner had left an enormous tepee behind which I quickly returned as playing Indians (as we used to call it – the term 'Native American' wasn't around then) was something I'd left behind, along with the cowboys, in the Mersey Park of my childhood.

I didn't physically dig the croquet lawn up myself of course: Sean, along with a couple of very handy men, and a JCB did the job. Sean, I should add, is an artisan builder who came with the house, and if he ever threatens to leave I'm going with him as the house and garden would fall into rack and ruin without him.

It was the perfect place for a pond and today it's as if it's been there for years. On a really hot day the Witch's House is the coolest place in the world to be, sheltered as it is by the shade of the trees. If I sit quietly enough with the door open I'm amazed by the variety of birds that visit the pond. Apart from the wild ducks, there's moorhens, woodpeckers, all manner of small wild birds who help themselves to the duck feed, the ubiquitous rook, robins and a magnificent kingfisher who occasionally comes to call.

The ducks have hatched countless numbers of ducklings over the years. Sadly not all of them survive, falling prey to crows, rats and magpies. There's also a snake that lurks in the depths of the pond. I've only ever seen it once, curled up on the bank enjoying the early-morning sunshine until it sensed that I was about whereupon it slowly and silently slithered into the water. It's not a water snake it's a grass snake, identified by the white/yellow collar around its neck. Grass snakes aren't venomous but if you pick one up it'll defend itself by letting off a disgusting fishy odour. Adders *are* venomous, and we have quite a few of them around here. One that was sleeping in the woodpile once bit me on the arm. I was lucky as apart from a little swelling the bite had no serious effect. The adder, on the other hand, ended up in intensive care on life support with toxic poisoning.

We planted all manner of water plants in the pond which the colony of wild ducks along with my collection of Aylesburys soon made short work of. We filled it full of fish but a heron, this enormous prehistoric creature, would swoop over the woods and treat my pond as a sort of fish and chip shop without the chips, helping himself to as many fish as he could get down his beak. I was told that this bird might have been a common crane, but whatever he was he was not only cunning he was hard-faced, for if anyone was about he'd sit on the chimney stack waiting until the coast was clear before advancing on the pond and helping himself to breakfast.

I'd watch this bird sat amongst the chimney pots and it always reminded me of the stork in *Dumbo*. Storks have always been associated with fertility, hence the legend of storks delivering babies in bundles from the skies. If only it were so easy, I hear all you mothers moan.

So I had the pond and the Witch's House, but something was missing, something every self-respecting magical landscape should have, and that little something was of course a well, and preferably one that housed a big fat toad that only came out in the moonlight.

A professional dowser was brought in, and on the spot where his little rods tilted violently downwards (this is not a double entendre) Sean and his mates got out the digger and went down twenty-five feet until they hit water.

'What sort of well do you want building?' Sean asked.

'One of those wells with a bucket and a handle to turn and a tiled roof that looks like it's been around for hundreds of years,' I told him.

A tall order, but *voilà*! One well made in no time out of Kentish ragstone, with reclaimed tiles on the wooden roof that make it appear as old as time itself. One of Sean's relatives had been a blacksmith and he recreated the wheels and handle that lower the wooden bucket. It was and is a masterpiece. Honeysuckle grows across the roof now, and while the water in its murky depths isn't potable, thereby rendering it useless, my well is lovely to look at and adds to the atmosphere.

Unfortunately I haven't got the toad that may or may not turn into a dashing young prince when kissed by a fair maiden, or even me for that matter, but I'd have to have a few drinks down me before I'd consider puckering up for a toad.

There's a china one sitting on the side of the well instead. It lacks mobility but looks the part if you're shortsighted, plus it doesn't mind being kissed.

My vision of how I wanted my place to look was almost complete. Now all I needed were some animals ...

Am I a Farmer?

Is a question I'm frequently asked, to which the answer is always a most definite no. Just because I live in the countryside and keep some livestock as pets it doesn't qualify me as a bona fide farmer.

Even though I come from a long line of farmers, it's not a profession that I ever considered as a career move. It's a hard life with no let-up and little reward and with the advent of Brexit, times are about to become even tougher for Britain's farmers.

It's a sad fact that the suicide rate amongst farmers is worryingly high and that a large percentage of farmers live way below the poverty line. Dairy farmers have been hit hard as it costs them more to produce the milk than they can earn from selling it, forcing families who have farmed for generations to sell up and call it a day. I find it very worrying to think that farming in this country may soon become a thing of the past. Thanks to trade deals with the US, instead of prime British beef for our Sunday roast we'll have to make do with chickens steeped in so much chlorine they'll smell and taste like the water in the old Livingstone Street Baths, as well as beef from cattle that have been pumped full of so many hormones that with a bit of CPR they would probably spring back to life.

Former farm labourers' cottages have become gentrified weekend retreats for those who can afford a second home, although, in my defence, I'd like to add that my house in Kent is the place I call my permanent home and not somewhere I visit occasionally.

I wanted to support my patch of the countryside and so I've planted a wild flower meadow, coppiced the woods and do my best to try to preserve and encourage wildlife.

There's a plot of land nearby that I spent a small fortune on at an extremely nerve-racking auction to prevent a company getting their hands on it and turning it into a site for motorbike scrambling and paintballing sessions. A local farmer grazes his sheep on it now, which is just how it should be.

I'm a city rat turned country mouse and, I believe, all the better for it. Oh, and on the subject of rats, you'll find they are mentioned quite a few times in the pages of this book. You'll also discover that country living isn't all about sitting on the patio sipping wine as the sun slowly sets – there's a little more to it than that, particularly if you're considering getting yourself some livestock. From the moment I emigrated from living full-time in London I vowed to keep a journal. Apart from a few entries down the years I never did fulfil that vow. One page in 2008 has written on it, 'Pipe burst in bathroom, front-room ceiling collapsed. Fuck it. Sean said he'll fix it.'

I can tell from the way I've scrawled that entry that it wasn't a good day.

Another states that on the 1st of January 2002, 'I woke up this morning to 18 people sleeping all over the place and the kitchen resembling the morning after the closing night of Studio 54.' I remember that particularly lively party well as after all these years I've still got the hangover.

I've included a few entries in this book that I've kept down the years in various 'journals'. There's a lot of talk about the weather as well as a fair share of moaning and griping, but at least they're honest and give a reasonably accurate, if not slightly warped, indication of what country life on a bad day can be like.

I've had a busy week as it's the summer holidays and I've had my daughter and her husband down for the week with the kids as well as assorted friends and their dogs. In short it's been bedlam, enjoyable but a bit full-on.

My grandson is animal-mad and can't wait to feed the critters. He's also very keen on learning about the countryside, whilst his younger sister is more content to sit and read and write little stories. Her latest epic, which she also illustrated herself, was about a family of squirrels and their constant clashes with a miserable old owl that lives in the same tree. She's only seven and I find it both amusing and a little poignant to discover that their interests and individual skills are a combination of mine when I was their age. They're spending Christmas with me this year – it's going to be a full house but we'll manage and I intend to exchange my Grinch's hat for one of a jolly Santa and make sure the kids have a memorable time.

In the last seven days I've baked nine apple pies, three blackberry and plum crumbles and a couple of lemon-drizzle cakes, I've also cooked stews, casseroles and soups, mashed endless spuds and made pan after pan of homemade chips and at this present moment in time I never want to cook again.

This house has a mood of its own. When it's full to the brim with people it seems to come alive, particularly at Christmas, but now that everybody's gone home and I'm alone the old place is still and at rest – even the dogs seem affected by the calming atmosphere after the hectic pace and rowdiness of the week. It's raining outside, but when isn't it bloody raining? And the dogs have to go out for their final walk, which will mean another soaking and the house reeking of wet dog.

However, I count my blessings that instead of having to trudge around the streets with a pack of dogs trailing behind me in the pissing rain I've got a big garden they can run around in and do whatever they have to before we all hit the sack. I couldn't go back to city life now even if I wanted to, and anyway, I'd have to find someplace to live first.

You see, I got married recently and for some reason the *Sun* newspaper saw fit to publish our marriage certificate with my London address on it for all to see. Irresponsible journalism doesn't come in to it, but then fair play and a sense of responsibility are not qualities that the morally bankrupt muck-spreaders at the *Sun* particularly care about. Tabloid journalism is a filthy business and I thank that editor of the *Liverpool Echo* daily for turning me down when, as a young teenager, I applied for a job as a junior reporter. Too many nutters hanging about the house meant we were forced to sell up and as fond as I was of that little house, using it as a convenient base when I was working in London, I've absolutely no desire to return to London on a permanent basis.

Olga's glaring at me now with her legs crossed, so I'd better get a move on and take her and the rest of the gang out before Eddy takes the easy option and pees up the leg of the piano.

I might watch a bit of telly before I turn in if I can find something watchable that doesn't involve a gang of pumped-up bimbos rutting on a desert island.

Goats and Other Animals

I'm always being asked, usually by the ladies and gentlemen of the press, if I prefer animals to humans, as apparently you can only like one and not the other. If you happen to be overly fond of animals then you're considered to be a bit of a nut, a reclusive misfit who wears handmade clothes, has no social skills and can only relate to anything with four legs. Tell that to Virginia McKenna.

There's lots of human beings that I like and respect, there are some that I love very much, there's others I can just about tolerate and then there's quite a few that, to coin a phrase, I wouldn't pee on if they were on fire, and I most definitely prefer animals to that last category.

There are very few animals that I dislike. I'm not wild about rats or mice and from the insect family I hate wasps, mozzies, bluebottles and fruit flies. Every other species apart from slugs are OK by me.

I've had dogs for years. They definitely enhance your life and I feel sorry for those who wouldn't dream of giving a dog a home despite having the time, space and funds to look after one properly, as they don't know what they're missing. Perhaps they're wary of getting involved, as inviting an animal to share your life will inevitably end in heartbreak when that last trip to the vet happens. Still, there's no point contemplating the hangover when you're at the party is there? If you went through life worrying like that, then you'd never leave the house.

Cruelty to animals is unforgivable and to say it makes me angry would be a gross understatement. A few years back my cairn terrier, Olga, was waiting for me outside a newsagent when a man jabbering away on his mobile kicked her out of the way. I saw all this happen as I stood in the queue, I also heard Olga's yelp as she was kicked and, turning a whiter shade of pale with fury, I marched out of the shop and gave this creep a well-aimed kick up the arse, telling him as he sat sprawled all over the pavement that if he ever kicked mine or anybody else's dog again he'd end up in the river. I make no apologies for kicking him as the arsehole deserved it, but I am ashamed of my gangster B-movie threat for which there's no excuse.

I'm not violent by nature, but cruelty to animals brings out the worst in me.

In the years that I've been filming at Battersea Dogs & Cats Home I've seen dogs that have been dumped and left to die, dogs that are nothing more than living skeletons, victims of unspeakable cruelty, abuse and neglect and it weighs heavily on me.

Then there's the dogs that have been used for breeding purposes by the puppy farmers – young dogs kept in atrocious conditions and used as breeding machines who have given birth to litter after litter and then, when they've outlived their usefulness, they're callously dumped.

Puppy farming is a cruel and disgusting trade and the sentences handed down by the courts to those criminals

Billy

who abuse animals is risible. Perhaps the Great British Judicial System has little or no respect for animals, and if that's the case then just like the bloke outside the newsagent it deserves a kick up the arse.

I've had a wide variety of pets over the years, ranging from guinea pigs to dogs, and after I'd been living in the country for less than a month I decided one morning that the time was ripe for me to get me some livestock.

'Shouldn't you get a decent couch first?' Murphy asked when I told him of my plans. 'You can't sit on a bloody goat!'

Of course, I ignored him. The battered old sofa that I'd brought with me from London would have to do for the moment, even if it did mean you had to crawl on to the floor to get off it as it was so low.

From a local farm I bought three kids, two females and a billy, who I christened unimaginatively, Billy.

Billy had left his mother far too early and turned out to be pretty sick with various infections including coccidiosis – a nasty disease caused by internal parasites that gave Billy constant diarrhoea resulting in weight loss and a high fever. He was close to death and the vet, seeing how anxious I was to keep him alive, took him away to his surgery and put him on a drip. Within a couple of days he improved dramatically and was able to come home. As he had to have medication every couple of hours, and to save me trekking out to their pen every couple of hours during the night, I brought him into the house and put him in a box next to my bed. After a few days Billy was finally better – I realized this when I woke up to find him standing next to me on the bed destroying a copy of the *TV Times* with what looked like a grin on his face.

I told Cilla this, who in turn told the viewers of *This Morning* that I slept with a goat.

Some of the tabloids picked it up and reported with great ribaldry that I shared my bed with a goat. No point trying to deny it so I just said, not without irony, that the only hassle was the horns as they kept shredding the sheets – and they believed me.

After Billy went back to his barn as it was clear he was now in good health, he grew strong, bossy and very friendly, particularly if he suspected I had food. Then he'd virtually climb up me, staring straight into my face with those yellow eyes that I swear had a hypnotic quality if you stared back at them for long enough.

*

Olive

Olive was an angora and with her beautiful snowy white coat she was the glamour girl of the trio. In the spring she'd shed this coat, assisting the removal of it by rubbing herself along the metal gate whilst a party of jackdaws sat observing from the fence like a crowd of hungry punters at a burlesque show watching the featured stripper peel off her clothes. The jackdaws would use Olive's discarded coat as material for building their nests and, suffice to say, there are some pretty fancy nests in the neighbouring woods.

Nan was brown and cream and a bit of a thug as, together with Billy, she'd bully poor Olive, driving her away from her feed and headbutting her at every opportunity. Nan and Billy seemed to have a bit of a thing going as they spent most of the day locking horns and leaping about in

Nan

what looked like an energetic if not potentially hazardous love ritual. Nothing was going to happen as Billy didn't have his bits – he'd arrived with an elastic band wrapped tightly around his tackle that caused an infection and must've been very painful for him. If done correctly this procedure causes a young kid no discomfort and his balls simply drop off (I'm crossing my legs as I write this), but my poor Billy's was a botched job and I kind of wish that he hadn't been 'done' as it would've been great to have had a few newborn kids about the place.

Goats are fairly easy to look after and the legend that goats will eat anything from a tea towel to a tin can hasn't been the case with mine. On the contrary, they're quite fussy.

Goats aren't grazers like sheep, they're browsers and they are also trained in the school of escapology as I soon found out when my three escaped and ravaged the garden, eating and trampling on almost every plant. They love brambles and bushes and are rather partial to the bark of trees. There used to be two trees in their field until the unholy trio stripped them of their bark, consequently killing the trees.

Mine are fed on a special goat mix and plenty of hay; they also get a block called a goat lick. Funnily enough I went to the farm shop this morning to get some. I'm not baring my soul here and admitting to a strange kink that requires a goat to lick me all over in the village shop. No, a goat lick is a small gooey brown block that's packed full of vitamins and minerals to help keep the goats in good health. Goats love them and lick them, hence the name.

While I was in there I bought a box of frozen chicks for the owls. The shop also sells boxes of frozen rats and mice but I can't quite bring myself to have a box of them in the freezer at home, nor could I bear to handle them dead or otherwise, so my owls feast on chicks and chicken livers and are thriving on this diet.

We were discussing rats in the shop and how we've all had trouble with them in our homes. One woman was telling the tale of how she went to visit a friend who had just bought a cottage. This cottage was as old as time and as it hadn't been renovated for donkey's years the flooring was rather primitive. As they were drinking their tea in the front room the woman saw something out of the corner of her eye, and after taking a closer look she saw that it was a mole tunnelling his way up and popping out of the ground underneath the telly.

A man suddenly piped up, telling us about 'a rat as big as a Jack Russell' running across his bed during the night.

Since I didn't have a rat tale to top either of these horror stories I bought a bag of mealworms along with the goat lick and left.

The weather today is like a rich woman's cat – contrary. One minute it's strong gales and torrential rain, the next sunshine and rainbows. I'd entered the shop in a maelstrom and left it in calm, sunny conditions. Weird.

There was a squirrel on the roof of my car. I know folk think they're cute but as far as I'm concerned they're nothing but rats with feather boas.

'Go on, sling your hook,' I told it as it scampered away and vanished over the roof of the florist's.

'Not keen then?' a man who was locking his car asked.

I told him that I wasn't.

'Neither am I,' he said. 'They carry the parapoxvirus you know, killing off all the native red Brits. Ever seen one?'

I had. Many years ago in Formby when we'd gone for a day out to get a 'bronzie' – the Liverpudlian term for a suntan. Unfortunately this bronzie turned out to be a bright reddie but despite the pain we were more than happy to have what we thought was a Mediterranean tan for when we went clubbing later that evening. I'd spotted a red squirrel then, in the woods, and was amazed at how much smaller they are compared to the greys. They're also pretty stunning with that rich russet coat and magnificent tail, and it's deplorable that they're being wiped out by the bigger, more adaptable greys.

'You can blame them Victorians,' he went on. 'Brought them here in the 1800s, all the way from North America by boat as something exotic for some rich bugger's country estate. Of course they bred, didn't they?'

'Well you can't blame them, can you?' I replied, giving a woman and her child a friendly nod as she opened the boot of her car parked next to mine. 'Cooped up on that boat all that time.'

'Well there's nearly three million of them now – they've taken over,' he said in a louder voice as he warmed to his theme. 'They shouldn't even have been here in the first place.'

'No,' I muttered, aware that the woman packing her purchases in her boot was frowning as she listened to all this.

'And now there's the blacks,' the man declared. 'They're starting to multiply by the hundreds. It's very worrying you know as it won't be long before the native Brit is extinct.'

'If you don't mind,' the woman said angrily, 'can you keep your voice down as I don't want my daughter hearing such racist talk. I'll tell you what's worrying,' she added, pointing her finger at the man, 'people like you and your ignorant views.'

The man and I just looked at each other.

'Have you ever seen a migrant camp?' she demanded. 'Well I have and they're a living hell. And as for these "boats" you're talking about' – here she shot me a withering look – 'do you realize they travel in rubber dinghys that are nothing more than death traps but they're desperate to escape and have no choice than to put their trust as well as their lives in the hands of traffickers who couldn't give a damn if they live or drown?'

It was quite a speech and I wasn't sure what to say to her until the penny suddenly dropped.

'Hang on a minute,' I told her. 'We're not talking about immigrants, we're on about squirrels – how the grey squirrel is killing off the red.'

The woman stared at us open-mouthed.

'And now black squirrels are increasing in numbers, particularly in Cambridgeshire, outnumbering the greys,' the man explained. 'We weren't being racist. It was squirrel talk, nothing more. You've got the wrong end of the stick, luv.'

'Oh my God,' the woman moaned, 'I'm so sorry, honestly I am. I just want the ground to open up and swallow me. Oh I can't believe it. Me and my big mouth! Oh my God.'

I thought it was wonderful, the kind of talking at cross-purposes that you couldn't make up if you tried, and obviously the squirrel man thought the same way as he was laughing as much as me.

'No offence taken,' he said to the woman, who drove off shame-faced still apologizing profusely.

'You know Charlie's going to sterilize them,' the man said after she'd driven off.

'Who?'

'The greys.'

'No, I meant Charlie who?'

'Charlie – Prince Charles.'

I had a vision of Prince Charles cutting the ribbon on his Grey Squirrel Sterilization Unit before donning a white coat and surgical gloves and performing demonic experiments on the reproductive organs of squirrels.

'He's going to put the contraceptive pill in Nutella,' he said. 'Clever isn't it?'

I wanted to ask how the squirrels were going to get the lid off but this was no time to be flippant as I wanted to get home so I simply said it was nice talking to him and drove off.

On the way home I spotted a lamb standing in the middle of the lane. Pulling over on the grass verge I got out and managed to grab it. It was a cute little thing no more than two weeks old. It bleated its little head off loudly at being picked up at first but then settled down, burying its head into my coat.

It was obvious the lamb had escaped from the big field nearby that was full of sheep and quite a few young lambs. After climbing the gate with the lamb under my arm I walked across the field looking for a ewe that was crying out. The lamb bleated loudly and a ewe wandering around at the other end of the field answered its call. The lamb, recognizing its mother's call, bleated again, only much louder this time. As it was struggling in my arms I reluctantly put the lamb down and watched him rush off to be reunited with Mommie Dearest.

There was a beautiful rainbow arching above the church spire in the distance. What with the sheep and the lambs and the smell of clean earth from a rain-soaked field it was the stuff of poets' dreams. Taking a deep breath, I folded my arms contentedly. And it was then that I discovered my sleeve was soaking and the lamb had peed all over me.

I wonder if that ever happened to Wordsworth?

I had these goats for years and they spent their days quite happily charging around their field, lying in the sun, eating and indulging in their favourite pastime of headbutting each other.

Nan was the first to go, from a cancerous tumour. Billy died a few years later. But Olive carried on until she was fifteen, until, riddled with arthritis and almost blind, I made the difficult decision of having the old girl put to sleep.

I missed these goats. They'd been around for so long that they'd become part of the family, and so it wasn't long before I brought another three home from Billy, who runs an animal rescue not far from where I live.

The new bunch is called Rosie, Beebo and Maleficent. Beebo is a pygmy goat, although he's not so Lilliputian these days, and he's shy with strangers whom he always suspects to be the vet. He only has to see someone dressed in green wearing a pair of wellies and he's off like a whippet.

Beebo has a bit of a skin condition that I've managed to control by feeding him an organic mix and treating the area with calendula cream, nevertheless the vet still has to be called in on the odd occasion. Catching Beebo takes a degree of low cunning that requires me going into his pen with some slices of white bread – which he loves – and standing around nonchalantly until he approaches me, whereupon I grab him by the horns and the vet, who has been hiding around the corner, rushes in to give him his treatment.

Holding a feisty young goat down is no easy task and in the early days he always managed to either escape or throw me to the floor in the struggle. However, I've got wise now and by trial and error I discovered the knack of holding a goat down.

Beebo's also wised up as well and seems to have developed a sixth sense as to when the vet's paying a visit.

Rosie and Maleficent

It's almost as if he can read my mind that I'm about to ring them, and not even the lure of a bit of Mother's Pride can stop him taking off across his field.

Maleficent is jet black with startling yellow eyes and a set of magnificent horns – hence the name. Yet she's the tamest and sweetest natured of the three of them and loves being stroked. Maybe I'll have to give her a name change to something less demonic like 'Cuddles', or then again, maybe not, as she's far too majestic for a cutesy-poo name.

If Rosie was human then she'd be one of those buxom wenches that Sid James would leer over in *Carry on Dick*. She's cream and brown in colour, similar to Nan, and extremely skittish and full of herself. She bossed and bullied poor old Beebo when they first arrived but now he's grown she's not quite so handy with the headbutts as she knows that she'll get a couple back.

I've only ever tried to milk a goat twice. The first time was on a smallholding in Wales and the goat I was milking had been contained in a small stall with plenty of hay to keep her occupied as I yanked on her teats. That was a successful, trouble-free milk, but the second time around, which took place on a farm in Kent, the goat wasn't contained and, being of a fiery temperament and unaccustomed to strangers milking her, I was rewarded with a teaspoon of milk and a headbutt. So, I've not much to say on the matter of milking goats except that for a nanny to produce milk she has to be lactating and as all you mothers out there know, to lactate you must give birth.

Milking also requires a certain amount of skill and isn't as simple as it sounds (see Cows), although I'm sure those who keep goats for their milk would disagree.

For a start, you'll need some equipment such as a stainless-steel milking bucket, a milk strainer complete with disposable filters, jugs, churns, detergents, a specialist chemical sterilizer and last but not least a very low milking stool.

Hygiene is of the utmost importance. The milking bucket needs to be sterilized after use by scalding it with boiling water and leaving it to drain.

In an ideal world you'd carry out these operations in the cool of your own personal dairy, the kind Marie Antoinette would've dreamt of for her Hameau de la Reine at the Palace of Versailles with delft tiling on the walls and freshly made cheeses lined up on cool marble slabs.

There'd be a milkmaid as well, dressed appropriately in a mob cap with a heaving bosom bursting out of her bodice, turning the handle of the butter churn and idly staring out of the window at the handsome herdsman stripped to the waist who was doing something masculine like wrestling a bull in the field beyond.

Sorry, I've slipped into Sunday-night historical drama otherwise known as Sunday Night Soft Porn, but you get my drift about the dairy. It would be lovely and cool on a hot summer day, a place of solace where one could escape from the lunacy of life to strain milk and churn butter. On the other hand, it would be bloody freezing in the winter.

Once you've milked your goat, which, depending on the goat's temperament, might either be simple or traumatic, you strain the milk and then cool it immediately. If you've only got a little bit, then put it in something with a lid and run the cold tap over it and once it's cool, store it in the fridge.

Goat's milk is supposedly better for us than cow's milk, although even though I like the cheese I don't fancy their milk. It's lower in lactose and cholesterol than cow's milk, rich in calcium and is known to reduce the symptoms of asthma, eczema and many digestive problems. Even so, I can't quite get it down me.

Goats love climbing, and we've put three sawn-off logs in their field that they balance on for hours, standing on tiptoe (or is it tiphoof?), like a music-hall tumbling act about to go into their big finale. They don't by the way – go into a big finale – they just stand there peering into space contemplating life.

Sean built them a wooden climbing frame, which they spend most of their time on, chasing each other around or just lazing in the sun. So if you're thinking of getting goats then make sure you give them something to climb on as well as somewhere sheltered and warm to sleep in.

Mine sleep in three breezeblock huts, positioned out of the wind and rain with a raised wooden floor for warmth and plenty of straw. And don't forget fresh drinking water. I've heard it say that a temperamental horse benefits from the company of a goat as they seem to calm a skittish horse down. On racing day, to calm a nervous horse, a goat would be put into its stable to relax it. However, an unscrupulous rival would steal this goat, leaving the horse unsettled and fretful, thereby scuppering the chances of it winning the race. Hence the expression, 'He gets my goat.'

Goats have long been associated with black magic and satanic rites. Esmeralda's dancing goat in *The Hunchback of Notre-Dame* was enough to have the gypsy girl branded as a witch, and if Hammer Horror were thinking of doing a remake then my Maleficent would be an overnight sensation: although I'd have to warn them that she can't play a tambourine.

The perverse Roman emperor Caligula was terrified of goats, and it was said that in the Middle Ages if a saint happened to come across a goat then the goat would sit itself next to this saint and whisper obscenities in the said holy person's ear. Why? I do not know.

So, if you don't mind the language, then I can highly recommend goats as a pet, although that's only if you've got the space. I wouldn't recommend them if you live in a high-rise flat with a balcony, and forget it if you're in a bedsit, sorry, studio apartment.

Concerning
Almost All Things
Feathered

You can't live in the countryside and not have a couple of hens as it doesn't seem right, plus these interesting little characters earn their keep in eggs. Poultry have made a comeback and I hear that lots of people are now keeping a couple of chickens in their urban back gardens, although I wouldn't advise getting a rooster if you live in a built-up area, not unless you want your neighbours to lynch you.

Then there's the universal problem of the fox, who loves a chicken dinner, not to mention the terms of your house deeds that might not allow you to keep livestock. It's a little more complicated than you might think so best check everything is shipshape and Bristol fashion before you introduce a couple of chucks into your back garden.

HENS

My first hens were three tiny bantams and an equally diminutive rooster, Solly. They lived in a little hen house in the garden and were free to roam where they liked.

I'd got used to having chickens around but before I got another batch I made sure that a secure coop was built for them. They could roam the garden all day but at night they were getting locked up, safe from any predators.

I literally started from scratch with my next flock of chickens as they came in the form of twelve fertilized eggs which I kept in a special incubator that very slowly rocked from side to side, gently turning the eggs exactly as a mother hen would do in the nest.

The farmer who gave me the eggs told me they would take twenty-one days to hatch but even so I couldn't stop myself from going into my bathroom (where I kept the incubator)

every five minutes to see how the eggs were progressing. I had contemplated playing these eggs a tape of hens clucking to prepare them for the outside world but that idea quickly fizzled out and they had to make do with the radio instead.

As the great day of The Hatching approached I made sure that I had all the right equipment to keep these chicks alive as soon as they'd hatched. I needed a box with a heat lamp covering it to keep them warm, a shallow dish of water, some food and, as a substitute mother, a piece of turkey-cock boa courtesy of Ms Savage's Wicked Queen costume.

Exactly as the farmer had predicted the eggs hatched on the morning of the twenty-first day. Cracks appeared in the shell and slowly a little beak would pop out until eventually the entire soggy, ugly-looking chick had emerged.

I left them in the incubator to dry off before transferring them to their new home. They all appeared to be quite healthy – not that I was an expert – and once their feathers had fluffed up and they became the yellow-blonde chicks beloved of Easter greetings cards they were irresistible.

After a few days I noticed that one of them had a slight limp. It didn't seem to bother her as she managed just as well as the others who by now were charging around their box and chirping their heads off. The chicken with the limp was given the very un-PC name of Gammy, and while she might've tilted to the left, that didn't stop her shoving the others out of the way to be first at the bowl of chick meal.

I'd kept the bathroom door shut tight at all times to keep the murderous Buster out and I'd let the chicks out of their box to have a run around. If I sat on the floor they'd all gather together under my legs and if I lay down they'd climb all over me until they'd finally form into a huddle on my chest whereupon they'd settle down and go to sleep.

What would the old crowd from the Vauxhall Tavern say if they could see me now, I thought, lying on a bathroom floor with twelve chicks on top of me fast asleep. I've lain on a few bathroom floors in the past when I was a teenager but only because I'd thrown up after too many ciders and thought it best to stay in close proximity to the lav in case another retching session was on the cards.

The chicks grew, and as they did they lost their yellow plumage, transforming into scrawny brown things with spiky feathers. I can't say they were particularly attractive at this stage and it would be a while before they blossomed into big fat egg-laying hens.

They settled down quickly in the new hen house, surrounded by an electrified five-foot perimeter wire fence which I'd frequently forget was turned on and absent-mindedly touch, giving myself a few volts to start the day. I had so many shocks off that fence that if I stuck a light bulb in my mouth I swear it would glow, just like Uncle Fester from *The Addams Family*.

The chickens grew quickly. One or two of them were getting quite aggressive but I put this down to them sorting out the pecking order. There's a definite hierarchy amongst chickens and the one who becomes 'top dog' so to speak isn't always the biggest and the bossiest. It seems to me to be the eldest that wears the crown, and since this lot were born at more or less the same time I reckoned there was going to be fisticuffs before they sorted themselves out. Gammy was high in the running for the title of boss hen as she certainly took no prisoners, limping around the garden like Jimmy Cagney in the film *Love Me or Leave Me*. She had a habit of roosting on top of the hen house instead of inside, but as soon as she'd nodded off she'd inevitably lose her grip and, sliding down the roof, she'd hit the ground with an angry squawk.

One morning I was woken up by a cock crowing repeatedly and assumed as I lay half awake in my bed that one of my hens had turned out to be a male. I was pleased about this as the transgender hen turned out to be Gammy, perched, a little wobbly perhaps, on top of the hen house crowing away like he/she was auditioning for Pathé News.

Good old Gammy, thanks to him I was going to have more chicks. And, asking a neighbour who knows a lot about hens if he'd come round to have a look at mine and see if there were any others who might be male, he told me with a wry smile that I had not one rooster but twelve. Every single one of my chickens had turned out male. There'd be no eggs, just a hen house full of testosterone-fuelled cockerels strutting around and squaring up to each other like a gang of drunken lads outside a club on a Saturday night.

What the hell was I going to do with twelve cockerels?

I put a card in the window of the local shop, careful of how I phrased it. For instance 'If you're looking for a young healthy cock then please ring ...' would in all likelihood encourage the wrong sort of enquirer and might even result in a police raid, so I put '12 Roosters to Give Away', and the phone number.

Nobody rang for over a week and I'd given up hope until I received a call from a woman who was looking for a cockerel so we arranged for her to come round first thing before she dropped her daughter off at school to pick one up.

The next morning when the woman and her daughter arrived I led them down the garden to the hen house, or should I say Cockerel Cottage, only to be greeted by utter carnage. The fox that had climbed over the fence and back again was obviously insulated as electric shocks certainly hadn't deterred him. All the cockerels were dead: the fox had taken what he wanted and killed the rest, I suppose because he could. While I appreciate that the fox has to eat, why does the swine have to go for my chickens when the surrounding countryside is bursting with juicy rabbits and pheasants?

The woman and the daughter, both shocked by the sight of the massacre, hotfooted it back to their car as I went to fetch a couple of bin bags and a shovel to clear up Mr Reynard's butchery. It was not a pleasant task, and even though it had solved the problem of having too many cockerels this was certainly not what I wanted.

It was heartbreaking to find what was left of Gammy, without doubt my favourite hen – sorry, rooster – but I consoled myself with the thought that he probably put up a brave fight and died a hero. I considered getting my bugle and playing the Last Post as a sign of respect but as I play it extremely badly my actions may have been taken the wrong way.

Sean bought me some more chickens, only rare breeds this time. The fence was raised and the voltage upped. He even put a wire mesh roof on the top. But despite these precautions the fox eventually got in, digging down this time and underneath the fence, killing the lot.

I was beginning to hate foxes.

It was decided that a new chicken run was to be built, one so secure that not even the Hatton Garden raiders could get in. A deep trench was dug and the new fence was sunk in a bed of concrete so nothing could dig its way in. As chicken runs go, this new one was Colditz.

It was enormous, partially sheltered, with freshly laid grass turf, a mulberry bush and a little pond plus an area of earth set aside for the hens when they wanted a dust bath. Three new hen houses awaited the arrival of my latest brood, ten ex-battery hens with hardly any feathers. These hens, no longer enclosed in cramped conditions and free to run around in a large space without fear from any predators, relished their new surroundings and within weeks their feathers had grown back.

They were also very friendly chucks, happy to sit on my knee and be carried, which was handy as that way you get to assess the chickens' health by giving them the once-over. These were seriously happy, healthy hens but sadly they lasted less than eighteen months as ex-battery hens have a short shelf life. At least they lived out the rest of their lives happily and in luxury compared to what they'd come from.

My next batch was six beautiful Orpingtons complete with an elegant rooster who were prolific egg layers – the hens that is, not the rooster of course. I called him 'Rooster' – unoriginal I know, but it suited him for he was a proud specimen and a gentleman to boot. He was the David Niven of cockerels, never aggressive and always standing back for the ladies to eat their feed first, watching over them as they pecked away at the grain and only eating himself when the last hen had finished.

Despite his gentle demeanour he was a raving stud in the hay as pretty soon I had two broody hens sitting on a clutch of fertilized eggs. Early morning seemed to be his preferred time for ravishing the women folk as when I

went into the run to give them their breakfast quite a few of the hens would be tottering about looking slightly dazed. Rooster would rise with the sun, wake the neighbourhood up with his crowing, have a quick scratch and then entertain the ladies.

The hens hatched sixteen chicks between them, and to protect these chicks from the others we put a temporary partition of chicken wire between Ma and her brood and the other hens. Remarkably, out of those sixteen chicks only one turned out to be a cockerel.

As we'd seen no sign of Mr Fox for a few years I thought I'd let them out to have a mooch around the garden. Tentatively at first they poked their heads outside the run before cautiously stepping into the big wide world and having a peck about, but careful not to stray too far from their run and always staying close to the ever-watchful Rooster standing close by protectively. A fox wouldn't dare attempt a daylight attack, not with people in the garden.

And indeed he didn't. But the wily bugger had obviously been watching unseen from the undergrowth and biding his time until the coast was clear, when he'd launch his attack.

That day came one afternoon when I foolishly went to the local shop. I was gone less than fifteen minutes but as I came back down the drive my heart sank as I witnessed a vixen running in front of me carrying a limp and very dead Rooster in her mouth.

Just as before she'd killed the other chickens too, the only survivor a tiny white bantam I'd acquired along with an equally tiny but fiery bantam rooster who had a habit of lunging at you when you least expected it, like Cato with Inspector Clouseau. And now here he was, lying dead, his head bitten off, leaving his missus a widow.

I was as annoyed with myself as I was upset for leaving my flock alone and went in search of the shovel, hating foxes more than ever now and vowing a dark revenge.

A few weeks later my attitude towards this vixen changed completely when I had the rare treat of witnessing her watching over her three lively cubs playing on the path close to the kitchen window. As I stood transfixed and watched these three beautiful cubs play-fighting I noticed that the vixen had spotted me and was staring right at me. I didn't dare move as I was afraid that she'd gather up her cubs and make a dash for safety, only she didn't, for after giving me the once-over she totally disregarded me and instead lay down on the grassy bank and yawned. The cubs, seeing that Momma was lying down, started to leap all over her, nuzzling into her belly in search of a nipple until she eventually had enough and with a sly glance at me she ushered them into the bushes and home.

Rooster had provided this vixen with a meal for all four of them, and I no longer resented her. After all, a mother has to feed her kids.

The white bantam seemed quite happy with her own company, which was just as well as I vowed that there would be no more chickens. Never again. That was it. Finished. Kaput. I was heart-sick at the continual sight of my decimated flock.

Two weeks later four fat black and white Brahmas arrived courtesy of Sean. They were soon put in their place by Madame Bantam despite them being giants in comparison. When two of these birds died of something nasty despite visits to the vet, the hen houses were fumigated and six brown beauties known as Isa Browns took up residence. The bantam, girding her feathered loins, soon showed these chucks who was boss too as she strutted amongst them, pecking their feet and defying them to retaliate, which they never did.

If I thought that the battery hens were friendly then the Isa Browns made them appear positively antisocial in comparison. One in particular can hold a conversation. She's called Ethel, and when she sits on my arm I chat to her during which she remains silent with her head cocked on one side and her beady eye on me. As soon as I stop she takes up where I left off, clucking away until I start speaking again when she shuts up and resumes the 'head cocked to the side listening position'. A typical conversation might go like this:

Me: 'How's tricks, Ethel?'

Ethel: 'Cluck, cluck, squawk.' ('Not bad thanks.')

Me: 'Laid anything yet?'

Ethel: 'Cluck, cluck, cluck, throaty squawk, cluck, cluck, treble cluck, squawk.' ('No, but there's a biggun on its way, that's if one of those bitches gets her arse out of the hen house and lets me drop it in peace.')

Me: 'Full up is it?'

Ethel: 'Cluck, cluck.' ('To capacity.')

Me: 'Hang on, here's Gladys coming out the hen house now.'

Ethel: a long series of clucks interpreted as 'She probably thinks you've got food as you know what a hungry old cow she is. Anyway I'm off. Better get in quick before Denise nicks me spot.'

Maybe I need to hang around with humans a little more often.

Over a short period of time I noticed that one of these hens, a big bird called Marlene, was slowly getting bigger and bossier. Her comb, as well as growing larger, was turning a deeper shade of red, and I wondered if she wasn't changing sex, but dismissed the notion immediately.

However, on the day she threw her head back and started to crow Marlene became Marlon. I mentioned this on my Radio 2 show and, surprisingly, lots of listeners got in touch to say that they'd witnessed the same occurrence amongst their flock.

What I found even stranger was Marlon's transformation back into Marlene. Obviously after a month or so of butching it up she'd had enough of watching football and *Top Gear* and quickly transitioned back into her original gender, laying eggs like a good 'un as if to prove she was all hen.

Hens can be vicious, suddenly turning on a weaker or sick chuck and eventually pecking them to death. One of the Brahmas is frequently henpecked and she has to be separated behind the wire barrier, her bare backside a bright blue after a squirt of antiseptic spray until she recovers.

But hens are good fun too. They also provide you with a never-ending supply of freshly laid eggs, perfect if you like poached eggs as the fresher they are the better. Murphy used to literally hang around the hen house waiting for the first drop for his breakfast. He reckoned that my girls' eggs poached within minutes of laying were the best he'd ever tasted, whereas the thought of it repulses me.

At the moment I have seven hens, including the little white bantam who I'm beginning to believe is invincible and will probably see me out. I couldn't recommend having a couple of hens as pets enough, providing you have the space and can keep them safe.

DUCKS

A friend gave me three Aylesbury ducks who certainly brightened the pond up with their snowy white plumage and bright yellow beaks. They'd gather together in a circle and noisily quack away, sounding – or at least it did to me – as if they were laughing their bills off at a dirty joke one of them had just told. They were quite shy and always ran when anyone approached but the fox, as always, got the two females when the pond froze over one winter, allowing him easy access to the island in the middle where the ducks slept. The male survived, and as he bore more than a resemblance to Donald Duck he was christened Uncle Walt after Donald's creator.

While not wishing for the Disney organization to come down on me like a ton of bricks, I have to admit that I much prefer Donald Duck to that anodyne Mickey Mouse and his prissy, nagging consort Minnie. Donald is a legend and a much more interesting character, and I can empathize with his volcanic temper and unpredictable behaviour.

Unlike the sickly Minnie Mouse, Donald's lady friend, the vampish Daisy Duck, is an outrageous flirt forever batting her enormous eyelashes and bending her knee coquettishly in the manner of a burlesque stripper. This sexy mallard is all duck, and just like Olive Oyl she's more than capable of bringing out her man's – or in Donald's case duck's – basic carnal instincts, reducing him to a drooling mass of jelly. Minnie is far too preoccupied with keeping house as a substitute for her non-existent sex life, but she lives in hope as once again she waves (she does a

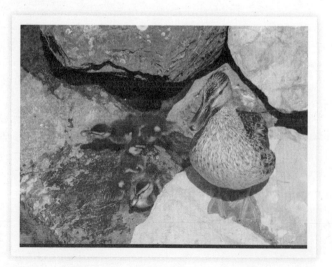

lot of waving – more than I had to do on *Blankety Blank*) her goody two shoes partner off for yet another day on the golf links, showing off in front of his showbiz mates Pluto and Goofy.

If I were evilly inclined I'd make unflattering comparisons to certain television personalities, but as I'm feeling charitable today I won't.

Uncle Walt became a confirmed bachelor, teaming up with a wild drake who remained unnamed but was always referred to as 'Uncle Wally's mate'. For a while I wondered if these two might be gay as they were inseparable, until the following spring, when Uncle Wally's mate took a girlfriend who became known as 'Uncle Wally's mate's girlfriend'. What else?

Uncle Wally was with me for quite a number of years. His mate left him not long after he hooked up with a mallard but Wally, a stoic duck if ever there was one, simply got himself another best friend and together this drake and Wally would stroll around the pond, Wally quacking incessantly as if recounting another chapter of his life to the silent drake waddling beside him.

Uncle Wally lived until he was ten and died of old age, expiring peacefully amongst the lavender bushes.

These days the pond is occupied by wild ducks, particularly during the winter when at one time I counted over forty, each and every one of them following me to the food shed at feeding time. The present count is four, and they choose to live with the pigs, ignoring their pond and preferring the pigs' waterhole instead. The pigs as yet have made no comment about these squatters. They seem happy to ignore them and go about their business as usual.

OWLS

Let me state here and now that barn owls, or indeed any owls, do not make suitable pets. However, saying that, I've now got seven, all of them living in perfect harmony with the hens in the Olympic-sized chicken run which, since the owls' arrival, has been upgraded to the grander title of 'The Aviary'.

I wasn't looking to keep owls as I knew nothing about them, but when I heard of a barn owl born in captivity and living in a converted wardrobe in the Midlands I knew I had to have her.

I'd say that she was half tame when she arrived as she had a little leather anklet strap that you threaded a thin leather leash into to enable you to hold her when she was sat on your hand. At first I suffered a couple of nasty nips. Owls have sharp beaks and claws and the ordinary leather gloves I was wearing weren't substantial enough to protect me so I bought a professional pair of falconry gauntlets that were as stiff as a board and wouldn't have looked out of place on one of the three musketeers. Still, they did the job, and the newly christened Minerva, or Minnie for short, would dutifully sit on my gloved hand – depending, of course, on her mood. When she was feeling what I called 'bitchy' she'd flatly refuse to grip my wrist; instead she'd allow herself to fall backwards like a bungee jumper falling off a bridge, her leash saving her from hitting the ground. This would go on repeatedly until I gave up and put her back in her nesting box.

We'd put a shed inside the run and cut a hole in the side for her to fly in and out of, and the nesting box was inside the shed – a vast improvement on her previous lodgings.

She also had all this space to fly around in and exercise her wings, and she was wonderful to watch at twilight.

Minnie is magnificent in flight, and watching her swoop around behind the wire fencing I always regret that she's not free and silently searching for dormice and voles high above the meadow, but apart from it being illegal to release an owl born in captivity, you are also condemning the bird to death as a captive bird has no idea how to hunt and would very soon starve.

Minnie is fed on day-old chicks and once a week she gets chicken livers, which she loves. I also give her a supplement once a month called SF50 to keep her healthy. The chicks come deep-frozen in a box from the farm shop and my freezer is not for the faint-hearted, stocked as it is with dead chicks on top of the ice cream. Owls rarely drink as they get all the moisture they need from their prey. They do like a bath though and they make regular use of the small shallow pool in the run. Lots of owls in the wild drown and that's why the 'pool' is no more than two inches deep.

Owls born in the wild have a life expectancy of four years – that's if they're lucky as many die not long after they're born. The owl's worst enemies are cars, lorries, trains, electric pylons, vermin that have been poisoned, dangerous pesticides and the loss of their natural habitat, the barn. On the plus side, owls born in captivity can live for up to twenty years so Minnie and co., just like the bantam hen, will more than likely see me out.

When Minnie was in the mood to play she'd not only willingly sit on my hand but had started to hop on my shoulder. The first time she did it I had no shirt on but I put up with the pain and the loss of blood as I was so pleased, not to mention surprised that she'd made the leap from wrist to shoulder. I wore a jacket the next time I handled her and she did the same thing again, only this time she took a liking to my ear, and while it's very touching to have a barn owl nuzzling your ear those little love pecks bloody hurt and once again I returned to the house minus a pint or two of my life's blood.

To tame an owl it has to be imprinted, or hand-reared, from the moment it opens its eyes.

Feeding it takes a strong stomach, as you have to dissect a dead mouse or day-old chick and then mash it up and get it down the bird's beak. I'll admit I could no more do this than I could show my bare bum in a Selfridges window as I'd probably never eat again: I know that with each mouthful I'd be thinking of a headless mouse I'd just skinned.

In the end I stopped handling Minnie as I always got the impression that she didn't much care for it, so I reluctantly left her alone. I was going to miss playing Maleficent, with Minnie on my wrist or shoulder as a replacement for the wicked fairy's raven, proclaiming to the hens that I was more than a little miffed at not being invited to the christening.

Barn owls are beautiful creatures with their snowy white heart-shaped faces and magnificent plumage. There's something ghostly and ethereal about them in silent flight. Contrary to belief they don't hoot, the tawny owl does that; the barn owl screeches and makes reptilian hissing sounds that can sound quite creepy.

Despite the owl's reputation for being wise I'm afraid to say I haven't found that to be quite true. Merlin may have had an owl as his all-knowing familiar and Minerva, the goddess of wisdom, might never be seen without one, but if mine are anything to go by the image of the wise old owl is a myth. They aren't particularly loyal either. A hand-reared owl will either see you as stiff competition in the mating game or as a prospective mate. Either way they can be aggressive and the males extremely noisy.

With the popularity of Harry Potter, there was a period when owls became every child's must-have. Forget ponies and dogs, to be the coolest kid in the class required owning a letter-carrying owl. I know this was not the intention of the author but such was the craze it was inevitable that every kid was hell-bent on having their very own Hedwig, and lots of unscrupulous 'breeders' were happy to flog them on the internet. But as I said, they make lousy pets and need careful handling, which the kiddies and their parents were very quick to find out, resulting in a lot of dumped owls, and owl sanctuaries and the RSPCA up to their necks in them.

*

Not long after Minnie arrived a neighbour of Sean's gave me a male who had also been born in captivity. At first Minnie resented this intrusion on her patch and gave this male, now known as Icarus, a hard time.

This state of play didn't last long as I went in one evening to feed them and found that he'd moved out of his nesting box and was getting very cosy with Minnie in her shed. On seeing me, Minnie started to hiss and, opening her wings, began to perform a threatening duck-and-weave movement similar to a boxer. During this display Icarus sat quietly behind his girlfriend nonplussed and quite clearly lovestruck, leaving the job of frightening off this intruder to Minnie. It was obvious who wore the trousers in this relationship.

Soon Minnie was sitting on two eggs, then four, then ten. Minnie the prolific layer was clearly intent on having a large family but as I didn't fancy being overrun with captive owls all of the eggs bar two were removed. This didn't bother her in the least, and if all the eggs had've hatched then the majority of chicks would've died, either from neglect or through being eaten by the alpha baby chick.

These two eggs eventually hatched, and the two healthy chicks couldn't have had a more devoted mother in Minnie for she never left the nest.

Now that Minnie had her chicks, Icarus was no longer welcome in the shed as Mummy instinctively knew that Daddy would more than likely eat them for lunch, and besides, that fleeting relationship was over. Poor old Icarus was now persona non gratis. I sang a bit of The Streets' 'Dry Your Eyes' to him as he sat on his branch in the corner of The Aviary but he just stared at me blankly before flying off to his nesting box, probably to sulk.

I wasn't up to date on how long it took before owlets left the nest but Minnie's twins, now all grown up and called Pollux and Casper, didn't seem in any hurry to fly the coop. Baby owls aren't particularly pretty at first, but when their bodies grow to match their beaks they're gorgeous, and Minnie's two, who didn't object to being handled even if their mother wasn't amused, were perfect.

They were still nesting with her over a year later, the equivalent of two teenagers who won't leave home and get a job. It was Icarus who soon put a stop to that as he and Momma were getting amorous again and quickly he booted them out to set up home together in their own nesting box. Well he didn't want the kids watching, did he?

Three more chicks arrived the following year and then I called a halt before my place turned into Hogwarts. Now when Minnie lays eggs I take them off her as seven owls is quite enough.

All my owls are fit and healthy, and Minnie has developed a very soft spot for one of her daughters who lives with her permanently, even when Minnie is sitting on eggs. Little Eadie (for that's the daughter's name) is a lot smaller than her siblings but it's not because she's undernourished or ill: the vet said she's simply 'a little one', and she's very beautiful.

As you've probably gathered by now I'm passionate about owls. They're very special and we need to think about doing more to make sure that these beautiful birds are protected for generations to come. But don't even consider getting one and keeping it in a cage in the front room no matter how much your Harry Potter-obsessed progeny harps on about wanting one as a pet. Get him a budgie instead and tell him he used to work in the sorting room at the post office.

Rural Idyll

I've lived in the countryside for almost two decades now and during that time I've seen many changes. Industrial parks and motorways and rail lines are cutting through land and villages, and housing estates are springing up on once open fields – there's a few in my village, with more to come. The once fairly quiet lanes now shake underneath the wheels of cement mixers, trucks and the massive machinery required for all this building, not to mention an increased flow of domestic traffic, and I fear that all this relentless overdevelopment will destroy rural villages for ever.

It seems that due to escalating house prices more and more people are abandoning city life and heading for the more affordable homes on offer in rural areas, hence the rise of these garden villages. I'm one of these migrants from the city but I bought an old house with more land than rooms as my main objective was to keep animals, and now, just like the trees I planted when I first moved in, my roots are firmly embedded in the countryside.

Or are they?

There's a lot more traffic on the lanes these days and these little winding B roads are in an appalling state. We haven't got potholes we've got craters, some of which have been there for years and are growing bigger. A couple of gentlemen from the council came round, not to fill them in but to very kindly paint little white frames around them so motorists and cyclists can see where they are and veer into the middle of the road to avoid them. Not that they needed to bother with the white frames as some of these potholes are so wide and deep they can be seen from outer space. I suppose they say it's all down to the cuts.

As the community grows, I wonder if the infrastructure can cope. What about the village school? Can it accommodate the growing influx of children? The same goes for the local surgery. Being granted a private audience with the Queen is easier than getting an appointment to see the doc these days so how is their already busy practice going to manage?

Of course people have got to live somewhere, haven't they, and there's still plenty of unspoilt land and stunning views around, but for how much longer? I've noticed that an entire field near to me has been given over to solar panels, and there's a couple more fields that have been earmarked for over a hundred new houses. I'm extremely worried that one day in the not too distant future my house will no longer be on the outskirts of a village, it'll be in the middle of a town, and that's not where I want to live. I'll go to the meetings in the village hall, sign petitions to protect our rural setting from excessive development, go on gov.uk and have a rant, join any protest marches there may be, but to what avail?

We managed to stop a proposed lorry park to accommodate the hundreds of trucks that can't get across the Channel because the French are on strike (again), so there may be a very slim chance – and I mean wafer thin – that development can be stopped.

I'm being optimistic here as I suspect that the deal was done and dusted long ago, but even so it's important for the little people to stand up to these big corporations and councils and make ourselves heard. I come from feuding stock and have always wanted to cock a rifle and say 'Git off my land', even if it is to a couple of fellas from the council wearing high-vis jackets as they set up their theodolites and not a gang of cattle rustlers.

I choose to live here not just for its outstanding beauty and the luxury of owning fields I can keep animals on, but also for – and I hope you'll excuse the sentiment here – its rural charms. If I find the fields are full of the same homogenized housing estates and I can't get to the village shop as I'm stuck in a traffic jam full of people driving to the supermarket then I'm off.

But I'd hate to leave this house and the privacy it affords and have to pack up twenty years of accumulated junk and a menagerie of animals and find alternative lodgings elsewhere. So I'm going to enjoy living in a rural community while I can, even if the reception is lousy on my mobile phone and I spend most of my conversations saying 'What?' and 'Can you hear me now?' Another teeny irritant is when the power goes out when we have electrical storms, and there's a good chance that during a heavy snowfall nobody can get in or out for days.

Well, I say teeny irritant. I rarely get past week two in a diary, but here's an entry I found from when the weather must've been particularly bad. I've no idea of the exact dates as it's the only entry and it wasn't written in a diary but in a book with the word 'Notes' stamped on the front so I've no idea of the year either; all I know is that it was written in January. These are the only notes I bothered to write. It's fairly short but certainly not sweet so excuse the language.

The bloody stand pipe was frozen over when I went to feed the pigs this morning and there was no water. I couldn't even turn the tap as it was frozen solid. The pigs came out of their shed as soon as they heard me swearing. The amount of steam rising from the heat of their bodies in the icy air would rival the Orient Express pulling out of the station.

Of course the pigs' water buckets were frozen solid, as were the goats' and the chickens', so I had to traipse back and forth from the house with buckets of hot water to thaw them out. That bloody bridge is a death trap. It's bad enough at the best of times but covered in a thick sheet of solid ice the f*****g thing requires Sherpa Tenzing to get across it. I fell over twice, once on that bastard bridge and again when I skidded by the well and dropped both buckets. I hate the countryside. What in God's name possessed me to move down here and live in the middle of a f*****g field? It's all that bloody Murphy's fault.

Anyway, I sorted all the animals out, the sheep included, and then went back into the house to try and thaw out as I was bloody frozen and couldn't feel my feet. One day I'll learn to dress sensibly.

The boiler had gone out and the house was colder inside than it was outside.

Why does it always turn itself off when you need it most? During the summer months it's all systems go but as soon as the weather turns cold the sodding thing allows its pilot light to go out. You only have to fart and that f*****g light goes out. It'll be the leccy next and then won't we have fun down on the farm?

Got the pilot light to work, thank God, but it took a lot of clicks before the flame finally appeared and the boiler roared up. I just hope it doesn't go again as it's started snowing. Sod this for a game of soldiers.

Lit a fire in the front room, and what with the snow outside and the roaring log fire it felt Christmassy and I'm regretting putting the tree away so early. Considering the state of the roads I won't be going anywhere so I might as well get on with it and watch a film. The snow is really coming down now so I rang Vera and Murphy to compare weather reports and it seems that out of the three of us I've got it worse. Never mind, I've got food in and the house is warm so I'm laughing.

The leccy goes right in the middle of *Batteries Not Included*. I was really enjoying it lying on the couch with the dogs on top of me when the bloody lot went. The snow's stopped at least but there's no point in ringing the leccy board up as you only get a recorded message telling you which areas are without power and how they expect to have it back on as soon as possible.

Didn't move off the couch, just lay there listening to the bloody burglar alarm beeping. I'll have to ring them up otherwise the cops might kick the door in. Rang them up and told them it was a false alarm so there's no danger of the police rushing to my rescue, although on second thoughts that might not have been a bad idea. They also told me what to do to turn the alarm off, thank God, as it was driving me crazy.

Made a cup of tea and got back on the couch. Louis snoring his head off and doing his best trying to drown out that wind outside. Wished Sean wasn't on holiday as I've got to brave the storm again to feed and water the critters which I'd better do before it gets dark. It gets dark around four o'clock down here and this leccy better bloody well be back on before then as I'm not sitting here in the bloody dark with a couple of candles like one of those Brontës.

Bored stiff. Haven't got any batteries for the radio and there's not much juice left in the laptop. Buster has peed up the leg of the piano as he won't go out in the cold. I don't blame him; wish I didn't have to. When is this f*****g leccy going back on?

The leccy came back on but I've missed the end of the film and there's nothing else on worth watching as per bloody usual. There's a couple of DVDs I haven't watched yet that I don't really want to watch as I'm not really in the mood for them but as they've sat there unopened for two years I feel that I ought to and get it over with.

I'm talking shit now. I'm going to make a butty and a cup of tea and then I'm going to park my arse and read that book I got for Christmas.

Leccy went out just as I was putting the kettle on. What the leccy board are doing is called a prick tease.

*

Leccy still off. Writing this in bed even though it's only quarter to four but it's already growing darker. I fed the animals earlier than usual and that was a bloody effort. There's lots of snow down by the pigs, lovely soft stuff that I kicked about, although the pigs aren't very keen. Dragged a bail of straw from the shed in the field for them. As I couldn't open the gate because it was jammed by a snow drift I had to climb over it which was surprisingly accident-free considering I've got a massive pair of wellies on.

There was a great bank of snow where the wind had swept it across the field and I had this terrible urge to roll in it as it was untouched by man or animal and was just begging to be messed up. I resisted this childish urge for all of ten seconds before cracking, and lunged into the huge mound of snow face down, instantly regretting my action.

Struggled to get up but I couldn't see as the snow was all over my face and glasses plus I was bloody freezing. Fell back into this mountain of snow a second time as I was seriously hampered by my wellies because the tops kept scooping snow up and pulling me down.

Soaked to the skin but vertical at last, I dragged a bale of straw from the shed and through the snow. Getting it over the gate was harder than I thought and by the time I'd dragged the bloody thing up to the pig pen I was sweating like a glass blower's arse. At least I wasn't cold, apart from my feet that no longer felt like mine, and the pig's shed looked very cosy with this bed of new straw. I could have quite happily got in with them myself.

Went back over the gate again to get some hay for the goats. Thank God the sheep have that great bale of hay and I don't have to hike across fields lugging bales.

It's started snowing again so I've lit a couple of candles and taken to my bed as there's bugger all else to do. The battery has died on my mobile and as there's no power I can't charge it up. I'm not standing in that freezing kitchen yakking on that antwacky [Liverpool expression meaning 'old-fashioned'] phone that I can't hear a bloody thing on – no, I'll die here in my bed.

The leccy came back on at about half four and I felt like primitive man emerging from his cave and into the blinding sun. God Bless the Omnipotent Leccy Board. Fed the dogs then made them go in the garden. Neither of them seemed fond of the idea but out they went and then behaved like maniacs, charging around in the snow, Louis in particular really going for it.

There's a few missed calls on my phone now that I've finally got it going again. Rang Murphy, he said he might come down tomorrow depending on the weather but in the meanwhile I'm to 'sit tight'. What the hell does he mean by that? What else am I supposed to do? Am I to 'sit tight' and await Sir Murphy to come to the rescue riding on a f*****g snowplough? The arrogance of the man. It's only a bit of snow. It's not like I'm in a chalet trapped underneath an avalanche.

Made a meatloaf for dinner with mashed spuds and spinach and realized that it's the meal they always have on *Family Guy*. Maybe it's because a meatloaf dinner is easy to draw but I think it's meant to represent the kind of meal white American suburban families eat all the time. Who cares? It's delicious.

Watched the telly and took the dogs out before calling it a day. It really is beautiful outside and as quiet as the grave. Not a sound. The virgin snow smothering the fields looks artificial for it twinkles in the moonlight as if lit by a million LED lights. It's a magical sight and an insult to compare it to the polystyrene efforts they create in department store grottos.

Do they still have grottos in shops? Would a few nodding dwarves and tinfoil impress today's kids? I suppose the tiny ones might enjoy it but older kids would no doubt dismiss it as rubbish and go back to their iPhones.

I don't suppose the practice of plonking the kids on the knee of an old man in a red suit is allowed any more for obvious reasons. Jaysus, if a teacher puts a plaster on a kid's knee these days and gives him a hug they can be charged with child abuse. Maybe the kids could just shake the old boy's hand before being moved swiftly on as it would be a shame to drop him as he's an important figure in a child's life. What I remember about sitting on Santa's knee in T. J. Hughes' grotto was that he stunk of ciggy smoke, but then everybody did in those days, even the kids.

I've given up on this book I'm reading set in a rural community as it's a load of crap. All the characters who are working class are painted out to be shifty skivers and have been given an ooh-aar accent whilst the others, who are frightfully middle class, are portrayed as superior beings and their dialogue is written as if they speak like a 1940s BBC radio announcer.

It must have something to do with this weather and being confined to barracks that's got my back up but I hate the way this author has the gardener constantly taking his cap off and scratching his head absently when the lady of the house asks him a question. None of the posh women go to work as all they seem to do is arrange flowers in the church and organize whist drives. Farmers' wives milk cows and have loads of kids and single women are either dykey or eccentrics. The working-class women go out to work as charladies, barmaids or waitresses and the single mums live in run-down cottages with scruffy kids and are branded as slatterns.

I've had enough now. I've been scribbling in this all day and I don't know why. To vent my anger at being housebound? Or is it just because I felt like putting pen to paper? Whatever the reason, I'm going to bed. What a bloody day.

Oh, and while I'm on the subject of irritants – the school run. It takes a brave man to drive down the lanes with a tank-sized four-by-four bearing down on you being driven by a mother in a hurry to drop the sprogs off. The village is filled with cars, tanks and trucks at dropping-off and picking-up times and I avoid it like I would liver and onions. By the time I was eight I was getting a train and a bus on my own to school. Looking back, I can see why I used to look forward to the journey as it was a blow for independence. I was very pally with the ticket collector at Green Lane station. The woman in the kiosk at the side of Olivieri's café where I'd buy a bag of pear drops was another mate, as was the bus conductor who used to sing and seemed to know everyone. It wasn't just a journey it was an adventure. Those kids strapped up in the back of Mummy's car aren't experiencing life. I sound like an old nit I know, and I don't blame parents for wanting to see their kids safely to and from school. Bus services aren't that plentiful and these are strange not to say dangerous times, and you can't expect a child to walk home alone on a winter's evening down a country lane, especially as these lanes are now teeming with speeding traffic.

If you live in a really rural area as I do, then don't expect to be able to order a pizza. There's no Deliveroo round here. Our chippy is miles away, as is the nearest Chinese takeaway, and I can remember that not so long ago such a thing as a cappuccino was unheard of in the cafés of the local town.

But really these are all niggles when you look at all the benefits that living in a rural area offers, and once you get your head around that and learn to adapt to country life then there's no going back to city living. I certainly couldn't. Unless of course I've got a new-build luxury housing estate on my doorstep, then I'm heading for the woods.

Sheds and Apples

If you read the Sunday supplements then you'll know that sheds are extremely fashionable these days, particularly these designer 'shepherd's huts' that are fast becoming de rigueur in the back gardens of the wealthy. Apparently David Cameron has a £25K hut, or it might be a £12K one depending on which paper you believe. Either way I think it's a bit pricey for a shed. I've seen one or two original shepherd's huts dotted around the marshes and while at one time they were a welcome shelter for a shepherd on a cold night, to me they smack of loneliness.

No longer seen as simply a functional construction, somewhere to stash the lawn mower and jam jars full of nails, the humble shed has taken on a new lease of life. For a lot of people their shed is a place of sanctuary, a refuge where one can escape from the hustle and bustle of the household, or (if eighties sitcoms are to be believed) a place where the man of the house can get away from his nagging wife.

Growing up in Birkenhead, nearly everyone I knew had a shed in his or her back yard. Mary-Next-Door's shed was very orderly: on one side she kept her weekly delivery of coal and on the other side, but only during the winter months, she stored her mangle with a clean dishcloth, wrung out and as stiff as a board, perched on top of the snowy white rubber rollers.

Our shed was a little more chaotic for as well as my dad's tools and my mother's gardening equipment it was also home to my menagerie of animals. In a large hutch lived two guinea pigs, with another hutch on top that housed a rabbit, blocking out the light from the solitary window. There was a decent-sized fish tank that the man in the pet shop on Church Road had given me because there was a small crack in it. Together with my mate Bob Carey we gingerly carried it back to the shed to serve as suitable accommodation for the ever-increasing colony of mice. To add to this collection of critters there was a hamster, a tank full of catfish, a ferret and our tortoise Hot Rod, hibernating for the winter just like Mary's mangle.

When the TV series *Batman* came on to our screens in the sixties and every kid became Batman-obsessed, the shed became the Joker's Hideout, the Bat Cave and the Catwoman's Lair respectively. It also served as a diabolical mastermind's headquarters when we played *The Avengers*, it substituted for the Tardis during our *Doctor Who* phase, and it acted as Dr Frankenstein's laboratory after I was given a chemistry set for Christmas.

We certainly got our money's worth out of that shed, and after my parents died and the house went back to the landlord the shed went to live in my sister's garden where it remained until quite recently when it finally collapsed in a high wind. I remember the day my dad dismantled the creepy old shed that had sat in the corner of our yard: it had been converted out of a wartime Anderson shelter and was falling to bits. Now it was finally being replaced by a brand-spanking-new shed made out of pine that came as a flat pack. Inside he wrote on the wall 'Erected in 1964', and it was still going strong forty years later. As I said, we certainly got our money's worth out of that shed.

There are competitions now for the proud owner of the best shed, and what people have managed to do with such a comparatively small space is astonishing. From fairy tale hobbit houses to mock Tudor mini mansions there are some remarkable sheds out there in the back gardens and yards of British homes. Reading about what people had done to their humble sheds inspired me to transform the two that I've got in my garden into something different.

I've already mentioned the croquet lawn hut that was renovated and transformed into the Witch's House; well, the other shed, situated in the garden and with wonderful views, was just an unremarkable modern inexpensive shed. It stayed that way for years until, inspired by the

multi-coloured wooden chattel houses of Barbados, I got Sean to give it a makeover and paint it in shades of blue, pink and green. It needs another paint job now as it's wide open to the elements but it's a great place to sit, listen to the radio and admire the view.

My old table from my flat in Victoria mansions is in there as well as a chair that used to belong to Murphy; there's also a small sofa from a junk shop, a battered old chest of drawers and a load of books. This humble shed is known by the grand title of 'The Summer House', possibly because that's when it's most used, although I'm sitting here now writing this and it's only April, yet the evening is warm. We badly need rain as there hasn't been a drop for God knows how long. There have been muted warnings in the media about an impending drought, plus worrying news that orchards around the country will undoubtedly fail to deliver the goods.

Last year my orchard, which was planted eight years ago with apple, plum, greengage, pear, peach and cherry trees, produced half a dozen apples, a solitary peach and a handful of cherries the birds had kindly left me after they'd picked the trees clean. We grow a variety of apples to aid pollination: Discovery, Red Devil, Bramley and my favourite, the Beauty of Bath, an apple that tastes sharp at the first bite before mellowing into sweetness. The flesh of the apple has a red hue to it that made me think I had bleeding gums at first as the snowy white flesh turned blood-red right after I'd bitten into it.

The year before that there'd been an abundance of fruit, and it's a wonderful feeling to be able to stroll around and eat a fresh peach straight off a tree followed by a plum and an apple.

As I'd been given an apple press we had a go at making cider. Unfortunately, when we opened a bottle at Christmas it had turned into vinegar. Still, looking on the bright side I had a plentiful supply to put on my chips all year.

But as I write there are great cracks in the ground around the fields and the orchard where the ground has split as it's so dry. Walking around the fields surveying these cracks and the dust that the light breeze is whipping up, I can't help comparing this scorched earth with scenes of the Midwest during the great American Depression.

The weather grows increasingly warmer over the coming weeks and I seem to be forever watering the allotment and hanging baskets. The summer solstice falls on what the media tells us is the hottest day since Noah first picked up a hammer and said I better get on with this ark. A slight exaggeration on my part, but then every time we have a hot day it's inevitably heralded as the warmest day since the year dot.

The dogs are exhausted and stay inside in the cool, all except for Eddie who persists in stretching out on a flagstone that's so hot you could fry an egg on it. It must be the Mexican in him.

The pigs spend their time lazing in the shade under the trees in the field, and when they come in for their dinner I cool them down by spraying them with the hose. Holly the sow loves it, as do the others, but Tom runs into the shed as he hates getting wet.

The heat seems to intensify and I'm grateful that I'm not in the city where I'm told sleep is an impossibility in this stultifying humidity. I've had no trouble sleeping as I open all my bedroom windows and keep the curtains closed all day so that come bedtime the room is cool and there's no need for the industrial fan I acquired years ago that's so violent I have to grip the mattress in case I'm thrown up the wall like the mother in *Poltergeist*.

Towards the end of June the hot spell is almost over, and now I'm wondering if that's all we're getting in the way of a summer. Thankfully it's started to rain, and not just a light shower either – it's coming down in buckets. It rains solidly for a couple of days and the difference in the fields, orchard and garden is remarkable. I love the fresh smell of the garden following a heavy rainfall, that mixture of damp earth and the pungent scent from the roses and the honeysuckle. The branches of the fruit trees are showing signs of a promising yield and the cherry trees are laden with fruit ripe for the picking. We've kept the birds away by flying two kites that resemble giant birds of prey over the trees. It's obviously worked: if I eat any more cherries I'm going to turn scarlet.

I decide I'm going to seriously study the rulebook this year and make a cider that's fit to drink. I also vow to make apple juice and promise to make a couple of apple pies every weekend. The windfall apples go to the pigs as usual and the ones that are left over after I've forced bags of them on everyone I know I'm going to store for the winter.

Stored apples last a surprisingly long time if they're put away properly. The apples should be healthy and without any sign of bruising or wormholes. Wrap each individual apple in newspaper and place them in a basket or a box. One rotten apple can spoil a whole box so the paper will protect the apples if one suddenly turns bad. Store the box in a cool place like a dry cellar or garage and they should see you through the winter months.

*

I'm sitting in the Summer House again, enjoying the scent from the two tubs of sweetpeas that sit by the door, although it's no longer warm and balmy; instead there's a bite in the air. Maybe it's time to decamp to the Witch's House and make use of the wood burner.

It's time to go back in the house, but before the sun sets I want to take the dogs for a last walk around the woods – those dogs that are willing to go that is. Bullseye, Conchita and Eddie are keen but Boycie isn't having any of it and he heads for the house to join Louis, who's too old to go on a lengthy walk, and Olga, who like Buster isn't very keen on thistles.

And while I'm on the subject of dogs . . .

For the Love of Dogs

I'd much sooner go to the village school fete
than an awards ceremony any day. They're
reassuringly old-fashioned with stalls and games
reminiscent of another era. The fire brigade turn
up and proudly display their highly polished
engine to the delight of the little boys who are
ecstatic at being able to touch and even climb
on the machine of their dreams. There's usually
a chap with his collection of birds of prey, and a
local band and a couple of girl singers, dressed in
full military uniform and belting out the hits of
World War Two. Dame Vera would be proud.

I always head for the home-baked cake stall as these village
women are expert bakers, and I never leave without buying
a quilt from one of the ladies who belongs to the Quilters
Group in the village hall. These handmade quilts are top-
quality and I keep telling them to put their prices up as
they're massively underselling themselves. But they never
do as they're too modest.

The tea, coffee and beer flows, there's burgers, cakes
and sandwiches, and everyone seems to be in a good
mood apart from the odd child throwing a gigantic wobble
because it can't have something it wants. Overall, the entire
experience can only be described as charming.

I've opened quite a fetes in the area now. They're short on celebrities around here, there's only a few, which explains why I'm hauled out to do the honours. I never know quite how to behave when opening a fete. Do I adopt the manner of a Lord Mayor and make a lengthy speech or do I go for the Lady of the Manor approach, waving graciously and announcing 'I declare this fete open'?

In the end I normally just say 'Hiya' followed by something totally inappropriate, forgetting there's children in the crowd.

Recently, a local village held a fete and Novelty Dog Show to raise funds for the village hall. The organizer wrote to me asking if I'd be a judge, which is a job I don't relish as you'll inevitably upset someone who thought their dog/baby/marrow/cake/horse deserved first prize. I couldn't help out on this occasion as I was filming in a certain dogs home, but looking at the programme of events I'll make sure I'm available next year. Amongst the categories was 'The Prettiest Bitch Award', 'The Dog with the Waggiest Tail', 'The Fastest Sausage Eater' and the 'Olga O'Grady Trophy for Best Rescue Dog'. A local lady won the latter and burst into tears when she was presented with the cup for her dog Albert. The afternoon was a great success and £400 was raised for the Village Hall Development Fund. See what I mean about events like this being charming? There's a marked absence of cynicism and everyone gets involved, including the dogs.

The first dog to enter my life was Bran the retired sheepdog, a Border collie brought home by my dad. I was too young to remember him but by all accounts he found it hard to adapt to his new surroundings having been a working dog all his life in the fields of Ireland and went a bit stir-crazy. Sadly, he died from distemper.

I plagued my parents for years for a dog until eventually Dad cracked and despite my mother's protestations he came home one day with a Border collie puppy who was named Bran after his predecessor. He turned out to be a sickly little thing and just like the original Bran he too died from distemper.

For a nine-year-old to lose his puppy after a few weeks is a devastating blow and I was bereft. However, thanks to the remarkable powers of recovery we're blessed with as children I perked up a bit when my dad brought home a white rabbit to ease my loss. My mother wasn't amused as this rabbit was quite a big buck and had a tendency to jump up at her, hitting her in the chest. The rabbit obviously didn't like her as he was fine with me but as soon as he saw my ma he'd go for her. Perhaps he knew that she wasn't a big fan of animals and was out to get her after he'd heard her remark that a rabbit belonged in a pot with carrot and onion.

It would be some years before I got another dog – thirty-one to be precise. Every morning at 3.30 a.m I'd drag myself out of bed and go to work on *The Big Breakfast* show as Lily Savage and then in the evening, matinees included, I was on stage in the West End in *Prisoner Cell Block H – The Musical*. The house I'd just bought was being gutted and I was living in a building site so the last thing I really needed in my life was a puppy.

One early December morning a litter of puppies were brought on to the show. They were shih-tzu/bichon frise crosses and one of them slowly mooched across the floor and sat on my foot, happy to remain there until I picked him up and plonked him on my knee. That was it, I was putty in his paws. This little tyke had picked me to stake his claim and without hesitation I announced I was taking this pup home with me. Barbara Windsor, who was one of that morning's guests, asked me what I was going to do with him while I was working. 'Take him with me,' I told her, and that's exactly what I did, for everywhere I went Buster went with me.

BUSTER

Buster was a city dog who loved travelling, especially if he knew there was a hotel and a theatre at the end of it. Show business was in this dog's veins and he made appearances in just about every theatre in the country. He didn't do much, he just waddled on and sat there. Occasionally he'd see something that excited him in the audience and then he'd stand, wag his tail and bark. He was a real scene-stealer, and to make sure that he got the last and biggest laugh, as he left the stage he'd cock his leg up the proscenium arch.

At first Buster took to country life like a duck to water as there were so many distractions. On the very first day he went missing – not that I noticed as I was too busy having a nervous breakdown unpacking. My next-door neighbour brought him round. She told me that he'd got through the fence into her field, chased the sheep and then, entering the house via the cat flap, terrorized the cat, ate her dinner, jumped on to the sofa and made himself at home. I made

sure that all the fences were secure after that and kept a very close eye on him.

Luckily my neighbour was very understanding and her sheep weren't lambing, as farmers are quite within their rights to shoot a dog that is running amok amongst their livestock. So keep your dog on a lead if you're crossing a field with livestock in it, or better yet, find an empty field, and don't forget to shut the gate behind you and take your rubbish home with you. I'm sounding like that public service advertisement that used to be on TV involving two animated characters called Joe and Petunia who incurred the wrath of an angry farmer for failing to follow the Country Code. Remember it?

The chickens fascinated Buster. He'd patrol the perimeter fence of their coop barking furiously at them, putting me in mind of one of the Japanese guards in the TV series *Tenko*.

'Chicken, bow or be punished!'

As you know, my first chickens were those tiny little bantams and Solly the rooster. He was extremely friendly and liked nothing more than to sit on my shoulder as I went about my business, and I grew very fond of him. They lived in a hen house in the garden and were free to roam. Buster, having been repeatedly warned off, had learned to sit and watch them from a distance – or so I thought, for his jealousy knew no bounds, and while I thought he was being a good lad by leaving them alone he was in fact quietly plotting his evil revenge on Solly.

Without warning he attacked one day and with one bite he snapped Solly's neck, charged across the garden and into the house and dropped his spoils of war triumphantly on the kitchen floor. Buster had turned killer, and for his crime he was banished to the bedroom where he spent the rest of the day sulking under the bed until I decided to forgive him. Solly's harem didn't last much longer, as a few days later the fox got them.

The long grass in the field that Buster hated so much hid an enemy I was unaware of. The tick. You've got to watch out for these disgusting parasites as they can transmit deadly diseases. Ticks aren't just found in fields and woods, inner-city parks have their fair share of the little horrors as well. In the case of vector-borne disease the symptoms are hard to recognize until it's too late so it's wise to have your dog screened annually. Thankfully there are quite a few preventative treatments available to safeguard your dog from ticks. I'm forever giving mine the once-over for any sign of them and I believe that all dog owners should do the same. Should you find a tick on your pet then your vet will sell you a little instrument that pulls it neatly out, but you must make sure that you remove every bit of the tick and don't make the mistake of leaving the head behind.

I've taken my tick remover on all my trips filming in Africa and Borneo and it proved itself to be invaluable as nearly every day I'd find a couple lurking somewhere on my body.

One day I noticed that Buster had stopped running around the garden chasing rabbits and instead he lay tucked away quietly in the laundry room. He definitely wasn't himself so off we went to his least favourite place in the world, the vet's, where he was diagnosed with fox mange.

He was very ill and it was obvious that he was in pain as he couldn't lie down. I sat up all night supporting him with my feet so he could sleep without toppling over on to his side and howling in pain. It was touch and go for a while and I was beside myself with worry that I might lose this little fella, blaming myself for moving to the countryside and exposing him to fox mange. Foxes were not high on the list of my favourite animals. They'd killed my chickens and now, it seemed, they were doing a good job of finishing Buster off. However, as much as I hated them at the time, nothing would induce me to support the evil blood sport of fox hunting.

Buster was a great actor and knew when to play the sympathy card. When he was with me he acted the part of the dying Camille but out on the green for a run with Murphy he was back to his old self. That dog could play me like a Stradivarius but I didn't care as he was getting better ... and while he made a full recovery I was in need of two weeks in a Swiss clinic as I was a wreck from a combination of worry and sleep deprivation. Dogs, eh?

Later on in life he developed a serious ulcer on his eye and spent three weeks in the care of the Animal Health Trust who managed to save the eye. I wasn't allowed to visit as it would only upset him but by all accounts he didn't seem that bothered as he became their star patient, showered with love and affection by the staff. I'll be forever in their debt.

During his absence from scene-stealing on the end of my desk on *The Paul O'Grady Show*, Buster received thousands of get well cards from the public, and the first thing every star guest who came on the show asked me was 'How's Buster?' The greatest of gentlemen the late Sir Roger Moore rang me frequently at home to check on his progress as he was besotted with Buster and insisted on sitting with him whenever he appeared as a guest on the show. Buster, equally in love, was more than happy to oblige.

The day Buster returned to the show as good as new – better, in fact, thanks to the skills of the vets at the Animal Health Trust – he was given a hero's welcome. Even the crew clapped, and there were tears in wardrobe and make-up. He 'todged' around the set, tail wagging, lapping up the applause, and I couldn't have been prouder to have this extraordinary little dog as a companion.

(It was Murphy who nicknamed him Todger. Nothing to do with the size of his tackle but because of the way he bounced around, which Murphy decided was called 'todging'.)

Buster had a sixth sense whenever the time was coming when I was going up to London. He'd follow me everywhere and any bag I happened to be packing he'd sit in it to make sure I got the message that he was coming with me. He'd wagged his tail on many a television programme but it wasn't until he started sitting on my desk during the first part of *The Paul O'Grady Show* that he really grabbed the public's attention and started a craze – Bustermania. We never sold the 'Nodding Busters', they were given away to guests and prize-winners, and soon everyone wanted one. They became much sought after. I once saw one that I'd signed on eBay that sold for £250.

Just as it had been for me, Buster's rise to fame had happened by accident as for the first days of the show he'd stayed in the dressing room until he realized that he was missing out and kicked off by barking at the door until I let him come with me. He loved sitting on that desk and showing off, and in the years that the show ran both on ITV and Channel 4 I'd play stooge to a dog who was an expert at drawing focus.

The show ran for more years than I'd thought it ever would and Buster was soon beginning to show his age. The day he declined to leave the dressing room was the day I retired him.

He was twelve years old when we discovered that he was riddled with cancer and obviously in pain. I had no choice but to do the right thing and have him put to sleep.

As a tribute, the producer made a video montage of his long career and it was played at the end of the show. I couldn't sit through it and left the goodbyes to the guest, who just happened to be a sympathetic Delia Smith. As I ran through the make-up department howling like a baby I could see that the make-up girls were in the same state, as were the crew, wardrobe and the audience.

His death made the papers, and one broadsheet described him as 'the greatest canine star since Lassie'. There's a bronze statue of Buster just inside the door of reception at Battersea Dogs & Cats Home with that quote on a little plaque on his plinth.

Sean built him a coffin and he was laid to rest with great ceremony in the garden, and in the tradition of every good funeral we all did the decent thing. We got blind drunk and maudlin.

I cried for months after Buster died and I'm not ashamed to admit it. He'd accompanied me every step of the way on what had been an extremely interesting decade and to this day I miss that extraordinary little dog.

BRUNO AND SWEEPEA

I got these two from a local breeder. Bruno was a beautiful golden retriever puppy who looked like a plump little teddy bear with his pot-belly and golden coat. Although he wasn't timid he was prone to worrying, especially if he had a toy in his mouth as Sweep, the tough guy, a tiny black Cavalier King

Charles poodle cross who was extremely affectionate but who unfortunately had a tendency to bully Bruno, would take it off him. Even at an early age Sweep would take his ball and his toys off him, guarding them in his basket as a sad-eyed Bruno stood back and watched mournfully, patiently waiting for Sweep to grow bored and wander off, enabling him to storm the castle walls and rescue his prized possessions.

Buster was obsessed with both of them when they first arrived, spending hours trying to hump the pups despite me constantly warning him that they were far too young and that he'd probably get five years. Thankfully his ardour was soon dampened by constant rebuttals and he finally gave up, pretending that they didn't exist.

As Bruno and Sweep grew older they became more adventurous, particularly of a night-time. Where once they'd been content to follow me off the lead as we walked around the garden and up the drive for their final chance to pee before we all hit the sack they were now jumping the wall and going further afield – much further.

The first time it happened Sweep had obviously picked up the scent of something interesting and in a flash he was off down the fields with Bruno in hot pursuit, Sweep letting out an annoying 'yip, yip, yip' as his war cry with Bruno's booming basso bark echoing in his wake. It's not fun walking around fields and woods in the dark with a torch that's next to useless thanks to a badly needed change of batteries. I'd hear them yipping and barking away in the nearby woods and despite calling them repeatedly in a voice that I reckon could have been heard in France they completely ignored me.

Returning to the house bloody and muddy I sat up waiting for them, semi-demented with worry, my inner voice nagging away at me.

What would I do if a farmer shot them for chasing sheep?

Or if they got lost or trapped somewhere, not to mention run over if they made it on to a main road?

Or even dog-napped?

Or if they fell down a well?

At four a.m. they returned, panting furiously, totally exhausted and full of themselves. I wanted to kill the pair of them but I was so thankful to get them back all I could do was hug them and cry tears of relief. They went out on the lead at night after that until stupidly, as I was taking out the rubbish one evening, I left the back door open and not being one to miss an opportunity Sweep made his escape with Bruno hot on his tail.

Another session of tramping around the fields at midnight followed, only this time in snow and ice. I could hear them but couldn't see them, nor could I predict their location as their yips and barks echoed confusingly in the cold, dark silence.

Once again I returned home dogless and colder than a fishfinger, and as Buster had selfishly let the fire go out in my absence I virtually sprawled across the top of the Aga in an attempt to get warm. Mine is a cold house at the best of times but it's positively arctic when you've left the kitchen door open on a winter's night and are sat waiting for the prodigal dogs to come home.

My friend Moira, who'd dog-sit for me when I was working in London, also experienced nail-biting nights waiting for the escape artistes to come home. The situation was growing impossible as they were no longer restricting their jaunts to night-time and consequently doors had to remain locked at all times and keeping an eye on them was bordering on an all-consuming obsession.

Eventually Moira took them to live with her in London. While walking them on the common they were still prone to take off oblivious to Moira's near-hysterical screams as she ran after them. And when they came down here, which was frequently, they still couldn't resist the lure of chasing a rabbit into the woods. But at least the all-nighters had stopped.

Each puppy that I brought home, Bruno would nurse it. He was the nanny dog who allowed them to sleep on his back, crawl all over him and chew his ear without ever losing his patience with them, unless they overstepped the mark and then he'd soon put them in their place.

When Eddie arrived, no bigger than a baby guinea pig, Bruno acted as chauffeur, carrying Eddie around in his mouth by holding on to his knitted jumper with his teeth while Eddie, contentedly dangling like a fancy handbag, would enjoy the ride. Bruno loved to pace, his ever-wagging tail clearing the coffee table as he walked round it with a slipper in his mouth. He loved to carry things and would always greet you with a little present – a blanket, one of your best shoes, a dog basket, or Eddie. He was very affectionate but he wasn't the brightest pup in the litter, which only added to this beauty's charms.

Sweep, on the other hand, was as smart as a whip, a daredevil, a charmer and a complete mummy's boy as he was devoted to Moira. When Sweep was around he was the top dog in the pack and all the others knew it, except Buster, who considered himself half human and didn't count.

Bruno went first, aged fourteen. Sweep lasted another year, then his heart gave out. Moira was bereft, as were we all, and they were both buried along with Sean's old black Labrador Jess in a quiet part of the orchard.

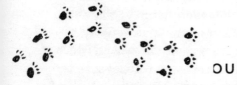

OUIS

In 2013 I was filming a series called *Eyes Down* for the BBC set in a bingo hall and we were on location in an old cinema in North London. There was a really good assortment of diverse but practical shops in the area, including a pet shop.

Foolishly I wandered in one day during my dinner break and came back with a shih-tzu puppy as a birthday present for Joan who had talked endlessly about getting a dog. She named him Barney and he turned out to be quite a character, and despite endless illnesses resulting in a couple of brushes with death and the loss of an eye the old boy is still going strong at the ripe old age of fourteen. He travels into work with her and spends his time plotting how to get out of her office so he can have a good root around the bins to see if there's anything nice to eat. He's another mummy's boy, devoted to Joan. His eye was obviously giving him a lot of trouble because since he's had it removed he's come into his own. His hearing's not what it was and he has moments of vagueness but I reckon he'll see us all out.

I'd never normally buy a dog from a pet shop as there's more than a good chance that the litter has come from a puppy farm. The pet shops of New York horrify me as the windows are stuffed with a variety of puppies, a cruel practice I'd stupidly believed to have gone out of fashion along with the sight of tortoises piled on top of each other. It surprises me that New Yorkers with their supposed love of dogs haven't taken action to stop this, or is it just me who lets my disgust be known each time I visit that city and pass a pet shop? I was escorted off the premises by two shop assistants after 'giving out' in one shop in Greenwich Village, and in another one on Lexington Avenue I was told that if I didn't leave they'd call the cops which shut me up as I didn't fancy being the bitch for some bald-headed twenty-stone killer in an orange boiler suit. I also had Cilla Black with me and I would've hated for her to face tabloid headlines blaring 'Cilla in Pet Shop Arrest' when she got home – that's if she didn't get sent down as an accomplice and carted off to the Women's Pen. So instead of chaining myself to the hamster tank and encouraging Cilla to lie on the floor, the pair of us made a dignified exit. Cilla later told a friend that she'd never expected to be threatened with the cops in a pet shop.

The puppies in the North London pet shop weren't in the window, they were at the back of the shop in a pen, and despite my reservations and out of pity for these pups I not only bought one for Joan but a couple of days later I went back and bought one for myself. He was christened Bingo, as it seemed appropriate since the series I was filming was all about that game, and despite having gastric problems he was a smashing little fella.

One morning after I'd fed the animals I noticed a black and white cat sitting on the wall at the end of the garden. I'd never seen a cat on the property before and as it didn't seem bothered having me in close proximity I assumed it wasn't feral.

I wish I'd chased it off as, searching for Bingo a little later, I eventually found him drowned at the bottom of the pool. The pool, which I never went near for years after, used to have a light cover that you rolled back. I can only assume that Bingo chased the cat and somehow slipped under the cover and drowned. I blamed myself and wandered around for days unable to get the image of Bingo's little body at the bottom of that pool out of my mind.

I vowed that I'd never get another dog, but unbeknown to me Murphy had paid a visit to the same pet shop and brought home another puppy.

'To stop you mithering yourself to death,' he explained as he handed him over.

I called him Louis – short for Lewisham, strangely enough, as we hit upon the name while driving through it. Just like Bingo and Barney, Louis suffered from gastric troubles. After a visit to the vet to check him over it was discovered that he had a deformed sternum as well as needing a special diet to control his diarrhoea. The vet,

having examined all three pups, confirmed my suspicions that they were from puppy farms.

But despite Louis now being deaf and arthritic, and coping with failing eyesight and a dicky heart, he's still the feisty little dog he always was, only he's just that little bit slower these days – but don't tell him I told you. Saying that, Louis, the only one of us who's brave enough to face the geese – I'll tell you more about them later – still has his moments of madness when he'll tear around the house or garden just for the sheer hell of it.

MISS OLGA

On the teatime chat show we frequently featured animals from rescue centres looking for a home. I'd always managed to resist temptation until the night a minute little scruffbag of a cairn terrier was brought in. She was called Olga, and I knew there and then as she sat in the palm of my hand that she was coming home with me that night.

I reckoned at first that Olga just might be part Tasmanian Devil as she was an unholy terror, falling through the stairwell and knocking herself out, falling in the pond, snarling at anyone who dared try and pick her up, and stealing Buster and Louis's dinner. Olga was a demon, yet when she was curled up asleep on your lap you forgave her everything.

As she got older she thankfully settled down; she still had an edge but she was far more friendly, even if it did take a brave man to attempt to pick her up. It's a different story when it comes to children as she'll sit lapping it up when she's mobbed by a gang of schoolkids in the park all wanting to stroke her.

She's also prone to attacking picnics, nicking the odd sandwich or biscuit, and once she snuck into the *Loose Women* production office and stole a purse from a handbag that was sat on the floor. The Loose Women swore that I'd trained her to do this but I didn't, she's just a natural pickpocket. Fagin would've loved her.

Buster had died and would no longer sit on the desk on *The Paul O'Grady Show*.

I was stood on a deserted railway station in the Midwest waiting for the last train out of the one-horse town we were playing in. I turned to Olga, sat sniffing a suitcase, and pointing at her declared in a loud voice, 'This time I'm going to do it for you, baby, this time I'm gonna make you a star ...' (cue orchestra).

'I had a dream, a dream about you, baby.'

I think I'm getting confused with the musical *Gypsy*, the scene where Madame Rose, down but not defeated at the news that the star turn, in this instance one Dainty June, has defected, turns to Louise, the soon-to-be Gypsy Rose Lee, and promises to make her a star.

Olga did go on in Buster's place, after a suitable period of mourning, and sitting bolt upright on the desk, imperious and aloof and acting as if I were dirt, she became an instant hit. Just as with her predecessor, nodding dogs were made in her image as giveaway prizes. We also had Olga pencil cases and moneyboxes.

She loved being on TV and there was no way I was ever allowed to leave the dressing room without her. As soon as the door was opened she shot out and headed for the studio.

After the show she could always be found in the green room begging for the cocktail sausages that had been cooked in honey, which she loved. Guests would fuss over her and the old pro that she is would roll over and look cute, hoping for a belly tickle and a sausage.

Just like Buster, Olga wasn't overkeen on the countryside. She was a city gal, so one day when she took to the cool floor of the laundry room I assumed she was sulking, as usual, but would soon get over it. I was due to fly out to South Africa to film a series of *Animal Orphans*, and since Olga was off her food I asked Moira to take her to the vet. I was worried about her and in two minds whether I should fly, but cancelling a big job that had already been set up at such short notice would mean not just opening a can of worms but a nest of anacondas.

I'd been in Africa less than a day when Moira rang. The reason Olga had been behaving the way she had was not, as I'd hoped, down to a simple stomach upset, it was something far more sinister. She had a large tumour wrapped around one of her kidneys. They'd operated and removed both the tumour and her kidney but the prognosis wasn't good and the vet thought it might be kinder if I had her put to sleep.

Needless to say I felt hopeless stuck out in Africa and unable to help her. I was also angry with myself and riddled with guilt for leaving her. After speaking to the vet in what was a lengthy phone call I was determined that she should be given a chance to live, so Olga went home to recuperate in comfort. Nursed by Moira, she made a full recovery.

I was never so relieved to see her than when I got home from Africa, but Olga being Olga she acted as she always did by completely ignoring me until she felt the time was right to approach me for a fuss.

Four years after her op, this tough little terrier is still going strong. She's twelve now and a grand old lady who is still as lively and feisty as she's always been. As I write this she's sat on the patio staring in at me as if she knows I'm writing about her. Maybe the offer of a gravy bone will persuade her not to seek an injunction.

BULLSEYE

Poor old Bully Boy is not university material. He's scared of stairs and goes through a bizarre ritual of turning around in a circle before attempting to climb them which, on a bad day, can take some time. He barks at planes and at the full moon, and each time an animal appears on the telly he goes berserk. It amazes me as even a cartoon dog will set him off – and they say dogs can't see images on the television? Well, I'm afraid Bullseye might disagree with the experts on that one.

He was another unwanted pup that turned up on the teatime show looking for a home. Small and plump with a rotund belly and skinny legs, I was assured that he would grow no bigger than Olga by the couple who brought him in but they got that wrong as just like Topsy 'he grew'd'. He's an unusual-looking dog with a long body and short legs; his tail looks as if it should belong to an entirely different breed altogether as it's long and thick and reminds me of an otter's; but he has the most handsome face with a reddish beard and the saddest eyes. We had him DNA-tested to see if we could determine what breed he is and it turns out he's a combination of a Newfoundland, a Scottie and a retriever, which explains his odd appearance.

He's also an epileptic. His fits started when he was around two years old, the first one occurring as we were taking the dogs up the path one evening. It was a full-on seizure that was very distressing to see and for at least an hour afterwards he was extremely disoriented. He had another one the next day, more violent than the first and twice as long.

Olga attacks him when he goes into a fit and I've been told that she no longer recognizes him when he's fitting. She's actually a good indication of when he's going to have one as she's snappy with him and sits studying him intensely from the end of the sofa, ready to pounce at the first sign of him deteriorating.

Following a series of tests he was officially diagnosed as epileptic (like we hadn't already worked that out) and consequently he takes seven tablets at different times during the day and night. He's still prone to the odd fit but thankfully his medication seems to have lessened them, although it's made him pack on the weight. He's been on a special diet which he doesn't seem to mind as he's not a fussy eater and already he's looking a little trimmer.

Epilepsy in dogs is not unusual and witnessing your dog in the throes of a seizure, frothing at the mouth and thrashing about, is very upsetting, plus the medication doesn't come cheap. I'm glad I took him home with me when he was a pot-bellied pup as I often wonder what would've happened to him if he'd gone to someone else who might not have been able to cope with the condition or been able to afford his pills.

More than likely he'd've been put to sleep, and the world would be a sadder place without Bully as everybody who meets him falls in love. I'm watching him now as he mooches around the garden. He's studying the grass with a mournful expression on his lovely face and I regret not naming him Eeyore for that's just who he reminds me of.

EDDIE

Sometimes known as Edouardo or Edward depending on his crime, this Battersea boy is part Jack Russell and part chihuahua. He's a breed known as a Jack-chi or a Jackahuahua. I prefer the latter as it sounds like 'Jackawowwah' and rolls nicely off the tongue.

Eddie's mother was a chihuahua who was found heavily pregnant and tied to the gates of Battersea Dogs Home late one cold night. Unfortunately finding dogs dumped and left tied to the gates of the home is not an uncommon incident. Uncaring owners who no longer have any use for their devoted pet because they suddenly find them an inconvenience usually neglect them, and then when they are weak with starvation and barely able to stand they callously chuck them out of their cars on to the roadside or ditch them in a wood. I've seen dogs that have been dumped in parks or locked inside a suitcase on a very hot day, as well as numerous dogs bearing the scars of unspeakable cruelty.

The staff at Battersea christened this tiny chihuahua Bourbon, and when she'd reached full term she gave birth to a large litter of pups, but as she didn't have enough milk to feed them a few were hand-reared by members of the staff.

Rachel, the head vet nurse, took Eddie, who was the runt of the litter, home with her. Hand-rearing a pup not only requires dedication, you also need stamina as for the first few weeks of two-hourly feeds you're not going to get much sleep. Eddie wouldn't take his bottle and grew sick and for a time Rachel was very concerned that he wasn't going to make it. It was touch and go for a while but, stubborn little sod that he is, he suddenly decided to live and began to drink his formula.

On the last day of filming at Battersea I went to say goodbye to Bourbon's pups as all of them now had homes apart from Eddie, which I couldn't understand as he was without doubt the cutest of an already unbearably cute litter. Being a mug of the first order and with the lyrics to the song 'The Little Boy that Santa Claus Forgot' running through my head on a loop tape I simply couldn't leave him behind, particularly as he'd be without the company of his siblings, and especially at Christmas. So he came home with me.

I took him everywhere as he was so small I could put him in my inside jacket pocket. He loved this mode of travel and would poke his head out to see what was going on, prompting people more than once to ask if he was a fox cub as he certainly looked like one.

He'd been called Custard Cream at the home, the whole litter having been named after biscuits, but I changed it to Eddie after the character Jimmy Cagney played in the film *The Roaring Twenties*. He suited this name as he was small and cocky and already showing signs that small certainly didn't mean weak and timid.

He's a loving little dog who likes to lie sphinx-like on my lap, but he also has a fierce temper and is more than capable of holding his own amongst my rowdy pack making his peculiar cat-like growling noise as he nips at their legs.

He's a right little character who likes to sleep with any guests who come to stay – not that they have much choice as he stands outside their door growling until they let him in. He lives in a little triangular house that was meant for a cat and clearing it out one day I found a bunch of taxi receipts, a half-chewed dollar bill, an empty yoghurt pot

and a rubber bath plug. He certainly has eclectic tastes does Eddie.

Small dogs are often unaware of their size and Eddie is a classic case as when he's in his cat-house guarding a scrap of paper from the others with a threatening look on his face they wouldn't dare go near him.

He's a determined little mite too. One day I took Bullseye for a walk through the woods and down the field. None of the others showed any interest in joining us so the pair of us set off, stopping for a rest in the middle of the big field.

Lying in the grass, I looked up to see this Lilliputian figure walking towards us. It was Eddie. He'd navigated the woods all on his own and then fought his way through the long grass in the field to join us. I was impressed with his bravery and determination to reach us and watched in admiration as he stood triumphantly on top of an anthill surveying his manor.

He's upstairs now, walking around a map of Europe with his Napoleonic hat on, wondering which country he should invade first.

BOYCIE

Apart from looking remarkably like Buster he also has most of his mannerisms and habits, which is uncanny.

This little fella doesn't really belong to me, he's officially Joan's dog. She was looking for a pal for her dog Barney and just before Christmas she discovered him at the Windsor branch of Battersea and took him home with her. He was a scruffy little thing and I fell in love with him on sight, and him with me. If there was anything that was going to convince me that reincarnation was possible then Boycie was it.

As soon as the annual gruelling stint in panto was over I went off on holiday to sleep and eat and it was while I was away that Boycie began having fits, sometimes five or six a day. Joan brought him down to Kent and after a trip to the vet's he too was diagnosed as having epilepsy. One epileptic dog in the family was enough and Battersea agreed to take him back but I told Joan to hold fire until I got home.

I couldn't stand to see this little dog go back to Battersea, and as Joan had her hands full with Barney and was seriously worried as to what would happen should Boycie start fitting on the bus or Tube he came down to live in Kent with me as his minder.

Despite medication his seizures became worse – one day he had fifteen in a row – and I was very concerned about him in case the severity of these fits caused long-term damage. Back to the vet he went and his medication was

upped. He's now on seven tablets at different times of the day, just like Bullseye. Olga's also on tablets, as is Louis, and to get all four of them to take theirs I wrap the pills in a bit of cheese. The first round starts at eight a.m., and as I also have to pop a couple of pills in the morning (prescription) I've found myself absently wrapping mine in cheese on the odd occasion. Well, the brain isn't functioning at that hour of the morning.

Boycie is a gentle soul who loves kids. Just like Buster he can be found leaning against the side of the house watching the day go by, or stretched out on the little brick bridge by the pond keeping an eye on the ducks and the rabbits. I love all my dogs equally but it's Boycie I feel the most protective towards as he exudes innocence and vulnerability and loves his grub.

Boycie still has fits although nothing like the ones he had pre-medication and, just as she does with Bullseye,

Olga attacks him when he goes into one. It's all go at three a.m when both of them have a fit simultaneously and I'm woken by the sound of the pair of them thrashing about and Olga barking. I shoot out of the bed in the dark with no glasses on, seek out Olga and drag her off whichever dog she is laying into. Making sure that there's nothing near them that could harm them as they thrash about I kneel in pee and stroke and talk to them until they come out of it, just as I used to do with the epileptic kids I used to look after.

I'm not complaining, I'm just explaining what it's like dealing with an epileptic dog. I wouldn't trade either of them for the world, but I do worry about both Boycie and Bullseye. Just how many fits can their bodies take?

Still, I'll cross that bridge when we come to it as right now I love their company even if Boycie pees up my bedroom curtains when he gets excited and Bullseye nicks my shoes, socks and underpants as well as Moira's bra and knickers and drags them up the path giving visitors the impression that they've just missed out on a bacchanalian orgy.

CONCHITA

This is another orphan of the storm from Battersea who doesn't really belong to me. While I was filming there one day I spotted a beautiful snow-white Maltese sat calmly in her kennel gently wagging her tail and staring with large brown unblinking eyes at every passer-by. She'd been brought in by the dog warden after being found wandering the streets late at night. As she wasn't chipped there was no way of contacting her owners so she waited out the obligatory seven days to see if anyone would come looking for her but nobody ever did, which made me suspect that she'd been dumped. If one of my dogs got out and went missing I wouldn't rest until I'd searched every single dogs home in the country, but obviously nobody cared enough about this little beauty, so I began to hatch a cunning master plan.

I casually dropped subtle hints about the charms of this dog over dinner with Andre my partner and by the time the dessert came he was completely sold and went straight down to Battersea the next morning to take a look at her. Of course, just as I'd planned it was love at first sight and he took her home.

She settled in with him immediately, and as she was the first dog he'd ever owned he was extremely attentive towards her. She travels in a special dog bag worn across his shoulders as he cycles around London. She also came on the Radio 4 show *Loose Ends* with me, travelling in her bag as I made my way into the studio on the back of a motorbike. She charmed everyone on the show, even Clive Anderson, and spent the duration of the programme fast asleep on my knee. As Andre travels a lot with work she spends a lot of time here with me in Kent and we've become very attached.

I'm often being accused of stealing the affections of people's pets. I don't do it deliberately, they just seem drawn to me. And it's not just dogs either. I've formed close bonds with elephants, orangutan, penguins and even a baby vulture. Animal experts have told me on countless occasions that I have a special way with animals that comes instinctively. Well if that's true then I'm extremely grateful as I could think of no better gift than to be able to gain the

love and trust of these beautiful creatures and spend my time with them.

I'm unable to sit down without Conchita jumping on my lap, and together with Boycie she follows me everywhere. She refuses to sleep with anyone else but me, always claiming the best spot – pressed against my side with her head on my chest. Not to be outdone, Eddie lies lengthways on my outstretched legs, and with Olga joining the love-in by stretching out across the pillows and pushing her paws into my head, I'm trapped.

She infuriates Eddie by sitting on the roof of his cat house when he's asleep inside and flattening it in the process. This sends Eddie into Donald Duck temper mode, squawking and kicking off until Conchita nonchalantly steps aside, allowing Eddie to wriggle out of his fur-lined, recently collapsed home fit to kill.

Recently two squirrels have taken to invading the chicken run by slipping in through the wire roof and helping themselves to the chicken feed. Conchita is fixated with these squirrels and will sit all day under the tree they inhabit like a teenage fan outside a hotel waiting for a glimpse of her favourite boy band. Considering she looks like a delicate little lap dog the gal's got guts and thinks nothing of sneaking in with the pigs who aren't the least bit bothered by her.

She's on my knee right now as I tap away at my geriatric laptop, making typing difficult as she has her head buried in the crook of my arm. Then there's Eddie, fighting for supremacy by crawling all over me, with Boycie at my feet grunting and growling for me to stroke him. I could do with a few more arms like the Hindu goddess Durga to please them all.

MILLIE AND FUDGE

Two more from Battersea Dogs Home, and although I see a lot of them they really and truly belong to Moira.

Millie is a black Lab. She's three years old and loves nothing more in life than playing with her ball. Her mother was found abandoned and heavily pregnant and she was so nervous a blanket had to be placed across the front of her kennel as people scared her. She gave birth to a large litter of healthy pups and was an excellent mother despite fears that if she was disturbed or felt threatened in any way she might kill them. Thanks to the loving care of the staff she slowly gained a little confidence and started to trust people again. Millie is a little like her mother, slightly wary of strangers at first but your friend for life once she gets to know you.

Fudge is a blonde cockapoo, two years old and a recent arrival, yet it feels as if he's always been here. He's extremely affectionate and well behaved and just like Millie

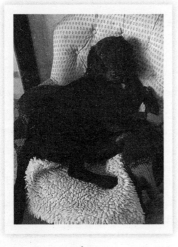
Millie

Fudge

he loves his ball. He was brought back to Battersea on two occasions after being rehomed with claims that he was unruly and had bitten a child. What utter bollocks. You couldn't wish to meet a more loving, good-natured dog. He is no trouble at all and great with kids. If he did snap at a child then I reckon it was because the parents hadn't taught their brat to show some respect and not to treat a dog as a toy, pulling on it and dragging it around the house. If a kid did that to me I'd bite it as well.

Dogs? I couldn't possibly begin to imagine life without one, or nine come to think of it, and I dare say that if I keep on filming in Battersea there's a strong possibility there'll be a couple more additions in the near future.

Pigs

They say pigs are more intelligent than dogs, and while I'll agree that they are indeed very clever I'm not so sure about them being smarter. Saying that, I can get my pig Tom to sit on command but I'm damned if the dogs take a blind bit of notice of me when the same is requested of them.

My first two pigs were a cross between a Tamworth and a Gloucester Old Spot, sows that I got as piglets from a rare breeds centre. I called them Blanche and Jane, the Hudson Sisters, and they were aptly named as Jane was the more dominant of the two and would bully Blanche, the gentler sibling. Both of them loved having their bellies rubbed and would lie there and let you do it all day if you had the time to spare.

They lived in a large shed with plenty of outdoor space and they even had their own pond to wallow in and coat themselves with mud on a hot day. I'd let them out to have a roam around the field and garden but pigs can do terrible damage to a lawn as they love to dig with their snouts. My two wrecked the field in less than a week.

Pigs can certainly communicate with you by means of a variety of different squeals and grunts, and I soon learned by their reactions what each grunt and squeal meant. Jane was the more vocal of the two whereas Blanche, unless she was being bitten and chased by Jane, which set her off screaming the neighbourhood down, always greeted me with a series of gentle grunts.

They grew to be a fair size and after a while their shed started to resemble the Crooked House as it leaned to the right and looked ready to collapse at any moment. The reason for this was because the girls had a habit of slamming themselves against the side every morning and rubbing their massive girths against it back and forth, enjoying a good scratch.

I kept these pigs for years, and despite their reputation for being dirty they were very particular about hygiene. Between them they designated a spot in the furthest corner of their pen as the toilet area. Nor do they smell, although pig wee can be a bit whiffy on a warm day.

Jane was the first to go as she suddenly became very ill and could no longer walk, so reluctantly I had to have her put to sleep. Blanche blossomed without her bullying sister and lived on for another four years until, old and a bit rickety on her trotters, she caught a chest infection and joined her sister in that pigsty in the sky.

It was eerily quiet without the girls and I missed having them around so it wasn't long before a couple more arrived to take their place. They were a pair of kunekunes, a young boar and a sow called Tom and Holly. Tom had bright curly ginger hair and seemed to be permanently smiling while Holly, who was heavily pregnant and not quite as hairy as old Tom, had a coat that was black and sleek as a seal's and without a curl in sight. Tom had two little tear-shaped bags hanging underneath his jaw that I later learned are called piri piri and are peculiar to the breed, and despite the vicious rumours going around the hen house he wasn't the father of Holly's piglets, he was just a good friend, and the two lived in perfect harmony together.

Kunekunes originate from New Zealand and are renowned for their good nature and love of humans. I sat with Tom one afternoon and taught him to sit and stand on his hind legs using food as a reward. He'll still sit when I tell him but due to age the standing on his hind legs bit has been dropped from his repertoire.

Holly gave birth to a litter of nine piglets one Saturday afternoon. I'd suspected they might be due as she'd taken to making a nest in the shed amongst the straw and lying down. I knelt by her side gently stroking her and sure enough after a short while out popped the piglets – and I mean popped out. The first one shot out with the speed of a missile, shook itself and started tottering about, followed closely by another, and then another ... she was like a machine, banging them out at the speed of light. 'No more, Holly,' I pleaded as I watched the shed fill up with piglets, 'that's enough.'

Luckily we were prepared for the birth – an area of the shed had been fenced off with a large heat lamp suspended over it to keep the babies warm – but gathering the piglets up was no easy task as they were all over the place. But after I'd finally managed to get them together it was a real treat to see them greedily sucking on their mother's teats.

The runt of the litter was tiny, and I named her Evangeline. She was a sickly little thing and despite the constant ministrations of both myself and the vet, just as Blanche had done she caught a chest infection and died. Joan cried and the rest of us were miserable all day.

The surviving piglets thrived, and by the time they were weaned and had no further need for Momma I gave four away to a local vet who wanted to keep them as pets and kept three sows and a boar for myself.

The boar is ginger like Tom so he was named Tom-Tom – not very original but you run out of ideas after a while. The three sows are known as The Twins and Squealer respectively. Squealer earned her name from the ear-piercing racket she made when she was small when anyone picked her up.

Every morning after they've had their feed they're let out of their pen and are free to roam in the big field. Kunekunes like to graze and love to munch on grass. They're also very fond of apples and cabbage, or at least mine are, and in the winter months we feed them a hot mash made out of their pig pellets and water which goes down a treat.

At 4.30 p.m. prompt they gather at the gate demanding to be let back in again for their evening meal. Tom is slightly hard of hearing these days and sometimes I have to go and fetch him from the corner of the field where he'll be quietly munching away on a tuft of grass oblivious that the others have gone off for dinner and left him. Both Tom and Tom-Tom

Squealer

have grown tusks, making them look slightly formidable, but don't judge a book by the cover as they are quite the opposite. Kunekunes are gentle beasts and easy to handle, which is why they're perfect for first-time pig-keepers.

Squealer is not only vocal she's a seasoned escape artiste, forever going missing. One afternoon she somehow managed to escape from the big field and by slipping through hedges and fences she got on to the road, sashaying slowly up the hill with a steady stream of traffic creeping behind her. My neighbour alerted me and I had to suffer the indignity of leading a pig home using a bucket of food as bait while every driver crawling past couldn't resist making a ribald remark.

'Taking your pig to market, Paul?'

'That's a big dog.'

'I hope you haven't nicked that!'

Catching an escaped pig, driving a cow out of the kitchen (coming later), dealing with killer sheep – it's all part and parcel of rural living, and for me it's been an education, what they always call on *The X Factor* a life-changing experience. Best thing I ever did, moving down here.

Spring

One of the many things in particular that you notice about living in the country is the change in seasons. Spring has got to be my favourite, and today it's clearly apparent that at last spring is nearly here.

Moira, who sometimes looks after my dogs, used to be terrified of birds, she had an absolute phobia about them. I remember when a group of us were on holiday together at the Venice Lido she'd go absolutely potty because my table at breakfast, outside on the terrace of the old Hotel des Bains, was always heaving with sparrows that I'd share my toast with. They were cheeky birds, regarding themselves as a tourist attraction unperturbed by humans who they saw as a source of food. One sparrow, the bravest of the lot, thought nothing of sitting in my hand pecking at the crumbs of a croissant. Poor Moira would be off like a shot, genuinely terrified of these little fellas. But nowadays it's a different story.

It started with the chickens. In the early days if she had to feed them she'd scream the place down if one so much as came near her. Gradually over the years she became used to them, and now she actively encourages them to approach her. She even feeds the barn owls, and despite Minnie the Matriarch of the parliament opening her wings and hissing threateningly when you approach, Moira is unfazed. Not bad for a woman who once fled at the sight of a tiny sparrow.

She loves birds now and is constantly attending to the wild ones that inhabit the garden. Half a coconut shell stuffed with a combination of fat and seeds hangs outside the kitchen window along with an assortment of seed feeders that the birds love. It's a joy to stand quietly and watch them flitting around and fighting over who gets the best spot on the feeders. Great tits and the smaller blue tits seem to be the predominant species here although the chaffinch hold their own as do the sparrows.

There's one bird in particular I always keep an eye out for and that's the robin. At the moment there's one particularly feisty little fella who's set up shop in the garden. If any other male dares to land on the patio then he appears as if from nowhere, legs astride, chest out, defiantly holding his wings in a way that makes him look like he has his hands on his hips, ready to defend his territory. I've seen bouncers adopt that position stood outside a club and I half expect the robin to point his wing and shout, 'Members only, mate.'

One male robin who is always chancing his arm (or should that be wing?) comes back repeatedly and my robin virtually bristles with indignation at the sight of this interloper, chasing him around the garden until his rival gives up and flies off. The battle won, my robin then stomps around the patio just in case any other foolish bird wants to try his hand, and then after he's calmed down he'll jump on the garden table where I've scattered a handful of mealworms for a quick lunch before vanishing into the straggling lavender bushes.

I've never seen him eat from the bird feeder or the coconut shell filled with fat. He's a solitary bird who doesn't mind the company of a crazy human but prefers to dine alone.

I've had chats with this bird, me sat on the bench and him at a safe distance perched on the back of a chair. He doesn't say much so it's a bit of a one-sided conversation although I have to say he's what they call a good listener.

Only once did I get a peep out of him and that was when I was reading a paper and asked him what he thought of Trump. He was silent for a moment before launching into a series of lengthy chirps and trills which by their tone and speed I took for being a distinctly uncomplimentary answer. 'You should go in for politics,' I told him, 'you've got a lot to say for yourself when you get going,' to which he replied with two cheeps that sounded uncannily like 'I might' before flying off. And no, I hadn't been smoking anything or drinking cough medicine.

The garden is slowly springing into life. The crocuses (or is it croci?) are starting to open up, clumps of wild primroses are popping up around the trees along the drive, and the banks are beginning to show an abundance of wild violet, although for me the most impressive sight is the veritable sea of daffodils that are ready to explode into life.

Of all flowers the daffodil has to be the cheeriest. They're such a simple design, and that vivid yellow radiates sunshine. It's considered good luck to bring bunches of daffodils into the house but a solitary daff is a big no-no as to bring one in will only result in bad luck (Molly O'Grady's book of superstitions, page 1,002). I can remember learning parrot-fashion Wordsworth's poem 'Daffodils' at school – you know, the one that goes 'I wandered lonely as a cloud / That floats on high o'er vales and hills, / When all at once I saw a crowd, / A host, of golden daffodils'. I learned that poem when I was eleven, not because I wanted to but because I had to, and at the time I didn't appreciate the words, I thought them meaningless and very old-fashioned, and it was buttock-clenching torture to have to get up and recite it in front of a class of your sniggering mates. These days I can fully understand why Wordsworth was inspired to write a poem after witnessing a field full of daffs in Ullswater. Shame he can't see my path down to the house: it's slathered with them.

Spring is a welcome break from winter. That's when living out in the sticks can be really tough, especially if it's a hard winter. This year it snowed just enough to cover the fields and make everywhere Christmas-card perfect before obligingly vanishing without trace a couple of days later. But a really heavy snowfall means being cut off from the world and a day or so without electricity as the power always goes down. It's a good idea when living out in the wilds to have a good stock of candles, lanterns and torches on standby just in case of a power cut. The obvious solution, of course, is to get a generator. I've been saying that I'm going to buy a cheap one for years but I always forget and typically it's only when I need one that I remember.

Feeding the animals on a cold winter's morning isn't much fun either. The goats loathe the snow, as do the chickens, and both parties refuse to come out of their respective accommodation, but the pigs are very curious, shuffling around and eating it until they realize that this strange white stuff is cold, then like the others they too retreat to the warmth of their barn. Sheep are hardy things and we make sure there's a plentiful supply of good-quality hay for them, but even so when the weather is extreme they also vanish into their shed.

Having said that, snowbound and stranded is actually good fun if there's a group of you. I once had a houseful and a heavy snowfall closed all the roads and plunged us into darkness. All of a sudden we were in an Agatha Christie play. Who was going to be bumped off first? Who was going to play who? With the aid of a lot of booze we spent a few happy hours re-enacting *The House on Haunted Hill* – not an Agatha Christie I know but there's no need to nit-pick.

The thing about these murder mystery games is that once a few people have been bumped off and are out of the game and the two remaining standing have decided who the killer was there's not much left to do.

As far as I can remember the highlight of the evening was discovering Vera lying dead on the bathroom floor having been strangled with her own tights, and after witnessing the spectacle of Vera with her tongue out and eyes crossed everything else that followed was a bit of an anticlimax. Still, at least some form of parlour game was taking place in a house where once upon a time such a form of amusement was commonplace.

Last week was bitterly cold. There was no snow but it was freezing. The air outside was biting and it almost hurt to breathe. I thought it could certainly do with snowing as then perhaps it wouldn't be so cold. The dogs were extremely reticent to 'go up the path' and they peered around the back door sniffing the air suspiciously. I couldn't blame them. I found it hard to drag myself away from what authors of romantic fiction describe as 'a roaring log fire' but the dogs needed to go out for a pee and as I'm not having Boycie cock his leg up my bedroom curtains out they went, albeit reluctantly, Eddie showing his displeasure by snarling like a little cat. That dog has got serious attitude. It was only when I was halfway up the path that I realized they'd all cleared off ages ago back to the house leaving me shivering in an ancient overcoat and a pair of wellies and talking to myself in the dark.

But as I said, spring arrived this morning, although I don't know for how long as the weather can change in the blink of an eye. Still, I'm going to enjoy this beautiful warm day for as long as it lasts.

Overheard today in the farm shop, said by one woman to another in hushed tones as they examined beetroots: 'When the swelling went down they just hung there so I said you'd best get yourself up the hospital, you might have an infection in them.'

I followed them around surreptitiously to see if I could discover what it was that was just hanging there as my imagination was running riot. Of course the obvious came to mind, but then she could've been talking about a woman who'd just had her ears pierced and been referring to her earlobes. Anyway, I never found out as the woman changed the subject to Brexit, paid for her eggs and sprouts, and left declaring to her friend, 'Well we'll just have to wait and see what happens, won't we?' I didn't know if she was talking about the long-term prognosis of whatever it was that was hanging or the impact of leaving the EU.

Either way the combination of this unexpectedly sunny early spring day and the conversation between the two women makes me feel quite jolly, and after buying a load of salad stuff which I know won't be eaten I go home and order online a couple of mulberry bushes and some comfrey, wormwood and marigolds for the hens' accommodation.

I'll put them in the greenhouse first until they are well established, in particular the mulberry bush, which will not only provide shelter for the hens but they love the berries too. They're also keen on comfrey and wormwood, and the marigold flowers turn the yolks of their eggs a rich deep yellow. I suspect that within hours of planting them out they'll be destroyed, apart from the mulberry bush which is sturdier than the other plants, but at least pecking away at them will provide them with a bit of a diversion as well as supplying them with lots of good nutrients.

As it's such a nice day I take the roof down on my ten-year-old Mini and go for a drive. Only two of the dogs, Boycie and Eddie, will come with me as Olga hides when I suggest she gets in the car, which I understand to be a slight on my driving. Bullseye is having one of his 'too shy to do anything today thank you' moods and slopes off apologetically to his basket in the laundry room looking more like Eeyore than ever. Louis and Conchita are enjoying the dizzy delights of London, so that just leaves the three of us for a jaunt around the marshes.

Romney Marsh has been described as 'the fifth continent' for it is indeed a remarkably beautiful place full of ancient churches and tiny villages, and it's a cyclist's joy as it's as flat as the Dutch countryside. There are also lots of caravan sites dotted around and I'm convinced that caravanning gives you the power of foresight when it comes to forecasting the weather as there are lots of signs of life whereas a couple of days ago the campsite was deserted. How did they know today was going to be a sunny day?

I came to a halt at some temporary traffic lights set up just outside the entrance to one of these camps and watched as a middle-aged woman in a pair of startlingly white shorts with a severe crease down the front and a blue and white halter-neck top watered a tub of battered geraniums. This was a woman who on the back window of her caravan not only had a pair of net curtains that were as pristinely white as her shorts but was wearing an outfit more suited to Benidorm than Dymchurch in late February. Looking up, she recognized me and waved.

'What are you doing in these parts?' she asked, shielding her eyes from the sun. 'You enjoying the lovely weather?'

'It's a bit early for the caravan isn't it?' I replied.

'Well,' she said, walking towards me, 'it's half term so I brought the grandkids down for a few days. And just look at the weather! Beautiful innit?'

I agreed with her and asked her if she was having a good time.

'I love it,' she replied proudly. 'Love me static caravan, love the countryside and the fresh air, love the beach, and so do the kids. Love it all – it's marvellous. I don't even mind if it rains. Next time you're passing pop in for a cup of tea.'

I told her I would as I drove off full of admiration for this optimistic woman who saw the joy in caravanning.

I drove to Sandgate as apart from being quite picturesque it has a decent chippy. I ate my fish, chips and mushy peas on the seafront, both dogs sat bolt upright staring at me, transfixed by the sight and smell of the snowy white cod and crispy batter I was shovelling down me. Of course I cracked in the end – who wouldn't under such scrutiny? – and gave them some fish, blowing on it first to cool it down as I would for a little kid.

Our meal eaten and thoroughly enjoyed we went for a walk on the beach, although neither of the dogs was very keen on the pebbles and stones, Eddie mincing about as if he was walking on broken glass and Boycie doing his best but constantly losing his balance.

The dogs attract a lot of attention. Usually it's Olga who causes a fuss. Walking through King's Cross station with her she gets as much attention as if I had Madonna on the end of a lead. A stout Italian woman came over.

'Chihuahua?' she asked, pointing at Eddie.

'No,' I told her, 'he's a Jack Russell chihuahua cross.'

'Ahh,' she cried, her eyes lighting up. 'I know you, you're the man off the telly! You're …'

I offered to tell her but she was having none of it.

'No don't tell me!' she squealed, flapping her hands. 'I know it.'

I was squirming with embarrassment by this stage.

'Oh, what is it?' she asked, thumping her chest and looking up at the sky. 'I know I know it. Let me think … don't tell me. It's … Jerry Springer!' she cried out triumphantly.

'No, I'm Paul O'Grady,' I corrected her, keeping my voice down.

'Jerry, Jerry!' she chanted.

'No, you've got it wrong,' I tried to explain, resisting the urge to strangle her. 'My name's Paul O'Grady.'

'Oh I love your show, Jerry,' she gushed, ignoring me. 'I must 'ave a selfie.'

As she was rooting in her bag, presumably for her phone, two elderly gentlemen joined us.

'Hello there,' one of them said affably. 'Lovely day isn't it? And who's this little chap then?' he asked, referring to Eddie.

Eddie growled and tried to climb up my leg, a signal that he wanted picking up.

'He's Jerry Springer,' the woman butted in, grabbing my arm. 'Off the TV.'

'Funny name for a dog,' the old man replied, smiling.

'No, not the dog,' the Italian woman shouted, '′im!' She jabbed me in the side with her finger. 'He's Jerry Springer.'

'No he's not,' the other old chap scoffed. 'He's that Julian Clary.'

'No he isn't, it's Jerry,' the Italian woman insisted, one hand deep in her bag as she searched for this elusive phone. 'Ah, here it is,' she announced happily, waving it in the air.

'You're both wrong,' the first old man said. 'This is Paul O'Grady. You know, the fella with the animals. And if I'm not mistaken, isn't this the little dog you brought home with you from Battersea?'

I was grateful that finally one of them had worked out who I was and I replied that yes, this was indeed the same Eddie from Battersea.

'He's grown a bit hasn't he?' he remarked, and Eddie growled again as he's a little sensitive about his weight.

The Italian lady, like so many before her, had no idea how to work the camera on her phone and started waving her arms in the air which made Eddie growl again and me tighten my grip on him in case he leapt out of my arms and went for her throat.

'Here, let's have a look,' one of the old men said, taking the phone from her and examining it with an expression of distaste that conveyed his disapproval of mobile phones. 'No idea,' he said eventually, handing it back. 'Why don't you get yourself a proper camera instead of relying on one of those things?'

'You're living in the dark ages, Bill,' his friend laughed. 'Everyone has a mobile phone now with a camera. You need to move with the times, mate, and get yourself one.'

Bill snorted in disgust and replied that the phone in the hall was good enough for him and if George was so clever why didn't he take the picture?

The Italian woman pushed the phone on to George, pleading with him to take the photo. George stared at it knowledgeably for a bit. After jabbing the screen repeatedly with his finger a few times he turned it around. Then he declared that he wasn't familiar with this type of phone.

'In other words, you haven't got a clue how to work it either,' Bill crowed smugly. 'Strange, what with you being so clued up on such things.'

It was Boycie, busy flirting with a young lad in a hoodie who looked like he might kill you, who solved this problem.

'I'd better get my dog,' I said apologetically, making my escape. 'He's probably driving that lad over there mad.'

''Ere,' the Italian lady shouted, spotting the youth, 'take a picture.'

The young lad walked over with his new best friend bouncing along beside him and, removing his hood, turned out to be not a mindless yob but a charming university student.

Don't judge a book ...

He took a number of photos ('take another, sweetie, just in case') with George and Bill looking on with another couple of kids who'd joined the party while I stood beet red and grinning like a fool with this little Italian lady clutching my waist.

'Thank you, Jerry,' she said when the photo session was over, pulling me down to her height to give me a kiss. 'I'll wave when I watch you tomorrow morning. I always watch you every morning.' She beamed at me, squeezing my hand. 'Every day, first Lorraine and then you.'

I tried to think who followed Lorraine Kelly in the schedules and was slightly dismayed when I remembered that it was *The Jeremy Kyle Show* as I didn't know if she'd mistaken me for the host or one of his toothless participants.

'Just one more,' this annoying woman demanded, pushing her phone into the student's hand. 'Say Tee-Veeee!' she said, grabbing me again.

In the hope that she'd piss off I duly obliged, grinning widely to show that I had all me teeth.

I don't know why I get embarrassed posing for photos. You'd think I'd've got used to it by now but I haven't. I know it's part of the job etc. etc. but I just feel daft grinning into a phone inanely and I believe you have to be an extreme narcissist to enjoy it.

The student was very laid back, thankfully not a bit impressed that I was off the telly, and recommended a pub to me that I'd already visited. We'd been to see the local amateur dramatic group perform *Blithe Spirit* in a church that had been converted into a theatre. We'd dropped into this pub for a quick one beforehand and I'd had a drop of their famous cider. We did the same in the interval, and by the end of the play, which was brilliantly acted by the way and very funny, I was more than a bit squiffy. One or two for the road before the pub closed and by the time they got me into the back of the car I was singing and continued to do so all the way home, much to Joan's amusement and Murphy's annoyance. Murphy cooked a fry-up when we got in which I devoured as only a starving drunk can, and a good night was had by all.

The weather remains warm and sunny and some of the daffs are in bloom. I can't bear to pick any of mine so I buy them at a pound a bunch, which probably doesn't make sense seeing as I've got hundreds of them growing all around the house, but I prefer mine to stay where they are – in the garden.

As I've got four days off (Thank you, Warden) I'm going to spend it working in the garden while I'm still in the mood. But first I'd better knuckle down to the job that's been on my mind for some time, and that's answering the post.

Three hours and twenty-seven letters later I'm standing in a small queue in our post office. I can't help studying the couple standing in front of me and come to the conclusion that they are mother and son. How did I deduce this? Easy, because I heard him call her Mother, that's how. I should be in the CID.

Anyway, he was middle-aged and towered over his ancient little mother who was studying a magazine on the rack and clearly not listening to a word he was saying. 'The mobile library is coming tomorrow,' he said. 'Do you want to change your book?'

'What?' she snapped as she leaned in to get a closer look at the magazine that had caught her attention.

'I said, do you want to change your book?' he asked again, patiently.

'Depressed? What's she got to be depressed about?' the old girl said suddenly, pointing angrily at the magazine. 'With all her money and education and a good job on the telly she's got no right to be depressed, she should be happy as a pig in shit.'

'Mother!' the man hissed, turning around to see if anyone had overheard her, which everyone had as the old lady had spoken in a very loud voice. Grinning sheepishly, he quickly turned back to his mum and started talking about her library book again.

'I haven't finished it yet,' she said distractedly, moving one mag out of the way so she could read the cover of another. 'It's a bit of a boring read really so I might just skip to the end to see what happens, save me wasting me time.'

They stood in silence for a while, and I wondered what Victoria Wood would've made of them. She once told me that she'd written sketches around a couple of snippets she'd overheard as like me she enjoyed eavesdropping on day-to-day conversations as they're always funnier than a contrived comedy routine.

This pair were no exception to that rule. I waited for Mum to start up again as she'd now taken the magazine off the rack and was holding it up to her face to get a better look.

'Well stop eating if you want to lose weight,' she admonished the celeb on the cover. 'Who are you anyway?' she went on, her voice growing louder as she became more heated. 'Moaning to all and sundry that you're fat just to get your big fat face in the papers. You want to try living on a pension, miss, you'd soon lose a couple of stone.'

Her son sighed loudly and tried to change the subject. 'It's warm today, Mum, isn't it?' he said, rubbing his hands in desperation. 'I bet it's not this hot in Dubai.'

Above: Before you start baking, lay out every single item that you're going to need – then you won't be wasting time charging around the kitchen looking for things as you mix your cake. And remember, clean up as you go.

Below: There's something magical about old trees and it's views like this that remind me why I moved to the countryside. Let's hope it stays this way and doesn't end up with a housing estate on it like so many others. Rural means Rural.

Goats love to climb, and Rosie and Maleficent spend most of their time on this climbing frame (**above left**). Beebo (**above**) is supposed to be a Pygmy goat although he's a fair size now. He suspects every stranger of being the vet and takes off like a whippet as soon as he sees them.

I've lost count of the number of ducklings and moorhen chicks that have been hatched on this pond over the years. There used to be fish in it but the heron soon put paid to that, just as the wild ducks destroy every bulrush and plant I've attempted to grow around the edge. Sean built the well (**right**) out of the Kentish ragstone that was dug up when he made the pond. As for the frog, I did try kissing it to see what happened and guess what? I got a wart on my lip.

Three of my dogs: Bullseye, Eddie and Olga. Miss Olga is no longer with us, neither is one of my other dogs, Louis. Both of them passed away this year. They do say that to invite an animal into your life inevitably means you also invite heartache, and the death of a pet is pure agony.

Buster loved television studios and he also loved touring around the country in a show. I always got the impression that, as much as he enjoyed chasing rabbits and barking at the chickens, he'd much rather have been hell-raising in the big bad city.

It doesn't get much cuter, does it? This is Bullseye as a puppy. He has epilepsy as does my other dog, Boycie. They're both on medication, which helps to control the seizures, but they certainly love the countryside and have a good life.

Above: This shed has been given the very grand name of The Summer House. It's somewhere to sit, listen to music, admire the view and forget for a moment about the state of the world.

Left: I've had many a good conversation with a hen, although they do tend to interrupt and can be very opinionated.

Evil incarnate – the dreaded Geestapo. Louis was the only one in the household brave enough to take them on.

All my sheep arrived as orphan lambs and were hand-reared – and they're not as stupid as people might think. Mine live a peaceful life without the threat of the butcher hanging over them. One of my proudest moments was delivering baby Raphael (**right**), and below is my first lamb, Waupie, in the early days, sitting in her favourite place by the back door.

Above: I love my pigs – they are all kunekunes, a breed which originates from New Zealand and are renowned for their good nature and love of humans.

Below: Holly and her piglets, you can see Squealer at the front. She's always been the most mischievous.

Growing your own produce can be very satisfying – if you've got the time and the know-how, that is (although I'll admit that I have help as I'm hopeless but getting better). It's good to know that everything is grown organically, but the yield can be unpredictable – some years I might only get a handful of strawberries and a parsnip and then other years I've got so much fruit and veg I could open a shop. The attack of the killer tomatoes.

Left: The Witch's House, the coolest place on the planet to sit or sleep when the weather gets unbearably hot. It also came in very handy during a particularly bad winter when I had no heating or electricity in the house: I moved in with the dogs and the lamb, heating up her bottles on the wood burner and making endless pots of tea laced with a drop of whisky to keep warm. The whisky was for me and not the lamb, you understand – she preferred a dry Martini.

Right: Dot with her calf in the field before she decided to go walkabout.

Below: I've always been a good, clean cook, cleaning up as I go. You wouldn't even know I was in the kitchen . . . still, the Dutch Apple Pie was nice.

'Never mind that,' Mum replied, 'ask her how much string I'll need to send a parcel to America.'

I love irascible old women like this and fully intend, if I ever reach her age, to behave in exactly the same way.

There's been a post office in the village for years and I often wonder what the postmistress of the 1930s thought when she was woken up in the middle of the night by a transatlantic call buzzing away on her tiny switchboard. Hurriedly sitting down and putting her headphones on she probably asked 'What number do you require?' only to hear a husky voice on the other end announce, 'This is Marlene Dietrich, put me through to Mr Noël Coward's residence please.' Dietrich had never met Coward but having just watched a production of his in New York she'd felt compelled to ring the great man and declare her admiration for him, and she tracked him down to the farm he owned in my neck of the woods. The pair became lifelong friends as a result. I wonder if the postmistress listened in? I know I would have.

The sun goes down and the evening turns into what a lot of folk would describe as 'chilly', whereas I would go as far as to say 'bloody freezing'. I hope the plants I spent the afternoon putting in will cope with the overnight frosts that the weatherman on the radio is promising us, but at least I won't have to water them: he's also talking of heavy rain tomorrow. Oh well, spring was good while it lasted.

The Geesestapo

After the pigs, goats, chickens and ducks had settled in I foolishly decided that what I really needed were a few geese to complete the farmyard setting I'd created. I wish somebody had warned me about their temperament before I brought a fine young male and a healthy pair of females home with me, as I was to find out that country life would never quite be the same again, not with the geese around.

I called them Mr Steed, Tara and Mrs Peel after characters in *The Avengers* and for the first few days they were quiet, timid and very shy, running away each time anyone approached. However, this happy state of play wasn't to last for very long. Within a month the gentle Mr Steed had turned into Dr No.

One rain-sodden morning as I made my way to feed the goats and pigs I passed the geese, busy occupying themselves by tearing up the grass underneath the washing line. They were so preoccupied with this act of wanton vandalism that they didn't even bother to look up to acknowledge my greeting. Seemingly oblivious to me they simply continued to tear up sods of earth.

The pigs were always pleased to see me as apart from enjoying human company they knew that I was about to dish up breakfast. They greeted my presence by charging up to the fence and grunting excitedly. As I leaned over the fence to chat to them, as I always do, I suddenly felt this excruciating pain in the back of my leg. It felt as if a chunk of my thigh was being squeezed in a vice. Turning around quickly to see what was the cause of this agony I found Mr Steed hanging off my leg with Tara lurking in the background with a mean look in her beady eye that signalled she was about to make a lunge in the region of my crotch.

Rule Number One: Never turn your back on a goose or else you just might get goosed.

Managing to shake Mr Steed off, I had no choice but to scramble over the fence and get in with the pigs to escape his fury. The pigs, being sociable animals, seemed delighted at this early-morning visitation and, rushing towards me enthusiastically, they managed to knock me over. I lay there in the mud. There'd been a lot of rain recently and consequently there was more than an ample supply of thick, gloopy mud mixed with God knows what else churned up by the pigs. I was covered in it, and Blanche, peering over at me sympathetically, grunted, a sound that in piggy language I took for an apology, which I gracefully accepted.

The geese hissed triumphantly at me through the fence.

As I was attempting to get up out of this mud swamp I was thwarted in my tracks by Jane casually backing up towards me, deciding at this moment to take a pee. A long warm one, straight down my back. The geese, watching this, honked appreciatively, as if they were laughing at me.

From that moment, war was declared.

Eventually this unholy trio wandered off, in search of some other poor fool to torture no doubt, and seizing my chance I ran back to the house slathered in mud, soaked to the skin and stinking of pig pee – and if you've never smelt it, it really reeks.

Buster was very interested in this array of aromas emanating from me as I stood in the kitchen and after a frantic sniffing session with my pig-pee-soaked jeans he obviously thought I had become the human equivalent of a Parisian pissoir, for he cocked his leg and peed up my sodden left leg.

'Thanks,' I muttered, staring down at him, at which he barked and wagged his tail happily, as if he'd just done me a good turn.

With what little dignity I had left I took myself off to the bathroom to clean myself up.

Rule Number Two: I've learned that coming into extremely close contact with animal effluence is to be expected when dealing with livestock. It's no place for sissies. I've now been peed on by almost every animal species from a baboon to a pig.

The geese grew more territorial and vicious by the day until a trip into the garden was akin to running across the Gaza Strip. Buster, having already had an unfortunate encounter with Mr Steed, had learned to keep his distance, but Louis, a sprightly young pup back then, delighted in teasing and taunting them. Fearlessly he'd charge them with a war cry of shrill barking, always managing to turn just in the nick of time and escape a nip from those deadly beaks. This made the geese furious but also a little wary of this foolhardy dog who didn't seem to be intimidated by them in the least. As far as Louis was concerned the geese were good sport and needed to be put in their place. For the first time The Avengers had met their match, and Louis became their most hated nemesis.

*

Just before Easter I went out one morning to feed the critters, wary as usual in case of a surprise attack, only to find Mr Steed wandering aimlessly around and Mrs Peel and Tara nowhere to be seen. There were no signs of a fox attack as there wasn't a feather in sight. After a while we came to the sad conclusion that they'd been stolen and had more than likely ended up as Easter lunch on the thieves' table.

There are just as many thieves in the countryside as there are in the inner cities. Farm machinery, dogs, livestock, lead from the roofs of the ancient Marsh churches, cars, even the copper wiring from phone lines or something more technical that leaves the entire area without the internet for ages are all stolen on a regular basis, and that's before you even look at the crime figures for burglaries. Outhouses, barns, garages et al. must be kept locked up and alarmed, and CCTV is advisable. The countryside isn't Trumpton. Forget roses around your cottage door, you need security lights and a set of decent locks.

Mr Steed was devastated by the loss of the women in his life and went into a deep depression. He was now so passive he'd allow me to stroke his long neck, but it was Sean who was the only human being on the planet he liked, whose knee he'd climb on, resting his head mournfully on Sean's shoulder for solace.

It was heartbreaking to witness the change in Mr Steed. He wouldn't eat, nor would he go near the pond; instead he spent his time mooching around mournfully, his head bowed in sadness, not uttering a single hiss or honk.

Eventually we got him a replacement, a beautiful snowy white female we hoped he'd take to. They ignored each other at first, the female taking off across the pond to sit on the island in icy solitude as Mr Steed watched disinterested from the bankside, as gloomy as ever.

Naturally this state of play didn't last long, and after a brief courtship Mr Steed was back to his old self – and his newly acquired lady friend, who at first had appeared placid and composed, was now beginning to show the same killer instincts as her boyfriend. I was going to call them Bonnie and Clyde until one day I looked at Mr Steed, who had been foraging amongst the trees at the side of the pond, and was shocked to notice that he bore a startling resemblance to Adolf Hitler, partly because he had a piece of woodchip stuck to his beak that looked uncannily like a moustache and the feathers on his head, having been ruffled during his search in the undergrowth, now sloped to one side, like a parting, and over one eye. Lowering that long neck and spreading his wings he went into attack mode, and I beat a hasty retreat.

He became the Führer from that day on, with his missus being christened Eva Braun.

It wasn't long before Eva commandeered the duck house on the island and was sitting on a clutch of eggs. God help any ducks that foolishly went anywhere near as the Führer guarded his missus day and night and would viciously attack and chase them off.

He was the same when the eggs hatched and three beautiful fluffy goslings took to the water with a proud mother in the lead: not even a crow was allowed near the pond. These goslings were christened the Hitler Youth. What else was I going to call them?

These cute little fluff balls pretty soon grew into mirror images of their parents with equally nasty tendencies and I came to the conclusion that geese are inherently evil. They ruled the roost. It was no longer safe to go in the garden unless you were armed with a bin lid and a yard brush. Of a night I'd lie in my bed listening to the five of them hissing menacingly as they patrolled the grounds and wondering how I would dispose of the body of any would-be burglar who was foolhardy enough to underestimate them.

If the back door was left open then the Führer thought nothing of entering the house in search of food. By now he was a considerable size and would just stroll in as if he owned the joint, attacking whoever happened to be stood in his way. It was left to Louis the Fearless to chase him out, who would duck and weave, snapping at the Führer's legs with the skill of a boxer until the Führer, knowing when he was beaten, would retreat back into the garden.

The day finally came when it was time for them to go. It happened on a cold winter's afternoon when the two male offspring, in a fight for supremacy, turned on their father and proceeded to tear him to shreds. There was already blood on the Führer's feathers by the time I got to him. He was lying on the ground, his head wedged in the fork of a low tree branch, defenceless against his treacherous sons.

As I rushed in to try and stop them the two of them turned on me, overpowering me and pulling me to the ground, dragging me towards the pond. 'They want to drown me,' I remember thinking as they yanked me across the mud. Starting to panic, I attempted to fight the furious and powerful pair off, which after a lot of effort I somehow managed to do. They retreated to the pond, sailing around triumphantly honking loudly to their mother and sister who were watching from the island. The Court of the Medicis had nothing on this lot.

Attending to the defeated Führer I saw, thankfully, that his wounds were only superficial. As a thank you for coming to his aid he bit me on the face.

A few days later they were rounded up and shipped out to a local farmer, not for the purposes of eating but as guard dogs in his extensive and much-plundered orchard, where I hear they did an excellent job and survived for years.

I was telling the tale of the Geesestapo to an old chap outside our village post office.

'They certainly are a hateful lot,' he said, nodding his head in agreement. 'My old dad used to keep them and I've still got a couple of scars from the nips they used to give me. Even so they never bit my mother, who they loved. She had a way with them, as did her sister. Maybe they prefer women to men.'

Mine certainly didn't. Apart from Sean, who they eventually turned on in the end, they hated every living creature on the planet. I was glad to see the back of them. Even the farmer who took them off me said he'd rather face a bull than the Führer and co.

There were to be a few more critters who would prove to be too hot to handle and had to be rehomed through no fault of my own, except inexperience, but that's how you learn – by trial and error. As one farmer put it 'There's no dealing with a rogue animal' and I've had a few of those in my time.

May

It's almost eleven p.m. and yet the house is still warm from the heat of the day. I've just spent what I can only describe as a Great Day, and a much-needed one at that. The murderous actions of a maniac in Manchester earlier this week sickened and saddened me. I'm also angry that a radical lunatic believed he had the divine right to murder and maim innocent men, women and children because they didn't follow his religious beliefs.

Filming at Battersea Dogs & Cats Home didn't do much to drag me out of my 'totally pissed off with life' mood as all week I've been involved with a steady stream of abandoned, abused and seriously ill dogs. My defences were down and I'd been more than tempted to take at least four dogs home with me, but the sensible voice in my ear kept telling me that six dogs, four of whom are on medication, is quite enough – for the time being anyway.

By the way, I wish people would stop referring to terrorists as 'animals'. Animals do not blow up children at concerts. Mankind is responsible for that crime.

By the time I got back to Kent from London last night I was worn out. Filming in hot weather all day is tiring. Getting dragged around a paddock by an excitable bull mastiff going at eighty miles an hour is pretty wearing as well. So all I wanted to do was have a shower, get something to eat, and collapse.

It was early evening, and going for a walk around the garden I was amazed to see that the plants and bulbs I'd put in last year which hadn't done anything impressive at the time had suddenly bloomed when I'd believed they'd all died. The poppies had exploded into flower, enormous scarlet petals so perfect that they looked artificial. The roses, too, were in full bloom, blood-red and velvety with a heady scent that could never be manufactured. Antirrhinums, foxgloves, lavender and plants I've no idea what their names are had taken over, and bursting through the catmint was a healthy crop of the exotic red hot poker. I was stunned, not by what a bit of decent weather can do but by my surprising proficiency as a gardener. I'd been running myself down all these years, declaring I was the crappiest gardener ever, the type who pulled up flowers in the belief that they were weeds, yet here I was stood in the middle of a beautiful garden that was all of my own making.

All right, there are a few weeds and nettles knocking about in the roses and the way I've positioned the flowers and shrubs is probably what a proper gardener would call a bit haphazard, but it's a blaze of colour, with wild flowers growing amongst their more snooty cultivated relatives, and it's my idea of a proper old-fashioned country garden, and that's what's important to me.

Upstairs there's a little balcony that normally resembled a wasteland until earlier in the year when I had one of my 'I'd rather do anything than sit down and write a book' days and I closed the laptop and set to tidying it up.

Of course once the deck was clear the gardening bug bit hard and I went berserk in the garden centre buying plants. These I put into pots, and the hanging basket, which was in a bit of a miserable state with nothing in it apart from a few weeds and a fag butt, has now been transformed into a masterpiece to rival the Hanging Gardens of Babylon. Well, maybe I'm going a bit over the top there, and anyway, as I've never seen the Hanging Gardens of Babylon I can't compare my basket to them. Whatever, it looks stunning – and the reason why? Because this time I did it properly. Instead of just chucking the plants in as I normally do and throwing a handful of soil over them before returning to give them the last rites a few days later I consulted books as well as the interweb for the best way to plant various herbs and plants. Lavender, I've found, likes a good soil with a bit of limestone in it. The nicotiana has flowered, and the hanging basket, which is now my pride and joy, is trailing petunias, lobelia and a lovely blue flower that I don't know the name of.

I'm amazed, gobsmacked and prouder than any Olympic gold medallist at what I've achieved. In fact I've just got up and had another look at the balcony in my bare feet and immediately stood on a big fat slug. No slug is going to dine on any of my plants. Telling it that there's only room on this balcony for one of us, I picked it up with a bit of paper and flushed it down the lav.

If by any chance you belong to that group of people known as POCTS (Prevention of Cruelty to Slugs) who stand outside garden centres with banners that proclaim 'Ban the Pellets' and 'Learn to Love a Slug' and are outraged by my actions then I have to say that frankly I really couldn't give a flying f**k. Anyway, that slug is probably still alive, lurking somewhere in the pipeline, slowly crawling its way up from the depths to wreak its revenge and strike when I'm at my most vulnerable – sat on the pan having a leisurely read.

I'm sorry, I seem to have managed to divert my attention on to the subject of slugs instead of getting on with the job in hand, so I'll get back to the point of all this.

Seeing the fruits of my labour in full bloom in the garden and on the balcony I got up at a ridiculously early hour this morning – half past six to be exact – and of my own volition and without a word of complaint I took three very bemused dogs for a walk in the meadow before seriously tackling the garden. (The other dogs are in London: two are having their hair cut and the other is doing an interview for *Heat* magazine.)

It really was a beautiful morning, and sitting in the meadow with a mug of tea I could see that my ordinary field was about to be transformed into a sea of wild flowers without any help at all from anyone: it was already giving a hint of things to come with stretches of daisies, buttercups and cornflowers.

The dogs sat staring at me, perplexed as to why I'd dragged them out of their beds at such an unholy time of day, as I sat lost in thought, remembering when the meadow was planted. The field was first ploughed, fertilized, and then sown with a variety of wild flower seeds. The first year nothing happened and we reckoned that the birds had eaten all the seeds. But come the following year, the meadow burst into a never-ending riot of wild flowers. It was stunning, a sight I'll never forget, and impossible to tear yourself away from.

I had my breakfast outside, and once I'd finished my Weetabix I went for a stomp around the flowerbeds looking for the best spot to plant my latest acquisitions, not forgetting the plants I'd grown from seed that were waiting in the greenhouse.

(I know, bloody remarkable, and they're strong, healthy plants as well.)

I came across a hole in the remains of an old rockery at the furthest end of the garden and noticed that bees were flying in and out of it. I kept my eye on it all day and I've come to the conclusion that they've set up home there. I just hope they don't swarm and end up in the house. I'll also make sure that the dogs keep well away. I wonder if a hole in the ground qualifies as a bona fide hive? I'll get some advice from a member of the local apiary group as to the best plan of action.

I spent the entire day outdoors, apart from a quick trip to the supermarket where I think I frightened the staff and customers with my dishevelled appearance. There was a time if I was going to 'the shops' when I'd put some clean clothes on, making sure that I looked reasonably presentable, but now I couldn't care less and wander abroad unshaved, unkempt and with soil under my nails, and to hell with it. I have to wear suits in the studio, and even on location I'm expected to wear appropriate clothing and shave every day, so being able to let myself go in the countryside is a joy after all that 'dolling up'.

I've got a T-shirt that has 'I'm up and dressed, what more do you want?' written on the front, but as I don't like T-shirts, especially ones with so-called witty slogans written on them, I never wear it, although I'm tempted at times as a response to some of the looks I get.

On my one and only trip to Las Vegas I witnessed a family of five whose combined weight was probably equal to two large elephants waddle through the hotel lobby wearing T-shirts that had 'We're The Johnsons!' written on the front and 'We're Having FUN!' plastered across their ample backs. They certainly didn't look like they were having fun as the daughter of the brood was complaining bitterly about wanting to see something while Daddy bear was hollering as he hurried his tribe through the lobby that not everything was about her and they were doing what Daddy wanted to do today, which judging by the route they were taking towards the food area I'd say meant eating. I quickly moved out of their way as they thundered towards me just in case they mistook me for a snack.

But back to the plot, which I seem to recall was about the joys of horticulture.

Well, I've finally learned to do things properly, use the right soil and dig a big enough hole when planting, and then, once they're safely bedded in their new homes, to look after them. I've also learned that over-watering is as bad as not watering. Lavender doesn't need much water, thyme and other Mediterranean herbs thrive without it, and the bougainvillea, which I never believed would grow in this country, positively hates it.

Gardening? It's like baking a cake: if you give the plant the right ingredients and follow the instructions then you're laughing. I'll be having a go at DIY next.

It's gone midnight now. The dogs are asleep and the house is quiet, and I find this time of night the best for writing as there are no distractions, apart from a solitary tawny owl calling from the spinney at the bottom of the field. My back aches, as do my legs and arms, and I've stupidly burned my shoulders and the back of my neck from spending the day digging and planting in the hot sun. Still, my face has a healthy glow and I know that as soon as my head hits the pillow I'll be in the Land of Nod.

I've always stupidly considered gardening to be an old person's game and I never wanted to hear anyone describe me as 'pottering around the garden'. Well I am old, but I certainly wasn't doing any pottering today, quite the opposite: I went at the garden like a whirling dervish, lugging bags of compost and ferrying a wheelbarrow filled with plants back and forth, but I enjoyed every minute of being totally absorbed in the job at hand. I might do it again tomorrow, depending on the weather that is, but if it's anything like today then there's only one place to be and that's outside, and if I'm spending the day outdoors then I might as well put the time to good use.

But for now, feeling very self-righteous and full of myself, I'm off to bed. It's been like a holiday today.

Goodnight.

Slept like the dead but woke up at a disgustingly early hour to thundery showers with Eddie sitting on my chest as he doesn't like storms. (In case anybody reads this page in years to come and you're not aware, I'd like to point out that Eddie is a dog.)

According to the weather report on the radio it was unbearably hot and humid during the night, not that I was aware of it being in an unconscious state, but now that the rain has stopped and the dark clouds have buggered off up north somewhere the air feels fresh and everything looks as if it's just had a good wash.

I feed the animals, give the dogs their medication, and then, as it has started raining again, I go back to bed – feeling quite justified in doing so due to the weather conditions – where I doze, listening to someone on the radio waxing on enthusiastically about a play they've seen which sounds to me like a lengthy, very meaningful monologue lit by a forty-watt bulb and therefore something to clearly avoid.

Feel guilty for lying in bed on my day off as it's a rarity and it would be a shame to waste it 'stinking in my pit' when there's nothing wrong with me, so I get up.

Have a Toblerone for breakfast and am bitterly disappointed to see the huge gaps between the triangles. I haven't eaten one in years, not since I bought a whopper of a Toblerone at Dublin airport and broke a tooth biting into it. I'd put it in the fridge and it was rock hard. That'll teach me for eating sweets in bed after staggering home from another night at the Vauxhall Tavern more than a bit squiffy. I've got a sweet tooth but now I always have a squeeze before I eat a chocolate just to make sure it's soft and not capable of causing dental damage. This 2017 model of Toblerone is fairly pliable as it's been sat in a warm kitchen and while it's not dangerous it neither looks nor tastes the same.

I don't know why I'm getting aerated over a bloody sweet – probably because I got up so early and I'm always a bit narky. Anyway, as I'm supposed to be an adult I shouldn't be eating sweets for breakfast in the first place.

As the rain has eased off a bit I go and have a look at the flowerbeds to see if they're still looking as impressive as yesterday. I'm pleased to see that they are, and imagine myself on the cover of *Homes & Gardens* leaning on a spade in a pair of wellies amongst the foxgloves and whatever these blue things are called, looking casual.

I haven't seen many rabbits around this year, there's certainly been none in the garden, and I wonder where they've all gone.

A few years back I was overrun with rabbits, and as endearing as they undoubtedly are they saw every single plant, flower and bush in the garden as their own personal smorgasbord. There were so many of them it looked as if I was running a rabbit farm. I gave up replacing plants in the end and left them to it.

I remember walking past the Summer House and from out of a hole in the paving stones surrounding it a fountain of kits literally bubbled up and on to the ground. Baby rabbits are called kits, short for 'kittens', and this lot were tiny. Olga, of course, was in like Flynn and snatching one up in her mouth she ran off with it towards the house. The remaining kits instinctively took off towards the bushes, and considering their size I was amazed at the speed of them.

Meanwhile back at the ranch, Little Miss Olga was holding the kit hostage in her basket, growling menacingly at any of the other dogs that came too close. She wasn't amused when I took it from her, nor was she going to give up easily: she danced around my legs, leaping up to try and reach it as I carried the poor thing out of the house, shutting Olga in behind me.

The kit lay limp and motionless in the palm of my hand, still warm but with its eyes closed and as dead as an audience on a New Year's Day matinee. I didn't know what to do with this delicate little corpse as it was too pretty to just casually sling in the bin, and after deliberating for a while over how I was going to dispose of it I came to the conclusion that I should bury it.

Olga was scratching frantically at the kitchen door to get out so, putting the dead bunny on top of the bin, safely out of reach, I fought my way back into the house to find the garden trowel. This normally lives in what used to be the coalhole but has now become a place for storing dog food, light bulbs and junk. The trowel naturally hadn't been put back in its right place and I cursed the person who had used it last, which of course was me, meaning it could be anywhere.

Putting my wellies on I went in search of the elusive trowel. But back outside the dead kit was now sitting bolt upright and probably wondering why it was perched on top of a bin.

'Bloody hell,' I said when I saw it, channelling Dr Frankenstein, 'you're alive.'

The kit didn't answer, of course, but neither did it flinch or run away as I approached, nor did it seem to be the least bit bothered when I picked it up.

Sitting on the garden wall with the bunny on my lap I wondered as I stroked its head if this 'back from the dead' act was only a brief revival and that after making the equivalent of a rabbit deathbed speech it would expire with a final sigh. But no, it seemed healthy enough. It even shifted itself around on my lap to get comfortable.

As it looked like this kit was now here for the duration I christened it Lazarus and, heaving myself off the wall, carried it back up the path to the bushes, to where the others had fled for cover.

'Go on then, Lazarus,' I told him, putting him down on the grass, 'off you go.'

Only he didn't. He just sat and stared at me for a bit before turning his attention to the grass, his whiskers quivering as his nose sniffed the earth.

'Go on,' I said again, giving him a gentle shove. 'Hop it.'

He shifted a little in response to the nudge but instead of running off he moved closer to me. I wondered if he thought I was his mother, or if his brain had been deprived of oxygen as Olga carried him off in her mouth and it had left him damaged. I knew that wild rabbits do not make good pets so despite the temptation to keep this little fella as he seemed remarkably tame I did the decent thing and walked away.

Lazarus, however, wasn't going to be easy to shake off. He followed me. I stopped dead, and he did the same. I told him to shoo and he ignored me. In the end I ran around the garden in circles to try and get rid of him but he ran after me. All we needed was a little bald man, a sexy nurse

and the *Benny Hill* music – it was ludicrous. Thankfully, before I collapsed Lazarus gave up and, running off in the opposite direction, vanished up the bank. Was I meant to follow him and fall down a large hole into another world or should I go in the house and have a whisky? I took the sensible option, went inside and reached for the Talisker.

What an odd experience. Curiouser and curiouser indeed.

Growing Your Own

It's true, fruit and veg that you've grown yourself really do taste better. Maybe it's a psychological thing that comes out of the sense of achievement you undoubtedly get from managing to produce something edible. Well that's how it is with me anyway. I'm bursting with pride when I sit down to a salad I've actually grown myself from seed. It's also good to know that whatever it is I'm eating has been grown organically and free from any toxic pesticides.

In supermarkets I always look to see where my fruit and veg originated from and if, say, the asparagus is from Peru I don't bother with it. I've nothing against Peru, apart from coming down with altitude sickness when I was on holiday there and seeing bugger all of the place bar the bedroom ceiling as I lay gasping for breath and chewing coca leaves. I don't buy Peruvian asparagus because it's not fresh. Oh I know all about how it's picked, packed and sent off via refrigerated trucks etc. etc. until it reaches the UK where it's unpacked, sorted, packaged and then transported to supermarkets all over the country before it's unpacked again and put on the shelves for you to store in your fridge for a couple of days before you eat it. In other words, that asparagus on your plate has had one hell of a journey before it reached its final destination.

I had a go at growing asparagus once, and not very successfully at that. All that appeared from the raised bed was a pale green knobbly thing that was christened 'ET's Finger'. It was never eaten as it didn't look very appetizing and besides, I wanted to see how big it would get. Day after day, despite rain and wind, ET's finger hung on in there and each time I passed what was laughingly supposed to be the asparagus bed I'd mutter, 'ET, phone home.' He never did – get to phone home, that is – as the finger eventually turned into a stick and vanished overnight, leaving behind as a memory a raised mound of asparagus-free earth that looked as if I'd attempted to bury a body in a hurry.

I ended up buying some instead as the asparagus season was over, thanks to me being an optimistic fool and waiting for months in the vain hope that a few healthy, edible shoots might be about to follow old ET, which they never did. So I bought some, and it came from Peru. I'm such a hypocrite.

When I first arrived here I set about making a primitive allotment without any advice. I managed to grow a few heads of lettuce, not enough to fill a stall at a farmers market but enough to fill, well, a very small trug. There was already a greenhouse when I moved in and I intended to make good use of that too, so 'growing my own' became my latest obsession.

There were many failures. My two tomato plants managed to produce one solitary tom between them which, when ripe, was carried into the house as if it were a precious offering to the gods and then shared out between four of us. Of course we all declared it was the tastiest slither of tomato we'd ever had in our entire lives until Murphy ruined the moment by asking if that was 'it' and where was the rest of the crop?

As usual I'd laid out a small fortune at the garden centre in the way of equipment, not to mention the time I'd spent nurturing what few fruit and veg I was growing, and all I had to show for it was a couple of lettuces, one tomato and a handful of strawberries that the birds had taken a bite out of. However, the family motto is 'Wounded but not defeated' so I soldiered bravely on and instead of turning my back on the greenhouse and my primitive allotment I did what I knew I had to do – I got a gardener in. Well, the other family motto is 'If at first you don't succeed – cheat'.

I wanted strawberries? I got thousands of them. In fact I grew sick of the sight of the bloody things, plus I hated crawling under the protective green netting to pick them as it felt as if I'd got myself involved in some awful game-show challenge. The same happened with the tomatoes: all of a sudden the greenhouse was full of them, the plants bursting out of the door like giant triffids with red blobs hanging off their leaves. The gardener had also grown a few obscenely sized cucumbers, slightly curved and threatening, as well as a plant heaving with chilli peppers that once eaten gave you the ability to belch flames and had the neighbours phoning the fire brigade.

I left him to it and concentrated on killing plants in the garden instead.

My allotment did well for a while; there were good years when I had more produce than I was able to cope with as well as times when all that came out were a few green spuds and an artichoke. I started keeping a

journal a few years back, which I quickly gave up on, but here's something I found that I'd written concerning the allotment during what I called the Year of the Slug:

> As it's been raining so heavily we are plagued by an infestation of slugs that can strip an entire row of cabbage in one night. On the night of the summer solstice I felt that I had to do the right thing in the way of a celebration even if it was wet, miserable and cold. I waited until it grew dark and, more importantly, the rain had gone off, and as none of the others wanted to leave the house I went off alone and lit a small fire in the fire bowl that I have on the patio to celebrate the coming summer months and to welcome the sun as it hasn't been seen since God knows when.

No sooner had I got the damn fire going than it began to rain, and turning to go back into the house I skidded on something slippy and fell over.

'I bet it's dog shit,' I moaned to myself as I lay there in the rain wondering if I'd broken a hip or something, which I knew I hadn't but I was being dramatic. As it appeared nobody in the house had witnessed my fall there was no point me lying there expecting sympathy so I quickly got to my knees and in doing so put my hand into something exceedingly unpleasant.

I expected the worst, and it was pretty revolting as on closer inspection the clammy, slimy, squelchy thing my hand had pressed into wasn't dog related but instead turned out to be a giant slug.

Huge apologies went out to the dogs as, turning my torch on the ancient flagstones, I was horrified to see the reason that I'd slipped was not down to one of Eddie's little accidents but because I'd stood on a slug, one of hundreds that were forming a vast carpet on the patio. I watched in disgust as they slowly dragged their slimy, pulsating bodies towards the house and wondered if I was about to become the victim of 'The Attack of the Killer Slugs'. They were even climbing up the front room window. Would I go into the house only to find that everyone had been eaten? With Vera, transformed into a heaving mass of slugs, sat writhing on the couch watching *Emmerdale*? How long would it be before they made it to my bedroom and into my bed as I was sleeping, looking for an orifice to slither into and turn me into one of the Slug People like Vera?

No, I'm afraid they have to go, every single last one of the buggers. But how am I going to get rid of such a vast invasion?

The strawberry beds are crawling with them, as I discovered when I was on my hands and knees picking what rain-sodden fruit they'd left me. They've eaten all the lettuce as well as the spinach and stripped the parsley bed down to the stalk. There's no stopping these monsters and it's high time I consulted the interweb to find the best way of annihilating them.

I'd braced myself and collected a load of slugs in a bucket as I had a notion that the hens would enjoy them as a tasty treat, but after a brief examination and a peck or two they left them alone to slither off somewhere dark and slimy and take over another part of the garden.

I've found out various ways to deal with them. In a small plot an effective way to dispose of slugs is to catch them in a beer trap, as I'm sure many gardeners will agree. Slugs and snails love the scent of booze (not spirits) and putting a deep container filled with beer or a mixture of yeast and honey into the ground will entice them to crawl into it where, unable to escape, they'll drown. Don't fret; it's a happy death as they're too pissed to notice. I'd try this method of extermination myself but due to the vast amount of molluscs that are crawling around my place I'd need a brewery.

You can also quite simply pick them up (wear gloves) and drop them into a bucket of salty water to dispose of them, but that requires a very strong stomach as what you end up with is a bucket full of a watery slimy mess. I'm trying not to retch as I write about it.

Copper is an effective deterrent, as slugs loathe it because it gives them an electric shock on contact. You could surround the premises with copper wiring or sheets of copper banding but I have a feeling that would work out to be very expensive, and besides, to keep the copper effective you'd have to clean it regularly to prevent it from tarnishing. You'd be forever on your knees with the Brasso polishing the brass. Then there's also the chance that all this copper will attract the type who like to steal such things, like the thieving scum who frequently strip the copper telephone wiring from somewhere down the road leaving us with no internet connection or phone line.

Now I've admitted that I'm not much of a gardener, although I've improved a lot since the days when I bought a plant from the garden centre and the poor thing, realizing where it was going, would top itself on the bus home. Hopefully if I stick at it I'll improve to the standards of Percy Thrower. (Ha! Who remembers old Percy from their childhoods? No one? Damn you all.) Or even my ma, who could make anything grow, as our tiny front garden proved, stuffed as it was with magnificent roses and an assortment of healthy plants that she'd taken as cuttings from the gardens of the stately homes of Cheshire.

I find geraniums easy to maintain as well as lavender and catmint, which probably explains why I have a profusion of them in my garden. I put in a whole row of lavender plants near the washing line and now that they've matured into bushes I take the advice from a member of the gentry who'd never stepped foot in a laundry in her life but nevertheless saw fit to write a book advising domestic servants to 'dry delicate undergarments on a hedge of lavender grown especially for such a purpose by the washing line as it will infuse the garments with the pleasing scent of the flower as well as keeping the moth at bay'. I can only imagine that this washing line was hidden around the back of the house as the sight of madam's drawers hanging off the lavender bushes as guests drove down the drive might've caused a bit of a scandal.

Now I promised you earlier, in Valerie Singleton mode, that I'd tell you how I make my own moth-deterrent bags, so here goes.

Simply cut some lavender, tie it in bunches and hang them somewhere warm like an airing cupboard with paper bags attached to the ends to catch the heads as they fall. Wash and dry some rosemary sprigs then put them in the oven on the lowest setting possible on a lined baking tray. Strip the leaves from some wormwood and dry in the oven in the same way.

Mix the lot together, tie up in a square of butter muslin you've twisted into a bag, and attach them to coat hangers. Put them in with any decent woollen clothing you'd like to remain unholey.

If you don't mind the aroma of lavender combined with rosemary then these bags smell a damn sight better than the stench of mothballs. Lavender is purported to have a soporific and calming effect so it's ideal for the bedroom as an aid to sleep, although personally I find the smell overpowering, and besides, I have no trouble when it comes to kipping, it's the getting up that's hard.

The bees that swarm around my lavender hedge aren't particularly happy at having to share their hunting ground with my washing but they soon get over it and move out of the way to parts of the hedge that are free of sweaters. (I regret to report that there are no 'delicate undergarments' on my lavender: I wouldn't describe anyone in our household's drawers as being 'delicate'.)

I've planted lots of lavender and catmint about the garden as they're wonderful for attracting bees, butterflies and some pretty exotic moths, as is the buddleia, honeysuckle and foxglove. On a hot summer's day a buddleia bush that I've allowed to grow wild is alive with butterflies – red admirals, cabbage whites and the tortoiseshell – but there doesn't seem to be the variety of butterfly that there used to be, nor do there seem to be as many bees.

I've mentioned already that I'm a bit obsessed about bees. You may or may not realize that the bee is an endangered species thanks, once again, to the poisonous insecticides sprayed on crops worldwide, and yet without these little marvels of nature who pollinate these crops the human race would quickly die out from starvation as there'd no longer be any food, resulting in global famine.

My Aunty Bridget kept a few hives in her small orchard in Ireland and I'd like to do the same here in my orchard, but I haven't got round to it yet as beekeeping is not as plain sailing as it seems. For a start, how do I avoid colony collapse disorder? I'll need a mentor to guide me through the process, and when time eventually permits I intend to approach our local beekeeping association and get started.

We badly need to encourage more bees, and the benefits from keeping hives means a supply of fresh honey on the comb and wax for making polish, candles and soap, which again is a lot easier than it sounds. I went through a phase of making candles and soap using shop-bought untreated beeswax. (Another short-lived obsession, it was interesting for a while, and the soap was surprisingly good, but the candles were in need of Viagra as some of them drooped. The ones I made in old jam jars were more successful but I soon got bored with churning out bars of soap and flaccid candles and, giving it all up, went in search of another 'hobby' that might keep me interested for more than a few days.)

It's September already, the first day of autumn, and yet the weather has suddenly turned unseasonably warm. As the week goes on the temperature rises until the mercury hits 35°C and the media declares it's the hottest September since the 1940s, adding, as they are wont to do, that it won't last and by the end of the week there'll be storms and heavy rain. The beaches are packed and Dymchurch springs into life with holidaymakers making the most of this late summer.

It's nice to sit out in the garden and feel the sun – the proper sun, not the weak miserable sun that's popped out from behind grey storm clouds now and then over the past year. This sun is Mediterranean, and as I sit on the bench with my face skywards 'like a lizard on a rock', as Murphy used to say, it's good to see that I'm not alone. The lavender bushes are full of bees again and there's a number of cabbage whites and red admirals careering around from bush to flowers like drunks on a pub crawl.

The dogs have stayed indoors, Olga pegged out on the tiles in the cool of the laundry, as is Bullseye. Boycie is sat in his customary position half out of the back door and Louis is under the kitchen table, but Eddie, as usual, is stretched out on the patio, roasting on a hot paving slab in the full sun. I chase him in, worried he'll get sunstroke. He growls like a cat to show he's not amused and is soon back out again flat on his back enjoying the sun.

The nights are hot and muggy, as predicted by Simon Parkin on *Meridian Tonight*, and despite having all the windows open and no duvet on the bed it's impossible to sleep.

While I've discovered that I'm not very good with tomatoes and the like, I do have a knack for growing herbs – the legal variety you understand, as this is Kent, not Denver or Amsterdam – and since doing so I've been able to explore their medicinal properties, testing my potions out on friends as guinea pigs.

I've always been fascinated by the use of herbs for treating ailments and with my newly planted herb garden thriving I put the theory into practice, with amazing results. Before I commence this crash course in herbs I should warn you that if you are taking any form of prescription drugs then it's wise to consult your doctor before knocking back any herbal remedy as they may interact and end up doing more harm than good. Understand?

Now then, pay attention, for here are just a few of the herbs that are simple to grow ...

PARSLEY
(*Petroselinum crispum*)

There's an old saying that claims only the wicked can grow parsley. Well that says a lot about me as I've managed to produce a healthy crop of both curly and flat-leaf, which I think is the tastiest of the two.

Culpeper the seventeenth-century herbalist reckoned that parsley was the best thing for the kidneys and bladder, and an infusion of parsley leaves (put some in a teapot and make it as you would a pot of tea, only allow it to steep longer) does wonders for women with irregular periods. Never ever use if you're pregnant as it could induce a miscarriage. This only applies to women by the way.

According to legend, parsley that you've grown yourself should never be given as a gift as you give away all your luck. It is also claimed that parsley water has the ability to weaken glass, which I seriously doubt, but just in case don't wash your windows or your best wine glasses in any.

Parsley should never be transplanted from one place to another or, guess what? That's right, you'll be plagued by bad luck.

On the plus side, parsley contains more iron than spinach and it's also high in vitamin C and important minerals, so try and chew a sprig every day. If you've been eating garlic or anything that makes your breath resemble a sewer rat's then chewing parsley is an excellent breath freshener.

You can grow this tough little herb in a window box, a tub or in the garden. Plant in a well-drained crumbly soil with some organic matter (manure), place it in the sun and keep watered. If you don't allow the soil to dry out, all being well you should have a healthy crop to prove just how deliciously wicked you really are.

DILL
(Anethum graveolens)

One of my favourite herbs. The word 'dill' hails from the Anglo-Saxon word *dilla* meaning to calm and lull, because long before the days of Calpol they used it as a sedative for the kiddies. If you have trouble sleeping then a cup of dill tea before you hit the sack just might help.

Chewing dill seeds is a good cure for hiccups, and the gripe water that's given to babies to relieve colic is made from dill. You can make your own if you're being kept awake all night by a screaming nipper.

Gripe water

Take about a tablespoon of dill seeds and crush in a mortar and pestle. Boil them up in about 15 fl. oz of natural mineral water until the liquid has reduced. Allow to cool, strain, and then give that screaming babe a little spoonful and put your feet up and watch *Doctors* as your colic-free child has a little snooze. This home-made colic water doesn't keep any longer than a day so make sure you chuck it out and brew up a fresh batch the next time you need some.

Witches are reputed to dislike dill, so if you happen to have any in your neighbourhood who you'd rather not communicate with then plant some by your door and they'll just fly straight past and won't bother inviting you to their party.

'Trefoil, Vervain, John's Wort, Dill, / Hinder witches of their will' – so said Sir Walter Scott's gypsy Meg Merrilies, who inspired John Keats to write one of my favourite poems.

Dill isn't fussy but it's best grown from seed, and it doesn't mind what sort of soil you use as I've found that it does as well in a rich soil as it does in a poor one.

If you're lucky enough to have an allotment then plant it next to your cabbages and onions as dill is a natural insect repellent. If you haven't got an allotment to pootle about in then it does equally well in a tub or window box, but it does like full sun. Nip the flowers off the plant if you don't want it to bolt.

Never plant dill near carrots or fennel for if the dill flowers they'll cross-pollinate producing a hybrid that might just attack you or eat a small dog.

Finally, if you suffer from flatulence and are inclined to let one go in a packed lift or while running to catch the bus then here's something I found in an ancient *Home Herbal*. Three tablespoons of dill seed bruised and battered in a mortar and pestle but not quite beaten into a powder. Add to that half a bottle of white wine and leave to infuse for a week. Strain into a clean bottle and take what the *Home Herbal* recommends as 'a small glass full as 'tis a powerful expeller of wind'.

CHAMOMILE
(Anthemis nobilis)

If you've got a plant that you're fond of and the poor old thing is ailing and starting to droop then plant some chamomile next to it and watch it perk up. Chamomile is the district nurse of herbs and has the ability to 'heal' sick plants so it's not surprising that my garden is full of the stuff.

If you want a sweetly scented chamomile lawn then use the Roman variety (*Chamaemelum nobile*) as it will form a carpet of tiny white daisies and wispy leaves that smell like apples. I managed to grow a chamomile patch in the corner of the orchard; it started off well and then just seemed to stop spreading, possibly because it had hit a different soil. I'd used a light soil mixed with some sand to plant it but the soil in the orchard is dry and mainly clay and my creeping lawn refused to creep any further. Nevertheless there was enough of it for me to lie on, and with eyes closed and the hum of bees in the air I lay there breathing in the scent of the chamomile and came to the conclusion that this was just another reason, one of many, why I could never give up country living. I suppose I could lie amongst the chamomile in a city park – that's providing the city had one – but I'd rather not as I don't want to end up in court for contravening the laws of behaviour in public parks and gardens.

The German chamomile (*Matricaria chamomilla*), or rather the daisy heads of this herb, are the ones you make the tea with that supposedly calms frazzled nerves and prepares you for sleep. Gather these flowers, dry them and put them in a jar, as they are handy for a number of things. You can use them to make a gargle for a sore throat, and as for that calming infusion of tea, well it will also help with indigestion, nausea and any other stomach problems you may have.

Natural blondes – and I stress natural – can go brighter without having to resort to peroxide by giving their flowing tresses a rinse with chamomile tea, so all in all I'd say this herb is versatile as well as looking good in the flowerbed.

You can plant this herb in any old soil as long as it's dry and not out in the roasting sun. I've discovered that it does best in partial shade where it's cooler. Don't feed it with super-rich organic fertilizer or overwater it as it's not keen on a rich diet and will sulk and not produce many flowers, so leave it to its own devices and fuss over some of the other plants instead.

CATNIP
(Nepeta cataria)

Years ago my garden had entire banks of catnip (or catmint) but most of it was dug up by the previous owner and replaced with some rather straggly, gaudy red roses. There's still some left and I'm slowly replacing it, mixing it with lavender as they seem to go so well together. Catnip has a lovely blue flower that the bees and butterflies go crazy over, as do cats, though not all of them it seems.

There's a cat that comes around occasionally, a big old feral moggy who doesn't seem to be bothered in the least by my pack of dogs trying to bash the French windows down to get at him. Nor is he the least bit interested in the catmint. His pal, though, a younger black and white cat, goes completely potty and throws himself into it like a teenager body-surfing at a heavy metal concert while the older cat lies on the lawn, lashing his tail and watching in bemusement. Maybe catmint only appeals to cats of a certain age, but then who can tell with cats?

Insects and ants aren't big fans of catnip so grow some in a pot on the window sill or near to the house to keep the little buggers out. Hanging a bunch over your door is guaranteed to attract the faery folk who will slip in through your letterbox and flutter about creating an air of harmony in the home – providing you don't mistake them for flies and swat them.

Both the leaves and the flowers can be used to make a tea that is reputed to 'calm hysterics, vapours and fits in children and gentlewomen'. I don't know what the men were prescribed if they threw a wobble; I suppose they just had a large Scotch, a pat on the back and kept a stiff upper lip. Catnip tea will act as a very gentle sedative, but beware, for according to another ancient herbal manual 'If the root be chewed it will make the most quiet and gentle of persons fierce, full of rage and quarrelsome.' So don't give any to your elderly aunt or your nan, not unless you're prepared to go down to the police station with your rent book to bail them out after they've been on the rampage in Boots.

FEVERFEW
(Tanacetum parthenium)

Do you suffer from migraines? Then grow some feverfew. It's not only pretty with its daisy-like flowers but a few leaves, eaten between a small piece of bread, is guaranteed to get rid of that thumping head. The leaves are bitter and can cause mouth ulcers if you chew enough of them but the bread acts as a barrier and makes the leaves palatable.

Feverfew is a hardy perennial, a distant cousin of the chrysanthemum (it took me ages to get the spelling of that right), and is often mistaken for a weed. It likes a sunny spot in well-drained soil, and although it's fond of a drop of Adam's Ale be careful not to over-water it as you'll kill it.

It's good for keeping moths away as well, so as soon as you've got rid of your thumping headache you could mix some with your lavender, rosemary and wormwood concoction.

HERB OF JUPITER
(genus Sempervivum)

There used to be a wonderful Greek shoemaker's in Chiltern Street, sadly long gone, owned by a Mr Savva who made ladies' and gents' shoes for theatre and television. Mr Savva was a craftsman who knew how to make a good pair of shoes and after years of wearing totally unsuitable, toe-crippling footwear bought from markets and usually just that bit on the small side Mr Savva changed my life. Thirty years later I've still got shoes he made for Lily Savage and I was still wearing them for the run of *Cinderella* at the London Palladium last Christmas. Talk about value for money.

Anyway, to get back to herbs, I was being fitted for shoes at a time when I had a humdinger of a corn on my little toe.

'Rub it with the juice of the Herb of Jupiter,' Mr Savva advised. 'It'll be gone by the time this shoe is ready.'

When I asked him what Herb of Jupiter was and where I could get some he simply answered, 'It's a plant that grows on walls.'

It wasn't until I moved to the countryside that I discovered what the Herb of Jupiter actually looked like and that it did indeed 'grow on walls'. It can grow from underneath a roof tile or a crack in the wall or between the cracks in paving stones as it doesn't seem to require much in the way of soil. It's a tough little thing, and people grow it in their rockeries not realizing that this is an ancient herb.

The leaf, if cut open, oozes a sticky sap so if you can cope with having one wrapped around the offending toe with a plaster or bandage to hold it in place for a week or so then you'll find when you remove the now rotting leaf that the corn has shrunk.

I never took Mr Savva's advice as I preferred to use another ancient method for corn removal as practised down the years by members of my family – a razor blade.

If you're not going to use the sap of the Herb of Jupiter for your corns then use it to treat cuts and burns, although personally I'd recommend the gel from a freshly cut aloe leaf for a burn.

VALERIAN
(*Valeriana officinalis*)

The Herb of Sleep, although I've stopped growing it as I've heard that it attracts rats. It's a shame as it grows quite tall and bursts into sweet-smelling pinky-white flowers. But now I have visions of a group of rats gathered around the plant sat on their haunches and telling each other to 'Inhale that vibe, dude'.

Swedish elves, by all accounts, were jealous little creatures who couldn't abide valerian. While preparing the groom for his march down the aisle, sprigs of valerian were hidden inside his wedding clothes to keep these angry and envious elves at bay, intent as they were on causing the groom harm for snaring himself a bride. One can only assume that Swedish brides must've been extraordinarily beautiful to invoke such reactions in the little people.

You can buy all manner of preparations containing valerian to help you sleep, yet the experts reckon that there's no conclusive evidence that valerian is a sedative. I'm afraid I disagree. Valerian has been used as a treatment for assorted ailments since the times of the ancient Greeks but I'll concede that you have to be careful when using it.

I said earlier that I was fond of trying out my potions on friends, Vera in particular. The dried root of the plant is the most potent part, and out of this I made a tea for Vera to try out. Within ten minutes she was out like a light and slept solidly for over an hour. I did wonder for a moment if I'd be tried for murder, but thankfully Vera awoke refreshed and there was no harm done.

A pregnant woman should never take valerian, and prolonged use of this herb can cause withdrawal symptoms if stopped. Best leave it alone I say.

FLAX
(Linum usitatissimum)

A beautiful blue-flowered annual that has a variety of uses. The long-stalked flax was used to make linen, but unless you've got a loom in the attic I wouldn't bother if I were you.

The seeds of this herb are a mild laxative so don't eat too many if you're planning on going for a long walk. The seed oil, which you can buy in supermarkets, is rich in omega-3 and excellent for the heart. It's also beneficial for the skin, so forget expensive face creams, the majority of which are a waste of money anyway, and take a teaspoon of flax oil daily instead. You'll have skin like a baby in a couple of weeks.

When you harvest the seeds, do as you would with lavender: simply cut the plants when the seed pods are looking like they're nice and ripe, then hang them upside down with a paper bag around the end to catch the falling seeds.

Flax is a sun-lover and prefers a well-drained sandy soil. It's easy to maintain and you'll soon have a decent crop.

In the olden days farmers would leap over midsummer fires to ensure a healthy crop. I doubt if they do that today, at least I've never seen any farmers around here doing it. One beautiful summer's eve we were all sat in the garden having a few drinks. The fire bowl was blazing away merrily, and Vera, having imbibed a little too much of the booze, staggered as she got out of her chair and fell into it. Remarkably she was unscathed, rising from the fire bowl like the phoenix from the ashes and, knocking back a lager, seeming not in the least bit perturbed. I think all those years working in that factory making flame-retardant overalls must have had something to do with it. Perhaps the chemicals used to make these garments flameproof rubbed off.

THYME
(Thymus vulgaris)

A lovely smelling plant that now comes in a variety of flavours: lemon-scented, orange-scented, chocolate ... you name it. But I prefer the plain old thyme-scented thyme, if you catch my drift. It's very easy to grow as long as it gets full sun, and it enhances a boring stew or casserole. Supposedly it was those Roman invaders who introduced this versatile herb to our shores.

I recently had bronchitis and an infection of the upper respiratory tract that left me sounding like a pubescent demon whose voice was about to break. Thyme is not only rich in beta-carotene, it also contains a potent antiseptic called thymol that has been used since year one as a cure for chest complaints. I made a tea out of the leaves, let it steep for fifteen minutes, and then with a slice of lemon and some honey drank a mugful. It certainly helped my breathing and eased my throat.

Thyme oil is reputed to be able to kill off the MRSA bug in hospitals, so why aren't they wiping surfaces down with it and giving the ward floors a thyme wash?

In parts of Scotland a sprig of thyme is placed under the pillow to keep you safe from nightmares, and it's said that thyme oil can help prevent hair loss, rejuvenate ageing skin and treat acne. Mix it with a little almond oil, as it's never wise to apply essential oils directly on to the skin.

ROSEMARY
(Rosmarinus officinalis)

If you like eating lamb then a few sprigs of rosemary dotted about the joint as you roast it will complement the meat.

I could no more eat lamb than I could a kitten, and I'm not over-fond of the pungent smell of rosemary either, yet like thyme, this ancient herb is extremely versatile. The ancients used it for magic formulas and love spells and it is often seen growing on a grave, as it is the herb of remembrance.

Herbalists of old would use it as a stimulant to 'dispel the Black Dog', meaning to lift depression. It's good for the heart and for blood circulation as it can strengthen the capillaries.

For centuries brunettes have been using an infusion of rosemary as a hair wash to give their flowing locks a healthy shine, and it probably kept the nits away as well. Rosemary is also great for treating dandruff. You could make your own shampoo from scratch or you can cheat by getting hold of an inexpensive bottle of rosemary shampoo, or any shampoo that professes to contain essences of herbs: put as many sprigs of rosemary as you want into the bottle and leave it for a few weeks to infuse. You can add a sprig of lavender if you fancy it and a few drops of rosemary essential oil.

Phew, if you walked down the street after washing your hair in this shampoo I guarantee that people will want to come up and lick you. Either that or mistake you for a leg of lamb.

So go on then, have a go at growing some herbs. They can liven up a bland meal, and the infusions and potions you'll knock up can be quite beneficial. Most garden centres stock herb plants now, as do some supermarkets, or you could buy the seed and cultivate your own plants which is far more rewarding.

An Interesting Concoction that's Not for Sissies

I mentioned this remarkable cure-all known as Four Thieves Vinegar in one of my last books but refused to give the secret recipe away for fear of reprisals. However, since the advent of Brexit the rules have changed and I'm now free to tell all without the European Alchemist and Necromancers Union kicking my door in.

There are numerous tales as to the origin of Four Thieves Vinegar but they all have one thing in common and that's its association with the Plague. During the 1600s the Black Death was once again sweeping across Europe and four robbers from Toulouse had been having a merry old time looting the homes of plague victims. They were eventually caught, and at their trial were sentenced to death by burning at the stake. The judge was curious to know what preventative measures these thieves had taken as in the years that they'd been robbing corpses the plague seemingly hadn't affected them. He struck a deal with the thieves: reveal the secret of how they escaped the plague and their sentence would be mitigated from the slow, painful death of being burned alive to a quicker though equally unpleasant death by hanging. Of course they agreed to the beak's terms and readily confessed to drinking a concoction of herbs steeped in vinegar.

The original recipe contains a wide variety of herbs and essential oils. The recipe that follows, simplified but equally effective, is just one of the formulas in use today.

Take a pint of apple cider vinegar and add to it the crushed cloves from two whole bulbs of garlic. To represent the thieves you add four different herbs of your choice. I use rosemary, wormwood, thyme and sage. I also add a few drops of clove and peppermint oil, a twist of lemon peel, a piece of peeled and crushed fresh ginger, and a teaspoon of honey.

Put it all in a decent-sized jar with a secure lid and give it a good shake. Place it somewhere dark for seven days, giving it a shake now and then.

Strain the contents through a sieve into a bottle or jar using a funnel, making sure you get every drop out of the garlic and herbs, and drink a shot glass of this miraculous cure-all if you feel you've got a cold coming on.

Everyone I know who has partaken of the potion swears by it and I'm constantly being pressured to 'make another bottle'. So after I've let the pigs out and had something to eat I'm going to do just that.

Superstitions and Country Lore

I was on the train one afternoon making my way up to London when a man who had been house-hunting in Kent started talking to me. 'They're a superstitious lot down there, aren't they?' the man said. Apparently one of the properties he'd viewed had a bag of rusty nails hanging by the front door 'to keep witches and evil spirits away'. I replied that while I couldn't speak on behalf of the good folk of Kent as to their superstitious beliefs, I was known to indulge in a lot of rituals myself to ward off 'bad luck'.

As if on cue, just as the train pulled into Ebbsfleet I spotted a solitary magpie on the opposite platform and spat in the palm of my hand as I've done for as long as I can remember.

Before we go any further, by 'spat' I don't mean one of those enormous throat-clearing missiles that young lads like to project on to the pavement to show that they're 'ard; mine is more of a symbolic gesture, a mere droplet if that, into the palm of the hand, though I've been given many strange looks over the years for doing so.

'Magpie,' I explained to the bloke on the train. 'One for sorrow, you know. Spitting gets rid of the jinx you see.'

'Oh,' he replied, looking at me as if he'd mistakenly got on the Hogwarts Express and was sat next to Professor Snape. 'Maybe I'll stay in London and the twenty-first century then.'

I didn't bother to tell him that in some parts of Ireland it was once customary to spit on a new-born baby to bring it good luck in life. Maybe that peculiar custom had something to do with a misguided belief that by exposing it to germs this somehow would strengthen the child's immune system. That custom has long since gone out of fashion – at least I hope it has as I couldn't imagine a proud mum being very happy at her chain-smoking neighbour leaning over the bassinet of her newborn and landing a yocker straight in the kid's eye.

Jesus, it was claimed, used his saliva to cure blindness by mixing it with dirt, making a paste and smearing it over the blind man's eyes, thereby restoring his sight. Ancient man (and woman) considered their saliva to be part of their very life essence so there was no casual spitting in the cave for them; spitting was a serious business and only done so as an offering to their gods who, I'm assured, greatly appreciated this gesture and as a thank you sent a solar eclipse. The big ball of all-powerful light in the sky suddenly vanishing and plunging day into night freaked ancient man (and woman) out and to protect themselves and to appease the gods they developed what we'd call superstitious beliefs.

There are those who spit in their hands before tackling a spot of manual labour – at least they do in the films – and I seem to remember spitting in my hand to seal a deal with a handshake, as many club owners from my past can testify. My Aunty Chris always spat on her money before she placed it on a bet on the horses. She also did the same if she won any back, which wasn't that often. When I was a kid, whenever I'd just had a haircut our next-door neighbour Frank used to spit on his hand and slap me over the back of the head shouting 'Firsty wets!' to bring him luck, an innocent and good-natured act that would undoubtedly be classed as child abuse now. Oh well.

Is it wrong to be superstitious? Are you? I grew up with it, having a mother and two aunts who could've given a very realistic performance as the three ladies in the Scottish Play. There's a perfect example for you – the Scottish Play, the name given to Shakespeare's *Macbeth* by actors who wouldn't dare utter the M-word during rehearsals or in a theatre dressing room as it's considered to be terribly unlucky and in doing so could bring unmitigated disaster to a production.

The last line of a play is never spoken during rehearsals either; it's only said when the company is in the theatre and on stage. I've heard tell of a few actors who got so accustomed to not saying the line in rehearsals that they omitted it from the actual performance as well.

Whistling in a dressing room is also a big no-no as in doing so the perpetrator is 'whistling up the Devil' who is guaranteed to blight the production, causing mishaps, mayhem and forgotten lines – or as the latter is called in the business, darling, 'drying', as in 'I dried tonight during the second act'. The person who has committed this unforgiveable act will be ordered out of the room and told to knock on the door, and as soon as you've invited them in they have to turn around three times and then swear. This ritual scares the Devil off and the show can go on without fear or threat from unwelcome supernatural mischief.

There's a far more practical reason why whistling in the theatre is frowned upon. At one time the crew who worked up in the flies of the theatre were former sailors who were used to complicated rigging and well suited to theatre life. When a scene change was due they'd communicate to each other by whistling, so a rogue whistler could cause confusion and possibly a fatal accident.

Stuck in the doldrums out on the ocean, sailors on small sailing vessels would whistle in the hope that this might whip up a wind, yet on other ships it was considered taboo as you might whistle up a storm and sink the ship. I can recall lots of businessmen walking the top deck of the *Mountwood*, one of the ferries that crossed the Mersey, whistling like budgies and we always got to the other side safely and on time.

It's good luck to touch a sailor's collar, by the way, but you have to do it without him noticing. There's a good reason for this: if he did suddenly feel a stranger's hand on his shoulder as he's walking down the street he might just turn round and belt you.

New shoes on a table would send my ma into a frenzy of panic, as would opening an umbrella indoors. It's thanks to her I've inherited these little foibles, and a lot more besides. The fear of putting new shoes on a table stems back to times when hangings were an everyday occurrence. The unfortunate victims would stand on a wooden scaffold and shoes on a table symbolized this, therefore to be careless enough to toss your brand-new pair of Jimmy Choos on the table will bring bad luck and quite possibly the death of a family member. When I lived in Yorkshire for a while, someone in a pub reliably informed me that when a coal miner died in a mining accident it was traditional to place his boots on the table as a mark of respect. Therefore flinging your brand-new Dr Martens on the table with gay abandon was seen as a gesture that was not only disrespectful to the dead but also a surefire way to kill off one of your loved ones. So the next time a parcel arrives containing those new stilettos you bought off the internet, be careful where you put them.

Funnily enough, the warning doesn't mention old shoes, which is strange, as surely having a pair of muddy boots with a smattering of dog poo and a lump of chewing gum stuck to the sole propped up against the sauce bottle is far worse than a new one, not to mention unhygienic?

BEES

A swarm of bees in May
Is worth a load of hay,
A swarm of bees in June
Is worth a silver spoon,
A swarm of bees in July
Is not worth a fly.

In other words, the weather is going to be lousy.

If a bumblebee flies into your house and buzzes happily about then you can expect a visitor, but if you're stupid enough to kill it then the visitor will be the bearer of bad news. The moral of this tale? Don't kill a bee unless you want the bailiffs, police or tax inspectors to come knocking on your door, or a neighbour to tell you your cat has just been run over.

The name Melissa owes its origins to the bee. In ancient Greece Melissa was a faery who protected the baby Zeus from his father Cronus, a god with a nasty habit of eating his children. When Cronus discovered that Melissa had been caring for Zeus he turned her into a worm out of spite, which I think was a bit steep. However, when the baby Zeus grew up he turned her into a bee as a thank you, although he could've done the decent thing and turned her back into a human being, but then there's no point trying to understand the actions of a god.

Melissa did get a group of priestesses named after her though as the hand maidens of Demeter, the goddess of the harvest, were called the Melissae in her honour.

Bee stings are said to cure rheumatism, and they were also said to have swarmed and left the garden of Eden as they were appalled at the antics of Adam and Eve and that business concerning the consuming of forbidden fruit.

SPILLING SALT

Well, according to my Aunty Annie, to do so, even unintentionally, is to invite the Devil himself into the house, and like a straggler at a party who should've gone home hours ago he's going to be hard to get rid of. However, there's always a bit of preventative magic to get shot of him and that is to toss a pinch of the salt over your left shoulder, and as Old Nick is supposedly peering over it this course of action will scare him and send him scampering off back to hell. I always remember thinking that it didn't take much to get rid of him considering his fearsome credentials, but I'm nevertheless tossing salt over my shoulder every time I spill any as I'm sure just about everybody else does, this being one of our oldest superstitions.

Salt has always been highly prized since day one. It was mined from the earth and gathered from the sea and paid out as wages to Roman soldiers (the Latin for salt is *sal*, hence the word 'salary') which goes to show how valuable it was. I can only presume they sold it on, thereby making a tidy profit in the process. What else were they supposed to do with it? They couldn't live on salt alone, not unless they wanted high blood pressure and an incurable thirst.

Salt was and is a preservative and a purifier. When I visited the Wieliczka salt mine in Poland I learned that there used to be an underground TB clinic there, which didn't surprise me as the air felt clean and pure and certainly cleared the chest.

Judas spilled the salt at the Last Supper, and it's used still in pagan rituals as a means of protection and cleansing. Salt is powerful magic, and people still go to any lengths to get their hands on it. Just drop by any trendy shop or market on a Saturday afternoon and you'll find hordes of well-heeled folk on the hunt for the much-prized Andalusian salt.

By the way, in case you didn't already know, salt is brilliant at getting rid of stains. Just soak the offending article overnight in a bowl of cold water laced with salt and it should shift it.

MIRRORS

Mirrors are a reflection of the soul, or so it was believed, and to break one will bring you seven years' bad luck. The antidote for this is to throw the broken pieces into flowing water such as a stream or a river but most definitely not your bath as you're running it. I once broke a hand mirror in a dressing room, which surely meant a double curse was coming my way. On the night of a full moon I threw the broken pieces in the Thames right by Tower Bridge. It made an awful clatter and a woman in one of the apartments above me came out on to her balcony to ask what I thought I was doing.

I told her the truth – what else could I say? 'I've just thrown some broken pieces of mirror into the river to get rid of the seven years' bad luck,' I explained sheepishly in my best telephone voice.

'Right-oh,' she replied, and went back indoors as if she encountered strange people chucking mirrors in the Thames every night, which maybe they do.

Who doesn't know the command given by Snow White's vain stepmother? 'Mirror, mirror on the wall, who is the fairest one of all?' Mirrors have long been considered to have magical powers. Witches use black mirrors for scrying (foretelling the future) and Catherine de' Medici, the much-maligned Queen of France known to her detractors as 'Madame La Serpente', was reputed to consult a magic mirror hidden in a secret circular room. She was a great believer in the occult and was also no slouch when it came to poisons, frequently offering her enemies an apple that was laced with something lethal 'for the journey home', or a pair of fur-lined gloves, the lining impregnated with a deadly toxin that would cause the victim to sweat blood. Well that'll learn them for calling her Mrs Snake won't it?

It's said that Catherine was the inspiration for the Queen in Snow White, but there's also a theory that Ms White was based on the sad tale of one Margaretha von Waldeck, a young German countess who fell in love with a prince and whose wicked stepmother forbade her to marry even though he was quite a catch and would eventually be promoted to King Philip of Spain. The marriage was doomed for political reasons and poor Margaretha was found dead from poisoning, some laying the blame at the King of Spain's doorstep, who didn't approve of his son hanging around this German girl; others pointed the finger at her stepmother Katharina von Hatzfeld, which was a bit pointless as she'd been dead for some time before Margaretha returned home.

Mirrors, apart from creating light and the illusion of space, were seen as a symbol of luxury and wealth, and come nightfall, reflecting the light from a myriad candles these elaborate mirrors must have appeared truly magical. Imagine the magnificent Hall of Mirrors at Versailles or the Catherine Palace in Pushkin, the summer residence of Russia's tsars, with its equally impressive mirrored halls bathed in candlelight. It's no wonder they considered mirrors to have powers.

I was in a shop in Amsterdam recently run by a woman who painstakingly restored old mirrors to their original condition. Staring into a seventeenth-century mirror that had once belonged to a member of the French aristocracy, I remarked to the owner that the people who had once looked at their reflections in this glass had in all probability lost their heads during the revolution. I don't think she used it as a selling point.

BERRIES

Early berries on a tree predict a cruel winter ahead, presumably because the trees very obligingly produce berries for the birds to stock up on, although with global warming and weird climate change I doubt now if this is a reliable indicator as a weather warning. I had daffs growing in the first week of January – now surely that can't be right.

HORSESHOES

You'll find a lot of these hanging over front doors and stables in the countryside as apart from giving the place a touch of rustic authenticity, a horseshoe is purported to ward off the Devil.

Way back in the year dot – 959 to be exact – St Dunstan, the Archbishop of Canterbury, had a part-time job as a blacksmith, which was handy as one day the Devil himself turned up asking Good St Dunstan if he could do something with his split hoof having hurt it after all that running around after people who had spilled salt. St Dunstan, being a saintly kind of chap, hammered a horseshoe none too gently into the Devil's tender hoof, only agreeing to remove it if the Devil promised never to try to gain access to a place that had a horseshoe hanging above the door.

Remember, the ends of the horseshoe should be pointed upwards to the skies and not the other way as its protective powers will pour out.

FLOWERS

Never bring ivy, lilac or hawthorn into the house as they are portents of death and guaranteed to bring bad luck. My mother wouldn't have lilies in the house, in particular Arum lilies as she saw them as funeral flowers; nor would she mix red and white flowers together as that too was an omen of death, the red flowers representing blood while the white symbolized bandages ...

Another feasible reason as to why lilac should remain outdoors might have something to do with the practice of bringing the corpse home and laying it out in the parlour for a period of time before the burial enabling the friends and family of the loved one to pay their respects and have a few whiskys and a boiled ham sarnie at the same time.

The lilac that would've been brought in the house on such an occasion was not just for decorative purposes but also to mask the smell of the decaying corpse.

Hawthorn is a sacred tree, and the faery folk who inhabit it don't take kindly to having their flowering branches stripped by a mortal who thinks that these blooms will look nice artfully arranged in a vase on the dining room table. Beware, for the faeries will follow you and cause havoc in your home as revenge.

The only time it was considered safe to pick the hawthorn blossom was on the first of May when those horny medieval lads and lasses would frolic and gambol in the fields, gathering the blossom to welcome the awakening summer.

To pick hawthorn after the month of May would be folly. Witches use it to make wands and besoms for flying, and as the old rhyme says, 'Hawthorn bloom and elder flowers will fill a home with evil powers'.

So there you go. Stick to roses – as long as you don't mix red with white.

ACORNS

An acorn in the window means that the house will never be struck by lightning. The oak is sacred to the Norse god Thor who once sheltered underneath a mighty oak during a violent electrical storm. That's why you'll find a carved wooden acorn as a blind pull on window blinds as lightning would never dare strike the oak.

Carrying an acorn around in your pocket is supposed to ensure long life, so forget Botox, just hang one around your neck as it will restore a youthful bloom to your cheeks and a sparkle to your eyes.

There's an old saying that goes 'Oak before ash, in for a splash; ash before oak, in for a soak'. Meaning that if the oak comes into leaf before the ash you can expect the odd shower, but if the ash comes into leaf first then you can guarantee it's going to lash down.

BESOMS (OR BROOMSTICKS)

A besom placed behind your door will mean that you will never be broken into – same with a sprig of fresh sage. A cinnamon broom hung on the back of the door will disperse negative energies and draw good luck towards you. Hanging a Henry Hoover will not have the same effect.

FIRST OF THE MONTH

The first words you should utter the minute you open your eyes on the first day of every month are 'White rabbits' as this will ensure that the coming month will be a lucky one for you. I always forget to say it, instead greeting the start of the day with my usual 'Bloody hell'.

Rabbits have the power of the evil eye as they are born with their eyes open, which is why it's fortuitous to give them a mention on the first of the month.

White rabbits have always been considered to be lucky, which explains the profusion of rabbits' feet hanging off key rings in the seaside souvenir shops of my youth.

During the witch-hunting craze any woman unfortunate enough to be caught with a brown rabbit in the house would instantly be accused of being a witch. Rabbits, like cats, were suspected of being familiars, and if it 'answered' to the name of Pyewacket then you were doomed.

Had the woman who used to run the launderette when I was a teenager been around during the days of the Salem witch hunt she would've undoubtedly had the finger pointed at her. And it would've been me doing the pointing, as revenge for not letting me use the tumble dryer to dry my home-washed jeans on a Saturday night when I wanted to go out clubbing.

She was fond of declaring darkly to any customer who brought in blankets to be washed during the month of May, 'Wash your blankets in May, wash a loved one away.' She was always happy if a customer's relative dropped dead after she'd chanted her prophetic warning at them as she'd been proven right; if it was the customer themselves who bit the dust then she was positively ecstatic, and amenable to allowing teenage lads to tumble-dry their wet jeans. I'm guessing that her gloomy prophecy might have something to do with the housewife being a bit hasty and stripping the bed of the winter blankets when the weather wasn't yet warm enough, thereby leaving the occupant of the said bed wide open to colds, flu and pneumonia, not to mention waking up perished with the cold in the middle of the night.

PICTURES

Just as a bird flying into the house meant there was sure to be a death, a picture falling unaided off the wall was also considered to be a portent of doom. If the picture happens to be a photo or a painting of a person then you'd better tell them to cash that private pension in and quick as they're not going to be needing it.

In my case, if a painting falls off the wall it's because the nail the picture is hanging on was given only a cursory tap with whatever heavy object was to hand at the time and has only ever been just about hanging in there. Consequently the chances are that if you pass a picture on the wall in my house there's a good chance it will fall at your feet.

MONEY

A basil leaf placed inside your purse or wallet will ensure that you will never go short.

Never give a purse as a present without first putting a coin inside to guarantee prosperity.

Money should be turned in the pocket on the night of the full and new moon, and never look at either through glass or the branches of the trees. There's a rhyme I was taught many years ago that should be chanted on the night of the full moon, preferably outdoors. You don't need to be naked for this, which is just as well if you intend to perform this moon spell in Birkenhead Park or on Wandsworth Common as the intention is to attract good fortune not a suspended sentence for indecent exposure, so keep your kit on.

You need to hold whatever notes you have on you in your right hand (coins won't do) and, staring straight at the moon, chant:

> *Moon, moon, oh beautiful moon,*
> *Fairer far than any star,*
> *Moon, moon, let it so be,*
> *Bring money and fortune to me.*

Good luck, and let me know if you win the lottery as you owe me 10 per cent commission and if you don't cough up I'll send the faeries round.

High Tea

Of all the meals of the day this is the one that I really like the best, and yet I hardly ever bother with it – although writing about it now on an extremely cold and windy Saturday night and reminding myself just how enjoyable a full-blown tea is, I probably will tomorrow.

I remember my cousin Maureen saying once, 'You can't beat one of Aunty Mollie's teas.' She was referring to the Sunday teas my mother used to dish up when the family came round. My mother's salad plate consisted of a slice of boiled ham, a spring onion artistically placed across said slice, and half a tomato served with a dollop of Heinz salad cream. Olive oil was never used to dress a salad as this was only obtainable in Boots and was solely for earaches. There was also a mountain of tinned salmon sandwiches, plus homemade apple pie, scones and cake.

If there was a lot of lettuce and she was in a hurry, my mother would wrap the freshly rinsed lettuce in a tea towel and then pop it in the spin dryer, sitting on top as it span because if you didn't the dryer took off across the kitchen floor spewing water everywhere. I use a plastic salad spinner these days. It provides quite enough centrifugal force to dry a lettuce and is less hassle than my mum's spin dryer.

There's two types of teatimes, Afternoon Tea and High Tea. My mother's teas were traditional High Teas, informal and sociable and served at the traditional hour of six o'clock, and if the food was plentiful enough, which it normally was, then unless you were a bit of a gannet you probably didn't need dinner later on.

Afternoon Tea was a much different affair. Ladies wore hats and tea gowns and nibbled on dainty cakes and sipped tea from tiny china cups, making polite chit-chat before moving on to someone else's house to do exactly the same thing. I wonder if any of them ever asked to use the lav considering all the tea drinking that went on or would that have been considered a terrible faux pas?

Apart from still being served in expensive hotels around the world the traditional Afternoon Tea has gone out of favour in a lot of homes. It's not surprising really as it is a bit of a palaver and who has the time these days, not to mention the funds, to be dishing out elaborate teas? I suppose eating a mountain of cake and sandwiches followed by dinner a few hours later isn't good for those worrying about their waistline either, nor in all likelihood is it particularly healthy.

Still, once a week on a Sunday won't kill you.

In working-class homes an offer to 'come to our house for your tea' didn't mean sandwiches and cakes, you were being invited to sit down for a proper meal. Lunch and brunch didn't exist; you had your dinner around midday and supper was a snack you had before you went to bed. But let's get back to the matter of tea.

If it's an Afternoon Tea you're serving up then you'll need to get the best bone china tea service out, as well as some starched linen napkins beautifully laid out in an elegant drawing room as you pour tea for your guests from a silver teapot that has been in the family for generations.

That's fine if you live in Downton Abbey, but in the real world you just have to adapt, and with a little imagination you too can serve an Afternoon Tea wherever you like as long as you make a bit of an effort and don't just sling a mug of builder's tea and a plate of curled-up sarnies stuffed with a dubious fish-paste filling under their noses.

High Tea, unlike the more refined Afternoon Tea, is not a rushed meal. It's a time to relax, to savour the variety of food on offer, and to chat about the day or tear someone's reputation to shreds, depending on the company and your temperament.

On the rare occasions I have a fit of madness and make a full-blown High Tea the kitchen looks like a thousand chefs on amphetamines have dished up for the Queen's Garden Party, but it's worth the mess, the preparation time and the clearing up afterwards – although for the more proficient and organized cook it's probably a stroll in the park.

HOW TO MAKE A DECENT POT OF TEA

First off always use freshly drawn water from your tap, well or fresh spring down the field, not water that's already been boiled and is sitting in the kettle.

Just before the kettle comes to the boil, warm the teapot with a little of the hot water and then throw it out – the water not the teapot.

The old rule is one teaspoon of leaf tea per person plus one for the pot. Loose-leaf tea definitely makes a better pot of tea than tea bags. I can't abide the wide variety of fruit teas on offer as I'm not an elf so I go for an English Breakfast or an Assam.

Don't let the water boil for too long as my dad used to reckon this tainted the tea. I don't know if this is true but nevertheless I let the water in the kettle boil furiously for no longer than five seconds before pouring it into the teapot.

Leave it to brew for about four minutes, give the pot a good stir, then pour out through a tea strainer.

Now, does the milk go in the cup first or last? The aristocracy added their milk last while us commoners put it in first, so who's right? I put mine in last, not because I fancy myself as Lord Snot but because I don't want it too milky. I like to be able to determine if the tea is strong enough. There is a theory, though, that the correct way is to put the milk in first. Each to their own, but remember this: tea definitely tastes better in a teacup than in a mug.

BOOZE

Is alcohol ever served at tea? The Edwardians as well as the Victorians would occasionally serve a claret cup, a potent concoction of sherry, claret, soda water and an assortment of herbs. Personally I think that's a bit much to be knocking back at 4.30 in the afternoon, especially if you're paying a lot of calls and are obliged to 'take a small glass' every time.

I'm surprised the pavements of Eaton Place weren't littered with aristocratic women out of their minds on booze.

The men, those who ever found themselves at an Afternoon Tea, that is, would be offered a whisky or brandy with soda.

A more pleasant alternative to the claret cup is a white wine and borage cup, particularly if it's a hot afternoon and you're taking tea in the garden and don't mind the wasps and flies. This would've been served in a cut-glass crystal punch bowl with a ladle and matching glass cups hanging off the rim as it was all about presentation, but as I haven't got one I use a large glass fruit bowl that Murphy picked up for a ludicrously cheap price in Prague.

Old-fashioned White Wine and Borage Cup

A bunch of borage leaves and flowers
A decent-sized sprig of mint
A bottle of your favourite white wine
Caster sugar to taste
Juice of half a lemon
A bottle of soda water, about half a pint

Find a nice big jug, or bowl if you've got one, bruise the borage and mint leaves, and place inside. Pour over the wine, add the sugar and stir well, then leave to stand for half an hour. Remove the leaves and add the lemon juice, soda water and some crushed ice. Float some of those rich blue borage flowers on top and serve immediately.

The sort of alcohol suitable for a High Tea would've either been a jug of ale or cider, preferably scrumpy.

However, as Joan Crawford was heard to say, 'If you're going to drink then drink what you like,' although fishing a flask containing 100 per cent proof vodka out of your handbag and lashing it into your tea will undoubtedly start a rumour that you need the help of AA.

Taking Afternoon Tea is an innovation reputedly attributed to Anna Russell, the Duchess of Bedford. Personally I doubt if she was the first person to ever eat a butty in the afternoon but I do believe that she was quite possibly responsible for making it fashionable.

Anna was a great pal of the young Queen Victoria and one of her Ladies of the Bedchamber. I'm not up to date in terms of what is required of a Lady of the Bedchamber but I suppose she laid out the Queen's nightie on her bed and helped her get undressed. She might also have given the old girl's back a rub-over with a flannel when she was in the bath and washed out her drawers for her in the sink, but I can't honestly say for sure.

Anyway, I'm digressing, for as well as being the Queen's mate and a prominent figure in court circles, the Duchess was also a vicious gossip, spreading malicious rumours about a certain Lady Flora Hastings who constantly complained of stomach pains and yet for some reason best known to herself refused to let the Queen's Physician examine her. Anna, encouraged by the Queen, started the rumour that Flora was pregnant after having an illicit affair with a man the Queen loathed, a certain Sir John Conroy. Being a single woman, poor old Flora's reputation was in tatters as a result of these two women's scandal-mongering for a child born out of wedlock was considered the ultimate scandal.

It transpired that Anna wasn't pregnant at all. The unfortunate woman was in fact terminally ill with a tumour, and after her death John Conroy and Flora's brother attacked both Anna and the Queen in the press for maligning an innocent woman's reputation. The public were suitably disgusted and the Queen temporarily fell from grace while the Duchess was shunned.

Anna was not only a scandal-monger, she wasn't shy at coming forward either for while visiting her pal the Duke of Rutland at his home in Belvoir Castle she declared late one afternoon that she was starving and needed a snack to keep her going before dinner, which was normally served at eight p.m. The cook sent up a pot of Darjeeling tea, a piece of cake and some bread and butter, and from that day onwards it became a lifelong habit of the Duchess to partake of a small repast every afternoon.

These snacks became more elaborate as the Duchess started inviting friends and acquaintances to join her (no doubt to spread a little more gossip), and so the Afternoon Tea was born. It suddenly became highly fashionable, and the cucumber sandwich de rigueur as it was suitably light and delicate for such a refined occasion. Ladies might remove their gloves but hats remained attached firmly to their barnets as they listened stiff-backed and pursed-lipped to the conversation.

Of course the working classes didn't go in for such pomp and ceremony at teatime, they got stuck into a hunk of bread and cheese or a pasty washed down by a mug of seriously strong tea.

So allegedly it was the Victorians who first thought of putting cucumber in between slices of bread. (They also put children up chimneys, but this isn't the time or place to start digging up the grimy side of their history.) The ultra-fashionable snack could even be found in India during the times of the Raj, when British officers would relax on their verandahs, sheltered from the hot afternoon sun, drinking Assam tea and nibbling cucumber sandwiches as an aid to keeping cool. Cucumbers are 95 per cent water and are capable of cooling the body down.

Cucumber sandwiches don't really belong on the menu of High Tea as they're a tiny bit delicate to be mingling alongside hearty fare but I don't care: rules are made to be broken and the cucumber sandwich is so moreish it's not hard to eat a plateful unless stopped.

So, if you're up for it, here's a recipe – one of many – for the traditional cucumber sandwich.

Cucumber Sandwiches

First peel your cucumber. Then, using a mandolin (the kitchen tool not the musical instrument), or if you haven't got one the bit on your cheese grater for slicing, cut the cucumber into slices as thin as cobwebs and place in a colander.

Sprinkle with a bit of salt then put a plate over them with something heavy on top to squeeze the water out. Leave them for about twenty-five minutes, and if you find that the slices taste too salty you can give them a quick rinse with cold water. Lay the slices out on a clean tea towel and pat dry.

The bread should always be fresh and white – no artisan breads or rustic wholemeals here, please, just an old-fashioned soft white loaf, cut into wafer-thin slices. This isn't that easy to do but with a good sharp knife and a steady hand it can be achieved.

When you've done this, butter the slices. Make sure the butter is soft and easy to spread otherwise you'll tear the bread.

Lay the cucumber slices on one slice of bread – two or three layers overlapping is enough. You've no need to add any more salt but you can give them a little dusting of white pepper. Cover with the other slice of bread, cut the crusts off, and then cut into three tidy fingers. Arrange these on a nice-looking plate and cover with a cloth that's been lightly dampened.

Pour the boiling water on the tea and then serve in the parlour as quickly as possible as nobody wants a warm, limp and soggy cucumber sarnie. That really is enough to have you ostracized from polite society and snubbed in the local Aldi.

Watercress Sandwiches

These were very popular with the Victorians, particularly the men, who approved of the peppery bite of the fresh watercress that for some reason they considered masculine. These gentlemen were also fond of a paste called 'Gentlemen's Relish', spread thinly on bread or toast. You can still buy it today, although I'm not very keen on its strong fishy/salty taste. Victorian men partook of it as not only was it butch but the salt gave them a thirst for knocking back the Scotch and sodas.

Watercress doesn't just taste good, it's also packed full of vitamins and minerals, and contains more vitamin C than oranges. It's also helpful for memory loss as it's high in vitamin K, which is known for assisting with preventing neurological damage from progressing.

Anyway, let's make some macho sarnies that are bursting with good health.

There's no need to strip the leaves from the stalk, just rinse the watercress well under the tap and dry with some kitchen paper. Butter some slices of wholemeal bread and lay the watercress on one slice. Season with salt, pepper and a bit of lemon juice, then cover with another buttered slice. Remove the crusts and slice into fingers or triangles. To really give them the stuff that sorts the men from the boys you can spread a little cream of horseradish on the bread.

Egg Mayonnaise Sandwiches

Nothing on earth could induce me to eat one of these as I don't like eggs served in any shape or form, but I will concede that these sandwiches are extremely popular, cheap and easy to make, and kids love them.

All you need is a couple of hard-boiled eggs mashed up with a fork with as much mayonnaise as you like, depending on your taste, and then seasoned with salt and pepper.

You can add finely chopped spring onions if you want, or add a teaspoon or so of creamed horseradish for a bit of a kick, but the perfect accompaniment to these foul egg sarnies is mustard and cress which I remember growing on a flannel at junior school.

You can use brown or white bread but once again the slices should be cut fairly thin with the crusts removed.

Then, if you're anything like me, get out of the room quickly as the rabble devour them because they stink to high heaven. Ugh.

Devilled Ham on Toast

My mother served this up as a snack one night just after Christmas when she was trying to find inventive ways to use up what was left of the cooked ham. I suspect it was something she picked up from her days as a domestic servant as two of the ingredients, Tabasco and Worcestershire sauce, weren't something that were commonplace in the larder of our house.

Years and years later I had something similar to eat when I was invited to take tea at the Ritz, and despite the opulence of the overcrowded tea room packed to the rafters with Japanese and American tourists I was transported back to Christmas in

Birkenhead at the first bite. You can make this with turkey leftovers as well.

Chop some lean ham, or use a tin of Spam if you prefer, and mix with a drop of Tabasco sauce, a good splash of Worcestershire sauce, plus a decent sprinkling of cayenne pepper. Fry this mixture gently in some butter for about five minutes – don't burn it.

When it's done, spoon on to triangles of toast and sprinkle with chopped parsley or a sprig of watercress.

It's quick to make and tastes really good.

Smoked Mackerel Pâté on Toast

This too is simple to make and tastes much better than anything you'll buy in the shops.

You need 250g or so of smoked mackerel fillets which you then flake into tiny pieces into a bowl.

Add to the fish 180g of cream cheese and a hefty tablespoon of thick double cream or crème fraîche. Throw in a teaspoon of good-quality creamed horseradish, either shop-bought or homemade, add a few squirts of lime juice and some salt and white pepper to taste, and then either mix by hand in a bowl using a fork or blend quickly in a blender.

It shouldn't be too sloppy so don't overmix or blend too much. Serve this on triangles of toast with a tart gooseberry sauce if you've got some. Or make it yourself.

Gooseberry Sauce

A hefty knob of butter
225g gooseberries
50ml of double cream
1 teaspoon of caster sugar
Pinch of salt and pepper
A good squeeze of lemon juice

Melt the butter and add the gooseberries, which
will have been topped, tailed and washed
beforehand by your kitchen maid. If you haven't got
a lackey then you'll have to do it yourself so sit
down, grab a bowl and a bit of kitchen paper and
listen to the radio as you pull out the stalks from
both ends, putting the goose-gogs in the bowl and
the stalks in the paper to be chucked on your
compost heap.

As I said, melt the butter in a pan and add the
gooseberries. Cover and cook on a low heat until just
tender and soft – about fifteen minutes, but keep an
eye on them.

When they are done, mash with a fork, adding the
cream and sugar plus a little salt and pepper and,
to finish it off, a good squeeze of fresh lemon juice.
Taste it, and if you want it a little sweeter then add
more sugar.

You can serve this hot or cold with the pâté
as it's the Ginger Rogers to the mackerel's Fred
Astaire.

Scones

The easiest thing in the world to make is a scone. They take no time at all and they taste even better if made with buttermilk, which you'll find in the cream section of good supermarkets. While you're there get a tub of clotted cream as you're going to need it if your scone is going to be worthy to join the table of a decent tea.

I've had this recipe for years, scrawled down in the back of my book of recipes. I have a feeling that it might have originally come from one of St Delia's recipe books, but then again I'm not sure as it could've been one of the relations. Whoever it was I'm indebted to them as these scones are the best.

225g self-raising flour
Pinch of salt
75g of butter (not rock-hard straight out of the fridge; let it soften)
40g caster sugar
A large egg
3 tablespoons of buttermilk

Sift the flour and salt into the bowl and add the butter, rubbing it in quickly with your fingertips. Don't manhandle it: you're not wrestling a pig, you're rubbing in, so be light and airy and lift the mixture up as you go until it looks a bit like breadcrumbs.

Add the sugar and quickly mix it in.

Then, in a separate jug, mug or bowl beat the egg with two tablespoons of the buttermilk and slowly mix this into the flour, butter and sugar mix preferably using a palette knife.

Once the mix has started to come together ditch the palette knife and use your hands until it looks like a ball of dough. Don't over-handle it. If the dough is still dry and crumbly then add some more buttermilk but be careful as if you overdo it it'll be a sticky mess. If you have been heavy-handed with the milk then you can add a bit more flour.

Form it into a ball and then roll it out on a clean surface you've dusted with flour. Don't forget to dust your rolling pin as well. Try and roll it into a circle, turning the dough around as you roll. It should be an inch thick (I've no idea what that is in centimetres). It doesn't matter if it's a little bit thicker but you don't want to roll the dough until it's flat as roadkill as you'll have workhouse scones.

Cut them out with a cutter. There's no need to shove it in the dough and then twist violently. All you need to do is simply push the cutter hard into the dough, then give the cutter a knock to release the dough.

Lay these circles on a baking tray, give them a brush with the buttermilk and sprinkle with a bit of flour.

Bake in a preheated oven at gas mark 7 (220°C) for about ten minutes or until the dough has risen nicely with a lovely honey-coloured top (not dark brown). Keep your eye on them after the ten-minute stage.

Leave them to cool slightly on a wire rack, split them, and then slather them in unsalted butter – that's right, slather them. Don't be skimpy as it's not as if you do this every day, is it? Or maybe you do, I wouldn't like to say.

Finally, pile on a dollop of strawberry jam and as much clotted cream as you think your arteries can take and enjoy the taste of a Cornish cream tea.

If you're worried about your figure or cholesterol level then you can chew on a celery stick instead – I've heard they're quite tasty. And after that culinary delight you can work it off by going for a nice long run and you can leave the rest of us to live fast and gorge.

After I'd finally settled permanently in London I found a job as a physiotherapist's aide in a North London hospital. The pay wasn't very good so to help pay the rent I'd work as a waiter of an evening handing out the drinks at private parties in the homes of the filthy rich.

One evening a poor unsuspecting lady asked me if I also cooked as she was having a small dinner party and needed a cook who would also wait at the table. I heard myself telling her in a surprisingly confident voice that I did cook and that I'd be happy to turn up next Wednesday to prepare and serve a dinner for eight.

The lady was delighted as she was entertaining some American business partners of her husband's and she wondered if I could suggest a suitable menu. Kebab and chips perhaps? I thought as I silently ran through my entire culinary repertoire in my head. Heinz Spaghetti Hoops on toast? Bacon butty?

I was starting to panic as I couldn't think of anything until I had a light-bulb moment and one of the few things I actually could cook sprang to mind.

'Since they're American, how about something traditionally British,' I suggested, 'like roast beef?'

Thankfully she liked that idea. But then she said, 'And as a starter?'

I thought again for a while, hoping she'd think I was flicking through the vast and varied recipe book in my mind when in reality I was just stalling for time hoping she'd come up with a suggestion first.

'Vichyssoise,' I eventually announced with a hint of panic in my voice since no suggestion from madam had been forthcoming.

I don't know what possessed me to say this as I had no idea what it actually was but I'd heard it mentioned in an episode of *Tales of the Unexpected* and it sounded impressive.

'Lovely,' she proclaimed happily. 'Served cold, I presume, since the main is quite heavy?'

'Of course,' I answered, grateful that whatever this thing was, I didn't have to cook it.

'What about dessert?' she asked. 'How about a fool?'

Well you've got one of them, I thought, you don't need another for dessert. 'I could make you an apple pie,' I suggested, as this was something else I wasn't bad at.

'Really?' She couldn't have looked more surprised if I'd suggested carving a swan out of ice. 'You'd do that?'

'Oh yes,' I bragged. 'I've been told they're not bad. But they don't look like the ones you'd get in a shop,' I added, hastily backtracking as I recalled the rough-as-guts pies

I turned out. 'They're a bit ...' I struggled to think of a suitable term to describe them. '*Rustic*, if you know what I mean.'

'Wonderful!' she exclaimed, 'Served with crème anglaise?'

'Oh no,' I jumped in. I didn't have a clue what crème anglaise was but it sounded French and that meant complicated. 'Double cream goes best with my pie.'

'Glorious,' she said happily. 'That's settled then.'

I went through every cookery book in Crouch End Library until I had my recipe for vichyssoise, which despite its elegant name turned out to be plain old leek and potato soup.

I experimented at home as the ingredients weren't expensive so if I messed up it didn't matter, but as I didn't have a food processor to blend the soup the bit I hated most was pushing it through a sieve as most of it ended up on the kitchen floor.

Thankfully the lady of the house did have a food processor, which of course I didn't have a clue how to work until she showed me, and my vichyssoise was a success. The gods must've been smiling down on me that night as the rest of the meal, thanks to a bit of help from madam and my sheer bare-faced brazen cheek, believing I could carry it off, went without a hitch.

I learned a lot from this lady, who taught me for instance that it's easier to chop herbs by putting them in a mug and cutting them with scissors. I'd love to be able to chop up a big bunch of parsley on a board with the speed of light like the pros but I fear I might lose a finger or two in the process.

I also recall her saying that if a soup or stew is too salty then put a large peeled potato in the pot which will absorb the salt.

She chattered away in the kitchen as I peeled spuds, passing on handy hints her mother had insisted would make her a better cook and therefore a better wife. I really liked this lady, and despite her being what I thought of as dead posh she was funny and easy to get along with, repeating her mother's advice on how to be the perfect wife with good-natured irony.

The reason I'm telling you this tale is because she also told me that scones will be lighter if cooked on a preheated baking tray, which I could've just said at the top, but brevity has never been my strong point.

Cheese Scones

I bought a book in a second-hand bookshop when I was on tour which turned out to be not quite as gripping as the effusive review on the front cover had suggested. I was going to leave it on the train for someone else until I discovered that in the back was written in pencil and in a very neat hand a recipe for cheese scones. I've come across a lot of recipes in the back of second-hand books, as well as personal letters tucked between the pages, and on one occasion two £10 notes.

I was serving up High Tea to some of my friends in my flat in Vauxhall and I decided to give these scones a go. The flat was tiny, as was the front room, but it had a grate and I could light a real fire.

However, once the table was folded out to seat six people there wasn't much room to manoeuvre and the heat from the roaring fire became unbearable. Eventually we abandoned ship and ate our tea in the kitchen standing up, but I remember them attacking these scones like a pack of gannets.

225g self-raising flour
A pinch of salt
Half a teaspoon of baking powder
50g unsalted butter
100g good strong Cheddar cheese, grated
1 egg, beaten
2 tablespoons of milk

Sift the flour, salt and baking powder into a bowl as in the previous recipe for scones and rub in the butter. Mix in the cheese.

Beat the egg, reserve a bit to brush on the scones before they go into the oven, and beat in the remaining egg with the milk.

Mix with the cheese and flour, then follow the recipe for scones.

Brush with the beaten egg that you've reserved and cook in a preheated oven at gas mark 7 (220°C) for ten minutes.

When the scones come out of the oven you can also sprinkle some grated cheddar mixed with a little cayenne pepper on top of them and flash them under a hot grill until the cheese has just melted. These really are the business.

Easy Strawberry Jam

450g fresh strawberries, washed and hulled

400g golden caster sugar

2 tablespoons of fresh lemon juice

A couple of small plates that you've put in the freezer
  to cool

Put the strawberries in a pan with a heavy bottom (if
this were *Bake Off* I'd be sniggering now, but it's not)
and mash them with a fork or a spud masher. I don't
mash them to a complete pulp as I like some lumpy
bits (I'd be sniggering again here) so leave a few of
the fruits only slightly battered. Add the sugar and
lemon juice and then stir continuously over a
medium heat until all the sugar has completely
dissolved. Then turn the heat up and bring the
mixture to what is known in the preserves trade as a
'rolling boil'.

   Stir it so it doesn't stick and burn, and if you have
a thermometer handy – not the type you stick in your
kid's ear or, even worse, the one that's used on a sick
pig, and all I'm saying about that is it isn't inserted
orally – once it's reached 105°C it's ready. There are
in fact thermometers on the market specifically for
sweet- and jam-making and one will save a lot of
hassle if you intend to make jam and suchlike on a
regular basis.

   If you haven't got a thermometer then drop
a teaspoon of jam on a cold saucer, leave it for a
moment, and if it's very runny then it's not done but
if you push it gently with your little finger and it feels

firm – not rock hard (snigger, snigger) but soft with what looks like a skin forming on the surface – then it's ready.

Put it in a washed and sterilized jar and store it away somewhere cool and dark like a cupboard or a trendy nightclub.

This really is a tasty jam and dead easy to make.

Right, well, that's me done on the subject of teatime. I could go on with a list of recipes for ice cream and glacé ices but it's fast approaching teatime as I write this so I'd best go and feed the critters as I can hear the pigs giving out, then when I get back I might just push the boat out and knock up a couple of scones and open a tin of salmon.

Halloween

Give me Halloween over Christmas any time of the year. I see the C-word as a trial to get through and can't wait for the first of the New Year when the whole bloody expensive palaver is over. I'm not a total Grinch. I observe all the traditions – the tree, sending out Christmas cards, buying presents and cooking the obligatory turkey dinner, although I've never tasted turkey and never will.

Occasionally I'll go to Midnight Mass, too. I find that infects me with the Christmas spirit more than pulling a cracker or the endless Christmas shows on the telly. I find it a very Christmassy thing to do possibly because Midnight Mass is a simple affair that lacks the excess and commercialism of the rest of the holiday celebrations. If you're a believer, Christmas is a time to rejoice at the birth of Christ after all. Isn't that what the festive season is supposed to be about?

When I was a kid, Midnight Mass was always packed out to the rafters, the back of the church full of latecomers and drunks swaying like bullrushes in the wind as they tried to act sober. These days there's less drunks but Midnight Mass can still pull a crowd. The ancient church not far from my village is always full on Christmas Eve.

This twelfth-century church has no electricity and the service is illuminated by candlelight. Sitting there in the soft light listening to the vicar it feels as if I've stepped out of the turbulent world of the twenty-first century and into another time. It's a pleasant, reassuring experience, cocooned in this medieval church that was built on ancient land and had once been a place for pagan worship. I leave feeling clear-headed and all the better for it and spend some time chatting to the regulars and turning down invites to 'come back for a mince pie and a sherry' as I seriously have to get home to deal with the turkey.

On reflection, there is something I like about Christmas: it seems to be Midnight Mass. Doesn't matter what denomination it is as long as the church is atmospheric and preferably old and not one of those monstrosities built in the 1960s. Oh, and I'll confess to liking Christmas trees. I hate unravelling the lights but love looking at it when it's dressed and lit. But that's your lot.

I've discovered to my shock that I'm actually a bit of a traditionalist, one who firmly believes that certain customs must be observed, and Halloween being one of those occasions, it gives me plenty of opportunities to go to town.

In the pagan calendar Halloween is known by the traditional name of Samhain, pronounced 'sow inn', and it's considered to be the most important of the four Great Sabbats on the witches' calendar. It's said that on this night the veil that separates the mortal world from the world of the spirits is at its thinnest, allowing us to communicate with loved ones who have passed over, not to mention the odd stranger who's tagged along for company on the journey down or up, as the case may be.

A candle should be lit in the window (mind your nets!) so the spirits can find their way in the dark, and you must always lay an extra place at the table just in case you have a celestial visitor.

The custom of trick or treating is nothing new. The practice quite possibly stems back to the Middle Ages when village folk dressed up as evil spirits to frighten away any genuine demons that might happen to show their faces. They'd knock on doors – the villagers, not the evil demons – and perform silly tricks and sing daft songs hoping that the householder would give them a drink and a bite to eat. It was known as mumming, and in the days before telly it was very popular, or so I believe.

Later on, after a little persuasion from the Church, the practice became known as 'souling', only this time they knocked on your door and promised to pray for your dead in exchange for something to eat. Not quite as jolly, you'll agree, and if the O'Gradys had lived during those times I daresay my ma would've ordered us to 'hit the floor' at the first knock on the door as she did when she was avoiding the Club Man.

When I was a lad Halloween was referred to as 'Duck Apple Night' as that's what we did. For the uninitiated, ducking or bobbing for apples involved kneeling on a cold stone floor with a gang of other kids and plunging your head into a tin bath filled with freezing water in the hope of catching an oversized apple in your mouth. Sometimes the older kids would hold your head under the water and you'd have to go home soaked on a cold late October night. Eeh by gum, we knew 'ow t'ave fun back in the good old days.

Nowadays Halloween is big business, for as usual the UK takes its lead from America when it comes to trends and consequently there's lots of kiddies out and about banging on doors trick or bloody treating. I wouldn't mind but some of them are well past puberty and threatening with it.

When I was living in London a gang of teenage lads knocked on my door once. I'd been trying to open a large box that had been sealed so tightly I'd resorted to hacking it open with a carving knife. When I heard someone at the door I ran down the stairs with the knife still in my hand but I placed it on the little shelf behind the door before opening it to what I'd expected might be little kids looking for sweets. Instead it was a gang of hairy-lipped lads with their hoods pulled up and heads bent, making it hard to see their faces.

'Posh round here innit?' their apparent leader said with a smirk. 'Now how about a trick or treat?'

I didn't like his attitude so I leaned forward and said in the voice I use for panto villains, 'You have to answer a riddle first.'

They sniggered and shuffled about, their hands stuffed deep in the pockets of their hoodies.

'OK,' the leader replied. 'But we don't accept sweets, only cash.'

His motley crew sniggered again, and one of them high-fived the leader for being so witty and upfront.

'Are you ready then?' I asked, adopting what I thought to be my best sinister smile. 'Listen carefully.'

I paused theatrically as they waited to hear what I had to say.

'My name is Insanity,' I told them calmly. 'Now tell me, how are you going to escape?'

And at that point I reached behind the door and produced the knife.

'Wanna come in?' I asked, grinning insanely.

You've never seen a group of lads run so fast and I made a mental note to adopt the same policy when the bible bashers knocked.

Personally I'd never let a young child go trick or treating without a couple of adults accompanying them as there's too many peculiar people lurking behind closed doors. Nor would I allow them to eat any of the sweets they've been given unless they're from trusted neighbours: I've heard of children in the States being given human excrement covered in chocolate and sweets filled with powdered glass or a razor blade. Sad times, thanks to the sick bastards who would do such things to children.

Down here in Kent I really go for it on Samhain Eve (Halloween to mortals) and prepare a meal suitable for such an occasion, always starting with a bewitching pumpkin soup.

Enchanted Pumpkin Soup

You'll need a large pumpkin – I grow my own on the allotment. Some years they're so big I need a wheelbarrow to shift them and then other years they're so puny I end up buying one from the farm shop. It all depends if they've been given enough TLC. Pumpkins are fairly easy to grow but if you want a decent-sized one then water and feed them well. A bag of horse manure works wonders, and as the tendrils grow nip off the ends so that all the nourishment goes into the pumpkin.

Once you've acquired your pumpkin cut a lid out of the top and scrape out the flesh from the inside. Discard the seeds unless you want to dry and keep them, and with the now empty shell of the pumpkin you can carve a jack-o'-lantern out of it.

So, for the soup:

A large carrot
A large onion
About 1kg of pumpkin flesh
A large potato (you can use a sweet one if you prefer)
A stick of celery
A large nut of butter
A litre of vegetable or chicken stock
A couple of strands of saffron
A few sage leaves
A teaspoon of chilli powder
Salt and white pepper

Half a pint of single cream
A good dash of sherry
Juice of two oranges

Peel the carrot and the onion, and chop all the veg. Melt the butter in a cauldron, or a large pan if you haven't got one, and gently cook the veg, including the pumpkin. Keep the veg moving and make sure the pieces don't brown. After about eight minutes add the stock, saffron, sage leaves, chilli powder and salt and pepper to taste and simmer slowly for three quarters of an hour. Leave to cool, then blend until smooth.

Return to a clean pan. Add the cream, sherry and juice of the oranges and slowly reheat, murmuring under your breath as you stir the soup widdershins – in other words, anticlockwise – this simple enchantment:

On this the night when the dead awaken,
Enchant this brew that I'm a-makin'.

Something tells me that this chant might be from the Kentucky Mountains region of America; either that or it's been lifted from an episode of the sixties TV show *Bewitched*. It's the 'I'm a-makin'' bit that gives it away. Still, it's a nice soup with or without the spell. Serve it with a swirl of cream or yoghurt and sprinkle with finely chopped chives.

Suitable booze for the occasion: cider, real ale, mead and champagne.

It's obligatory to dress up on this night and the traditional colours are black and orange, the black representing the passing of summer while the orange welcomes in the autumn.

We all dress up down here. It's compulsory, and guests are forced into cloaks and the traditional pointed hats. I might throw my Maleficent outfit on, although I keep forgetting about the horns when I'm going through doorways and almost drag my head off my shoulders.

I light a fire in the fire bowl on the patio and those with worries can write them down and burn them in the flames – a symbolic gesture that will hopefully improve your lot. In days of yore, as the fire was dying a burning ember would be taken back to the home and placed in the hearth to ensure good fortune in the future.

These days I wouldn't recommend putting a red-hot coal in your handbag or suit pocket as you'll probably burst

into flames on your way home, and anyway, most homes no longer have open fires so where would you put it?

If you're still sober after all this feasting and celebrating you can spend the rest of the night telling ghost stories, although we never do, nor do we hold seances or get involved with Ouija boards either. The jury's out with me when it comes to the paranormal and I wouldn't want to invite anything worthy of a horror film into the house by messing around with things that should be left well alone.

Instead of calling up the dead we might take a trip down the woods with those large wax garden candles substituting for burning torches. We don't actually do anything when we eventually get there after untangling cloaks from brambles and retrieving shoes that have come off in the mud; we normally just sit in silence, half canned and listening to the peculiar sounds of things creeping about in the dark, spooking ourselves in the process. Above all Halloween is a time for both young and old to have fun, so let your hair down, grab a broomstick and go for it.

Cows

'What do you want for Christmas?' Murphy asked.

'A cow,' I replied without any hesitation.

'Of course you do,' he said, raising his eyebrows. 'I shouldn't have asked.'

I've always loved cows, ever since I was first introduced to them as a child on my family's farm in rural Ireland. I particularly used to love bringing them in at the end of the day to be milked, traipsing across the fields behind my Uncle James and his herd.

It was my uncle who taught me how to milk a cow by hand, which is difficult to explain how to do in print except that it involves a sort of rhythmic pull-and-squeeze motion. I'd have to physically show you, but since I've no longer got a cow and I haven't heard of any cow-milking competitions lately it ain't going to happen.

Thanks to Uncle James's expert tuition I became quite good at milking and when the devil got in me and my uncle wasn't around I'd fire a teat full of milk in the direction of the cat, or at my cousin Maureen, standing watching me in the cowshed doorway.

It was after announcing on my Radio 2 show that I was desperate for a cow that my plea was answered by my neighbour Cathy, known in the area as 'The Heroic

Horsewoman' after she bravely chased two armed robbers who'd held up the post office across the marshes on her trusty steed à la Margaret Lockwood in *The Wicked Lady*. Cathy got in touch to tell me that she had a very friendly house cow she'd be happy to sell me called Dot. In my ignorance I wondered if Cathy meant that this Dot actually lived inside the house, and if she did where the hell was I going to put her? I suppose she could have bedded down in the dining room as we hardly ever used it, although I didn't fancy getting up every morning and having to shovel up a mountain of cowpats. Countrywoman Cathy was quick to explain that a house cow was one kept solely to provide milk for the household. At one time every rural cottage with a bit of land kept a cow as it not only kept the family in milk but also in butter, cream and cheese. I had visions of the same fantasy dairy I'd mentally cooked up for milking goats, with me churning butter surrounded by bowls of cream and slabs of butter. Ha, dream on, neophyte, dream on.

Now, buying a cow isn't a simple matter of toddling off down the hill and after exchanging a few groats with your friendly neighbourhood farmer you lead your cow home; there's a lot of red tape and formalities to deal with first. In fact I swear it's probably easier to adopt a child than it is to purchase a cow as DEFRA are very, very exact.

Paperwork sorted out, Dot eventually arrived, and for the first few days I kept her in the barn until she acclimatized to her new surroundings and didn't take off back to Cathy. She really was a prize specimen, a black and white Jersey/Dexter cross with big brown soulful eyes framed with eyelashes that would've done a Mary Quant model proud. Dot was also in calf, expecting not only one but two.

After a couple of days I let her out of the barn and she settled down quite nicely in the field in front of the house, munching grass and staring into space. She was familiar with the field by now as I'd left the top part of the barn door open so she could inspect it.

Waupie, who I'll introduce you properly to in the next chapter, was very put out by the arrival of this newcomer in the field and she spent a lot of time peering over the garden wall and creating a racket that I took to be her way of complaining. Cows belong in a herd, and I hoped that Dot and Waupie might team up and become pals, at least until the calves were born, but so far they didn't seem interested in each other and kept themselves at a respectable distance. This stand-off didn't last long and they were soon grazing alongside each other with Waupie, who was still a young sheep and prone to bursting into the odd bit of what they call 'gambolling', leaping and bucking around the field as if to impress Dot, who stood silently chewing, seemingly unmoved by this display of acrobatics.

Pretty soon they were what you'd call BFs, going everywhere together, Dot unfortunately picking up some of Waupie's disrespect for boundaries.

I'd been led to believe that cows are highly unpredictable animals but Dot seemed to be a very placid cow who enjoyed human company. Occasionally, egged on by Waupie, she'd jump the small wall that separated the field from the garden and help herself to some flowers but she never objected when I led her back to the field by her bridle. Cows are excellent jumpers, as I was to find out; they're also inquisitive creatures. But I never expected her curiosity would lead her *into* the house.

I was in the downstairs lav reading a two-week-old Sunday paper – a practice that I consider to be quality time well spent that should never be disturbed by anyone – when I heard Buster and Louis barking frantically in the kitchen. Annoyed at this disturbance, I affectionately shouted out my normal request for them to cease barking.

'SHURRUPP!!!!!'

Only they didn't. Instead their barking grew louder so, reluctantly hoisting myself off the lav and shuffling down the hall towards the kitchen with my pants still around my ankles, I went to see what they were kicking off about.

I wondered at first if I was hallucinating for there, in all her glory, stood Dot, calmly licking the remnants of some smoked haddock off a plate in the kitchen sink.

'Dot!' I exclaimed, for what else could I say?

The cow lifted her head out of the sink and headed towards me. I shut the kitchen door smartly as I didn't want her in the front room or, worse, upstairs, which given the chance I wouldn't now put past her. How would I get her down the stairs again if she did venture up to the bedrooms? I'd probably have to ring the fire brigade, and then how would I get them to believe I was genuine and not a crank caller? Would they really believe a caller who claimed to have a pregnant cow in his bedroom? And if they did, would they contact the police and the RSPCA suspicious as to what I was doing with said cow? Did it sleep with me?

Oh God, I could just imagine the headlines in the gutter press.

The many books I'd read about all things bovine didn't give any advice on how one persuades a cow to leave the premises, and Dot didn't seem keen to move. In fact by the look of her I'd've said she'd got her hooves well and truly under the table.

I put the dogs in the little laundry room and set about luring this invader back into her natural habitat. She showed no interest in a Weetabix, nor was she particularly impressed by the offer of a slice of bread.

It was then that I made the big mistake of opening the fridge to see if there was a lettuce or something green to entice her with: I was shoved quickly out of the way by Dot who stuck her head inside to take a look, scattering a tub of cream, cartons of milk and a large pot of yoghurt all over the floor in the process. Dot clearly didn't approve of dairy products that weren't of her own making, and to impress on the world at large just exactly what she thought of her rivals she raised her tail and peed with the force of a fire hose.

Somehow I managed to drag her away from the fridge – not easy when you're standing in an inch of pee with your trousers around your ankles, soaking it up. Realizing that my movements had been reduced to the tiny steps of an elderly geisha there was only one thing for it and that was to step out of my trousers and hope nobody came in unexpectedly and found me naked from the waist down with a cow in the kitchen.

It was a pot of parsley growing on the kitchen window sill that proved to be the bait to persuade Dot to leave, and once I'd got her attention it was surprisingly easy to manoeuvre her down the short passage and out of the kitchen door, the only casualties being a couple of pictures that she managed to knock off the wall. Barefooted and bare-arsed, I led her towards the field – a painful experience as Dot now seemed keen to get back to her manor and had gathered up considerable speed, and as I didn't want to let go of her bridle I had to keep up with her, trying to ignore the agony of the small stones and tree roots cutting into the soles of my bare feet.

Once she was safely installed back in her field with the gate firmly closed behind her I made a mental note to ask Sean to build a bigger wall or erect a fence to keep her out. He did better than that: he put a wire across that was electrified, which didn't stop Dot but gave me and a few of my friends frequent unexpected shocks when we forgot it was there.

Life with Dot was rosy, though. She became very attached to me and we'd go for walks together in the big field along with Waupie and Buster who she didn't mind at all, although when he ran between her legs I still worried that he might get a kick, which thankfully never happened. If the heavily pregnant Dot had what you could call cravings then it was for nettles: she couldn't get enough of them, and we made frequent stops so she could slowly munch her way through entire clumps of the things. There wasn't a nettle to be seen in my fields during Dot's pregnancy. When we finally got to the bottom of the big field she'd lie down and I'd lean against her with Waupie at my side, all of us watching Buster chase rabbits in the long grass that we knew he'd never catch.

Without wishing to sound as if I'm over-romanticizing, it was moments like this that convinced me I'd done the right thing by moving to rural Kent.

The view was stunning, the only sound I could hear were the birds and the gentle rhythm of Dot breathing, and as I leaned against her, chewing on a long piece of grass as you're supposed to do when lying in a field, I realized that there was nothing in sight to indicate that I was living in modern times. I felt completely detached from the present day, as if I'd accidentally come across an ancient portal that had transported me back in time and now here I was with my cow, my lamb and my dog in another century.

Closing my eyes, I settled into Dot's hind flank to enjoy this illusion that I'd taken a trip into the past until an explosion of methane gas out of Dot's substantial rear end shattered my idyllic bliss. Sitting up sharply, I told her what I thought of such unladylike behaviour but she seemed nonplussed and didn't even turn to look at me; she simply shifted a bit to get comfortable and carried on chewing the cud.

It was time to go home, and walking back up the field I wondered what my Uncle James would think of his now grown-up relation bringing his own cow in and I silently thanked him for his influence over me at an impressionable age.

The length of a cow's pregnancy is a bit longer than a human's, about nine and a half months. Cathy predicted the exact date when Dot would give birth, and she wasn't wrong.

I was doing two a day at the Bristol Hippodrome when Dot, after an uncomplicated labour, gave birth to the twins. I would've liked to be there for the birth but even so I couldn't have been prouder, and at the curtain call I announced their arrival as if I'd given birth to them myself. The audience cheered politely while the kiddies probably wondered what the hell the Wicked Queen was talking about.

Dot had calved in the field, which is healthier than giving birth in a barn or stall, and as the weather was mild for December we left them outside. Even so, good mother that Dot was, she would return to her barn every night of her own accord taking her twins with her.

She was extremely protective of her calves and I made sure that neither Buster, curious as he was, nor Louis went anywhere near her. You might be surprised to hear that almost a hundred people have been trampled to death or crushed by cows as Momma Cow will charge at dogs and people who get too close. A dog should never be off the lead amongst a field full of livestock, particularly in a field that has cows with newborn calves. You might as well step into an arena with an angry bull.

Now that Dot had given birth it meant that I could finally milk her. I was a bit rusty for it had been quite a

few years since I'd milked a cow but with the help of Cathy, who'd proven to be a godsend since I'd got Dot, I was soon filling the bucket. Cows have to be milked twice a day, morning and evening, and as all this was new and exciting to me I didn't mind getting up at seven a.m. to do so.

As soon as a calf is born it should be encouraged to suckle immediately as the milk that Mummy provides during these early days is full of colostrum, which is vital to the health of the calf as it contains all the antibodies it will need as an immunity to any infections and diseases. Colostrum is also reputedly beneficial to humans, boosting the immune system and improving stamina in athletes. It's even said to be an aid to anti-ageing.

I've never eaten veal, nor would I, as the practice of taking a calf away from its mother the moment it's born and locking it in a dark enclosed space where it's fed on synthetic supplements instead of its mother's milk is unspeakably barbaric.

Believe it or not, milking a cow, if done properly, is a pleasant experience and one worth getting up at the crack of dawn for. I love the smell of cows; the odour is one of warm earth and milk with a whiff of Eau de Cowpat thrown in as a subtle undertone. For me the smell of the country isn't new-mown hay or anything floral it's the rich beefy smell of a cow. You can't beat it.

Dot was reluctant to give this foreigner pulling at her teats any milk at first. I'd tethered her to the barn with a big hay bag hanging off the wall to keep her occupied but try as I might she wasn't giving me anything but a drizzle of a thin watery substance. I rang Cathy for advice.

'Put one of the calves on her teat,' she told me, 'and she'll let you have the good stuff.'

Dot was keeping this 'good stuff' for her calves and as soon as I had one suckling on her teat the floodgates opened. In no little time I had a large bucketful.

In case you're worried that by milking Dot I was depriving the calves of their milk I wasn't, as even though Dot was producing enough milk for both calves she still badly needed milking.

Soon, after milking her morning and night I was getting nearly one and a half gallons a day and anyone who came near the house was made to drink a big glass of the stuff whether they liked milk or not as I was desperate to use this never-ending well up. I and these enforced drinkers would stand in the kitchen drinking glasses of ice-cold colostrum-laced milk passing judgement on it as if we were drinking a fine old wine, everyone agreeing that it tasted far better than the milk you get in supermarkets. Well they had to, didn't they?

After milking Dot I'd strain the milk through muslin into sterilized jugs and put it in the fridge for the cream to rise to the top and settle. As we are constantly being advised by health experts in the newspapers to avoid such fatty foods as cream I did the wisest thing and completely ignored them. Instead I bought an ice cream machine and soon the freezer was full of ice-creams ranging from lavender flavour to strawberry and black pepper. The eggs for the custard-based ice creams such as the rich creamy vanilla came from my own hens, who thankfully were good layers and seemed to be working overtime, as if they'd cottoned on that a small cottage dairy industry had started up in the kitchen.

What really surprised people was that I made my own butter, which, if you have the cream, is dead easy.

Butter

Double cream, as much as you like
A food blender, mixer or, if you've got the time and
   strength, a balloon whisk and a bowl

Mix the cream in the blender until it gets past the whipped-cream stage and starts to solidify. I start off slow in my ancient Lytham St Annes KitchenAid and then build up speed. What happens is the cream starts to separate until the fat has formed a lump sitting in a pool of buttermilk.

Strain off the buttermilk – don't chuck it away as you can use it for baking – and then press the butter in the mixing bowl with a wooden spoon to squeeze out any excess buttermilk.

Strain through a fine-mesh sieve.

You could eat the butter at this stage but it won't keep for very long unless you get rid of every trace of buttermilk. To do this, add some iced water and mix again to rinse out the remaining buttermilk. Drain the water off and rinse again until the water runs clear. This will take three or four attempts.

Give the butter another squeeze with your spoon and add salt or herbs if you want. Pat into a tidy shape and then wrap in greaseproof paper and put in the fridge.

Fresh homemade butter goes well with a hunk of strong cheese, a red onion and some crusty bread that you've made yourself.

If you want a good bread recipe then I suggest you consult Paul Hollywood as he's the expert. My early attempts at bread-making were a dismal failure. I'd bought one of those bread-making machines that folk raved about yet I didn't have much luck with it, as the bread always tasted more like cake.

The traditional way to make bread is far more satisfactory, although the first loaves I made in the Aga came out resembling that knobbly fungi that grows on trees. You also needed a metal jaw and dinosaur teeth to eat it as it was so hard.

It took trial and error to finally produce some half-decent breakfast rolls and a wholemeal loaf, but the kitchen looked like there'd been an explosion in a Peruvian cocaine factory. Everything, including me and the dogs, was covered in a fine dusting of flour.

Nowadays I'm more organized and not so messy but I'm damned if I'm getting up before sunrise to knock up some rolls for breakfast, not when there's a farm shop down the road that sells perfectly good fresh bread. After all, I'm not in domestic service.

On the rare occasions I do make these really very tasty rolls I'll dish them out for Afternoon Tea, stuffed with tinned salmon that's been mashed up with vinegar and white pepper plus a dollop of mayonnaise – reminiscent of the lunchtime rolls I'd buy with my luncheon vouchers from Cousins Café in Liverpool as a young teenager.

If you haven't chucked the buttermilk down the sink then here's something easy to make. My Aunty Bridget used to knock a batch of these up at teatime. You eat them slathered in the butter that you've just made with a big dollop of strawberry jam – homemade of course.

Irish Buttermilk Farls

✶ ✝ ✶ ✝ ✶ ✝ ✶ ✝ ✶ ✝ ✶ ✝ ✶

Farl means 'four' in Gaelic as the dough is flattened
into a circle and divided up into four.

250g plain flour
Half a teaspoon of salt
A good-sized teaspoon of bicarbonate of soda
250ml buttermilk (if you haven't got buttermilk
   then use full-fat milk with a good squirt of lemon
   juice in it)

Sift the flour, salt and bicarb into a mixing bowl.
Pour the buttermilk in (you can make a well in the
flour mix if you feel so inclined) and then quickly mix
it all together into a dough. Don't play with it, get a
move on, and if you think the dough is too sloppy
then add a bit more flour.

Tip it out on to a floured surface and knead
quickly and lightly. Flatten into a circle about half an
inch thick.

Cut the farl into quarters and cook on a
preheated griddle or in a heavy frying pan
sprinkled with a little flour on a medium to low
heat for about nine minutes each side. Don't let
them burn and the middle has to cook so don't
have the heat on high.

When they're done, remove and leave to cool
down slightly. Eat hot or cold.

Ulster Farls

These are made with spuds, so if you've got enough mashed potatoes left over then this is a good way of using them up instead of putting them in a little bowl covered in clingfilm and 'popping' it in the fridge 'for later', which means they'll sit there at the back uneaten and forgotten. That drives me bloody mad.

The very first time I worked in the north of Ireland my budget didn't run to a night at Belfast's Europa Hotel so instead I found a small, inexpensive B&B not that far from the city centre and the club I was appearing at.

In the morning the lady who ran this establishment served me up a full Ulster Fry for breakfast comprising bacon, sausage, tomatoes, black and white pudding and these potato farls, all washed down with endless cups of strong tea. It was cooked to perfection and I ate it in the kitchen with her kids as she chatted away ten to the dozen. I could've stayed for a week.

There's a lot to be said for a decent B&B, especially ones that serve gut-busting breakfasts unlike the congealed beans and undercooked bacon that's doled out at some supposedly quality hotels.

Here's the recipe for the farls. Give them a go.

4 large spuds (you can't go wrong with a King Eddy), or approx. 400–500g

50g melted butter

Salt and pepper

50g plain flour

Half a teaspoon of baking powder

Wash the spuds but leave the skins on, then slice into quarters and put into a pan of boiling water. (You really don't need me to tell you how to boil a spud do you?) When they are ready – and by that I mean tender not mushy – drain in a colander, and when they are cool enough to handle, peel the skins off. The best bit of the spud is just under the skin and we lose these vitamins by peeling them, however, I think these vitamins might be annihilated during the boiling process, but at least we've made an effort at healthy eating, haven't we?

Mash the spuds really well with the melted butter and salt and pepper to taste.

Sift in the flour and baking powder and combine the ingredients into dough. If you feel it's a bit wet and clingy add some flour; if it's too dry, add a drop or so of milk.

Knead on a lightly floured surface for a couple of minutes and then divide into two pieces. Make a ball out of one of them and lightly roll out into a circle about a quarter of an inch thick, and cut into quarters. Lightly fry in a bit of butter for about four minutes each side. Serve hot with an Ulster Fry and sod your waistline.

Now back to the lovely Dot, who was producing enough milk to keep the Co-op Dairy afloat. I still enjoyed milking her by hand even if it was time-consuming, but because of this I thought it might be a good idea to invest in a milking machine.

Does anyone want to buy a second-hand milking machine used once and then only very briefly?

Dot seemed quite content as I fiddled about, trying to attach the metal and glass tubes to her teats (that took some effort). Once attached I turned the damn thing on and stood back, expecting to see the glass bottles the tubes were attached to slowly fill up with milk.

With the speed of light and wearing what I can only describe as a look of outrage on her face, Dot took off across the field, dragging the machine behind her, until it eventually came loose and bounced into a ditch.

Needless to say I never used it after that and it's sat in the barn ever since – a waste of money and time but a lesson learned: don't try to mend what isn't broken.

Thankfully, once the calves were weaned Dot finally stopped lactating. Our cholesterol levels dropped and I started buying milk and butter from the local shop again.

I'd always brought Dot and her twins in of an evening, and after milking the three of them were quite happy to stay in their barn overnight, although lately I'd noticed Dot preferred to stay outdoors but always in the field close to the house. However, after a while Dot developed wanderlust, and soon I was traipsing miles every evening across neighbouring fields looking for her.

One morning I was woken up by a garden full of cows that Dot had gathered together and brought up the fields. There were over forty of them surrounding the house, with Dot at the helm. Hitchcock would've loved it. To make matters worse, each and every one of them was mooing and bellowing with Dot, glaring up at the bedroom window, leading this dawn chorus with gusto.

I had no idea where these cows had come from nor who they belonged to. The dogs were going crazy at this unaccustomed disturbance at such an unhealthy hour so, opening the window, I stuck my head out and asked Dot quite reasonably what the hell she thought she was doing. An illogical reaction I know, but then I was half awake and you don't really expect a bovine protest at 6.30 in the morning, not just noise but trampling the flowers and running amok amongst the lavender beds too. Nice way to start the day.

Dot looked up at me and, snorting angrily, stamped about as if to convey that she was a woman on a mission and that she and her comrades were not to be messed with, although I had no idea what this demonstration was about.

I did the best thing possible and sat it out until Sean came in, ignoring the herd of cows peering at me through the kitchen window as I filled the kettle. Sean couldn't get the car down the drive for cows but he rang the local farmer who came and collected them. Dot was unmoved as she watched them go and began grazing as if nothing had happened at all.

I noticed that her bridle was missing. Was this symbolic, I wondered, a bovine equivalent of burning her bra? A fight for independence and freedom? I made a mental note to keep a close eye on Dot as I had a feeling she was up to something and she needed reminding just who was boss around here, which at the moment appeared to be Dot.

A few days later I was bending over to fill up the water trough when I felt a thud in my back and saw a hoof appear over my shoulder, knocking my glasses off and sending me head-first into the trough. The speed at which I scrambled away not only surprised me, it obviously threw Dot off her guard as she backed off and then, almost as if she were embarrassed, she slunk off down the field.

I rooted around, half blind, looking for my specs, which thankfully weren't broken, and while stomping back to the house I became aware that Dot's hoof had given me a blow near my eye which would probably turn into a beautiful shiner.

'You won't believe this, Murphy,' I said dramatically, marching into the kitchen. 'Dot tried to mount me.'

'Well there you go,' he replied as he made toast. 'You've still got it, Savage, you've still got it.'

He wasn't quite as casual a few days later when, while walking in the field with our friend Chad, Dot suddenly decided to charge them. They ran, looking for a place to hide, but all they could find was a small sheet of corrugated iron, holding it up as a makeshift and totally useless shield together with a puny branch to fend her off with. Dot backed off, but she was only toying with them, for after a bit of stamping and snorting more suited to a Spanish bull than a Kentish house cow she charged again. Hearing their screams for help I ran out of the house to see what was going on although I already had a sneaking suspicion that whatever it was, Dot had something to do with it.

I hung over the gate and called her and instantly she turned from mad cow to friendly, passive Good Ol' Dot again and came ambling over to me, licking my hand as I stroked her head. Murphy and Chad, visibly shaken, made a hasty exit.

Dot was a powerful beast and her behaviour was becoming very worrying as her tendency to bounce around like an overgrown puppy was proving to be dangerous. Seeing me one day in the field with a bucket she charged, thinking it contained food. I literally had to throw myself over the gate as she would've seriously injured me. That's if she didn't kill me. Those horns were deadly.

Finally, on Christmas Day, I accepted the bitter fact that Dot was no longer welcome. I wasn't experienced enough to deal with a house cow turned feral so she had to go.

After devouring a massive Christmas dinner we'd collapsed on the sofas in the front room to watch a bit of telly. Olga, my cairn terrier, had joined the ever-growing pack of dogs at this stage and she'd been perched on the arm of the sofa growling for some time, and we couldn't understand why. I went to the window, and there was one of the twins staring back at me, wide-eyed.

It took some time for Vera and myself, armed with only a branch and a broom for protection, to get them back into the field and into their shed. It would be raining of course, and the wind would have to be of the gale-force variety, and Vera, not blessed with the best of eyesight and struggling in the pitch dark, thought she was pushing Dot's rear when in reality she was pushing her head and Dot wasn't in the least bit amused, refusing to move and ready to charge at any moment.

Thankfully she didn't, and after finally getting this unholy trio back into the field we returned to the house soaked to the skin, battered and bruised, still wearing our paper cracker hats but now drenched and stuck to our foreheads, the dye running down the sides of our faces. I made the decision there and then that Dot and co. were leaving for pastures new.

I rang Cathy and thankfully she happily took Dot home. Cathy has a way with cows for as soon as Dot saw her walking across the field her attitude changed. She put me in mind of a terrible schoolgirl who had been unexpectedly caught out for some misdemeanour by the headmistress.

Cow-free once again it was safe to walk the fields. I'd had Dot for over a year and she and her twins had been a lot of fun, but when a cow gets out of control then expert help is needed. As much as I missed having cows it was good to be able to go walking again without fear of being trampled, or worse.

Now there was just the sheep gently grazing, as friendly as the dogs and nothing to be wary of. Sheep aren't violent by nature. Or so I believed, until Christine arrived on the scene.

Sheep

My first lamb was a four-day-old orphan whose mother had died. She came from a local farmer who'd got in touch as he'd heard that I was looking for a lamb that needed hand-rearing, and once the paperwork was sorted out there I was sat in the back of a van with a lamb on my knee that was happily christening our relationship by peeing all over me.

I named her Waupie after Gypsy Rose Lee's pet lamb of the same name. Gypsy's lamb would appear on stage alongside a performing pig wearing a comedy hat as part of the 'Baby June and her Newsboys' act, but so far my Waupie was showing no signs of any showbiz aspirations.

She was a confident little thing though and beyond beautiful with her heart-shaped face and permanently wagging tail. Waupie was a Romney Marsh lamb, known for the distinctive flavour of their meat, although there was no way Waupie was going anywhere near an abattoir.

Originally Waupie was going to live in the barn but as she screamed the place down if left on her own she moved into the house. That's a downright lie. The real reason was because I couldn't bear to be parted from her so I brought her in, and she settled down quite happily to life on a dog bed in the kitchen.

Buster loved her on sight, and when he wasn't trying to hump her he would spend ages licking her all over and giving her a good wash – not that she needed one as the first thing I did was give her a bath. Waupie was the cleanest lamb in Kent. I was obsessed with her.

A lamb of that age needs lots of care and has to be bottle-fed every four hours including throughout the night. I'd set my alarm for four a.m. and as soon as it went off I'd hear her giving out in the kitchen, as she knew that the alarm meant feeding time. I'd make up her bottle with her special milk formula, feed her, and then take her out into the garden where she'd obligingly pee before returning to her dog bed with Buster at her side and going straight back to sleep.

Just as with a human baby all bottles and teats had to be sterilized as the young lamb was still prone to infection, although Waupie seemed to be bursting with good health. In fact it wasn't long before she was ruling the roost. Wherever I went Waupie was behind me. If I went to the loo she was there; if I sat on the sofa she was beside me;

and every morning when I took a shower Waupie would insist on getting in with me by banging on the shower door with her hoof and creating a terrible racket. On the odd occasion I'd give in and let her in but she'd get very excited and start jumping up and down, which can be a bit chaotic in a small shower, not to mention painful if a hoof catches a delicate place.

Soon I couldn't imagine life without Waupie. She seriously brightened up the day, and I was convinced that she hadn't caught on that she was a sheep. I think she saw herself as part human, part dog, for when I'd take her for walks she'd show no interest in neighbouring sheep and made no effort whatsoever to approach any, preferring to stick with me and Buster.

By the time she was eight weeks old I started to wean her off the bottle and try to encourage her to eat her lamb feed and learn how to graze. Of course she was having none of it and would create merry hell until I cracked and gave her a bottle.

How do you teach a lamb to graze? Easy, you get down on your hands and knees and pretend to nibble grass. Waupie, thinking this a great game, would climb on to my back and stand there, making me wonder if maybe she was a natural performer after all. I'd spoken about her so much on my teatime chat show that in the end I had no choice but to bring her in for the folks to meet her.

Once again paperwork had to be filled out to transport her, and Waupie made her TV debut, running straight up to me behind my desk and giving out until I gave her a bottle. She had a little collar by now and was quite content to walk on a lead. The sight of me strolling down the corridors of the London Studios with a dog and a lamb on a lead caused some raised eyebrows from the bosses, one of whom was heard to complain that I was 'turning the place into a bloody circus'. Gypsy Rose Lee would've been proud.

As Waupie grew she started to spend more time in the garden until eventually she gravitated to the field, although she remained just as friendly as she had been when she was a lamb and still enjoyed a bit of fuss and going on walks with me.

Fifteen years later I've still got her. She's an old girl now but still hale and hearty even if she seems to have forgotten the early days and has become a proper 'sheep', which is how it should be.

More lambs arrived, a black one and two white ones, and like Waupie they too lived in the kitchen until it got a bit much having three of them tearing around the house. The one thing that did manage to calm them down seemed to be the television, and the three of them would sit next to me on the sofa glued to *Des and Mel*, which they absolutely loved.

By the time they were old and strong enough, and despite their noisy protests, they went to live in the barn with plenty of hay and a shallow bowl of fresh water, but they'd seize every chance they got to be out and straight back in the house. They'd sit on the sofa, hoping, I suspected, to see their idols Des O'Connor and Melanie Sykes.

Every spring I seemed to inherit a couple of orphan lambs. It wasn't long before I had a flock of nine sheep, and once they were of the right age for breeding, a ram was brought in. He was an impressive beast and certainly wasted no time in doing his job as all the sheep fell pregnant, except for one – Christine.

Now when Christine was a lamb she loved to sniff flowers and showed a great interest in the garden so I named her after the gardener Christine Walkden. In retrospect Christine should really have been called Attila the Hun as she grew to be a bit of a thug. No, not a bit of a thug, a full-on raging, charging, stomping ewe.

When Denis Healey famously remarked that being attacked by Geoffrey Howe was like being 'savaged by a dead sheep' he'd obviously never met Christine.

The ram was terrified of her after she beat him up when he foolishly attempted to mount her, and when she wasn't terrorizing any poor soul who ventured into the field to pass the time she'd spend a happy hour headbutting the side of the barn.

Just like Dot the cow, Christine was becoming a hazard. She charged and nutted everyone and everything, and once when Sean was out in the tractor she even attacked that, headbutting it furiously.

One afternoon as I was minding my own business in the kitchen my peace was disturbed by a woman banging frantically on the window.

'Your sheep's attacking my daughter!' she was screaming. 'She's knocked her over!'

I pointed out rather snottily to this woman that neither her good self nor her daughter should be in my fields or my garden in the first place but, worried about the damage Christine could do, I braced myself and quickly went to see what carnage this crazy sheep had caused.

The woman had opened the gate that led into the garden from the field and consequently the sheep were all over the place. The teenage daughter of this stupid woman was screaming her head off as she lay in a bed of lavender with a furious Christine standing guard over her like a police dog with a burglar. I was bloody livid, not with Christine but with the gormless lump of lard crushing my lavender. Not surprisingly the girl was hysterical and I heard myself saying, 'Back off, Christine,' which to my surprise she obligingly did and started to amble back into the field as if nothing had happened.

'You've trained that sheep to attack!' the girl's mother shouted accusingly as she pulled her gibbering daughter out of my beautiful lavender. 'It wants putting down!'

'You and her want putting down,' I shouted back. 'Look at my lavender!'

'F**k your lavender,' she snapped. 'If my daughter's hurt, I'm going to sue you.'

As the sheep wandered about we had a lengthy argument about trespassing on private property. Christine, hearing this altercation, decided to return to the garden just in case I needed back-up and the sight of her set the daughter off screaming again. The mother grabbed her roughly by the arm and dragged her off up the path towards the gate still banging on about how Christine should be 'put down'.

They haven't been back.

I managed to round up the flock by banging a bucket that they foolishly thought contained food, luring them back into the field and locking the gate.

Eventually, after terrorizing us all, Christine went to live on a farm as a 'guard sheep' (seriously). A local farmer said she was just what he was looking for as he'd been having trouble with intruders breaking into his outhouses. Christine is still going strong, although I hear she's mellowed a lot with age and is content to put her violent past behind her and mooch around munching grass instead. Despite her savage outbursts I was very fond of her and, just like it was with Dot, I was sorry to see her go as she was a character. A psychopathic one, granted, but full of personality nevertheless.

The pregnant ewes duly gave birth and whatever that ram had inseminated them with was mighty powerful stuff as one of the sheep gave birth to two lambs and another to four, which I'm told is quite rare. The other sheep thankfully only gave birth to one lamb each, but poor Waupie's baby was stillborn, and despite trying to get her to bond with one of the other lambs she rejected it and went off to mourn under a hedge. She refused food and despite endless coaxing from me she wouldn't budge from her spot and remained there, silent and sad, for two weeks.

Who said animals don't have feelings? Whoever it was didn't have the first idea about them as watching Waupie grieve for her lost baby was heartbreaking.

As Doris the sheep didn't have enough milk in her to feed four lambs I took two to be hand-reared, and as the other ewe (who went by the name of Joyce) didn't seem to have enough milk for both of her lambs one of those came into the kitchen as well. This little one was tiny and undernourished and to give her a boost I made up a substitute for colostrum using an egg, cod liver oil, cows' milk and glucose, and kept her in a box near the Aga to keep warm.

I really bonded with this frail little lamb and, as she was extremely reluctant to take her bottle, feeding time took for ever as I encouraged her to suckle. I called her Alice, and gradually she began to thrive until one afternoon I suspected there was something not quite right, as she seemed to be having trouble breathing. The vet was called, and he diagnosed bloat – not uncommon in sheep and lambs but potentially dangerous. Bloat is caused by a build-up of bacteria in the rumen (stomach) that thrive on lactose and as they quickly ferment they produce excess gases that can cause the rumen to rupture and kill the lamb.

The vet inserted a rubber tube into Alice's side to dispel the gas and I spent all night massaging her to force it out. It was a long, worrying night as she was very ill, and trying to get her to take a syringe of castor oil was near on impossible. I'd squirt it in and she'd spit it out. Eventually we got there, but not before both of us were soaked in the foul-smelling stuff.

By the morning Alice was showing major signs of improvement, and by the time the vet came back in the afternoon, half expecting to find a dead lamb, she was hopping around the kitchen and creating a racket. The vet was amazed and said it was all down to my perseverance, which gave me a big head and had me going round all day proud as punch that I'd helped her pull through. Like many of the others, Alice is still holding court with the other sheep in the big field.

If you're going to hand-rear a lamb then here's a couple of tips to avoid bloat.

Don't let the lamb guzzle the bottle all at once. Let them have a suck, then stop and take the bottle away for ten seconds before carrying on.

Make sure the hole in the teat isn't too big, and mix a little bit of natural plain yoghurt in with their milk as the probiotics will help the growth of good bacteria and fight off the baddies.

Good luck, and if all goes well you'll find hand-rearing a lamb one of the most rewarding experiences of all time.

After reading in the news about a lamb that had been found dumped in a wheelie bin in Manchester I immediately offered him a home. The RSPCA brought him down, but before they left him with me they were obliged to check me out to see if I could accommodate a lamb. Satisfied that I could, Winston – for that was his name – stayed, and he turned out to be quite a character who constantly demanded, and got, attention.

He didn't bother with the other sheep. They didn't exist as far as he was concerned. All Winnie craved was human companionship – mine in particular.

He grew into a comical-looking sheep with long gangly legs that didn't look strong enough to support his wide girth, and a melancholic but expressive face. Every morning he'd appear at the garden wall calling out for a Weetabix, which he loved, as well as a bit of fuss, which he enjoyed even more, while the rest of the flock looked on, slightly bemused by his behaviour and considering him to be a bit of an oddity. Just as Waupie had done in the past, Winston loved to go on walks with me, surprising any walkers we might meet on the way with his total lack of fear and dog-like devotion.

I was lucky enough to have Winnie for three years before he was found dead one morning in the field. He'd died from blowfly, a scourge for sheep during the summer months. I was glad that I was away filming in Africa and didn't have to witness his corpse being slung into the back of a van and taken away.

A rampant ram had escaped from a nearby field and unbeknown to me had impregnated half of the ewes in the area including three of mine. Two of them gave birth without any trouble but the third was late and seemed to be experiencing some difficulty. It was a Saturday afternoon, and knowing that she was due to lamb any minute as she was showing all the right signs I put her in the barn to get on with the business in hand, going out every five minutes to see how she was getting on.

The ewe had been lying on her side each time I looked in but so far there was still no sign of any action. The next time I popped in she was standing with what looked like a large bubble of water hanging out of her rear end. The bubble burst, and once I'd got over the shock of this unfamiliar sight I thought this is it, any minute now a newborn lamb will pop out – only it didn't.

The ewe was bleating loudly and she seemed distressed. Quelling the urge to panic I danced around in a circle flapping my hands, wondering what to do. I braced myself to take a look at what they call in the business the birth canal, even though I wasn't quite sure what I was looking for. Should I have a feel around? Or should I just leave her to it?

I went back into the house to see if nature would take its course while I was away, but just in case it didn't I filled a bucket with warm water and Dettol, put on a pair of surgical gloves that I kept for washing dogs' posteriors and went back out, praying that she'd managed to give birth on her own.

She hadn't, and she was now lying on her side seemingly having trouble breathing. There was nothing for it but to get stuck in. My sister Sheila was a midwife and I hoped that there might be something in the genes that would help.

The first thing I did was remove my jumper as it was a good one and I didn't want it covered in whatever was going to come out. Then I washed the ewe's rear end with the Dettol and water before taking a deep breath and tentatively sliding a gloved hand in, my eyes tightly closed during the procedure. I could feel what I assumed to be a pair of curled-up legs that I had a strong suspicion needed straightening out. Once I'd managed to do that and a set of hooves started to appear, the lamb slipped out backwards fairly easily with me shouting 'Oh my God!' as I tugged on its legs.

The lamb lay on the straw before me, a shiny, slimy mess, and I wondered if it was stillborn. I panicked. Then, remembering something I'd read, I quickly cleared the mucus from its mouth and nose, gave it a brisk rub with a towel, and much to my delight it started to struggle.

I could've cried with relief that it was alive but instead of howling I left Mum to it.

Standing in the field, stripped to the waist and covered in all manner of sheepy fluids and blood, I felt reborn. 'I've just delivered a lamb!' I wanted to shout, close to tears of elation that the birth had been successful. It was a special moment that I'll never forget, another one of those many experiences that remind me to count my blessings and open my eyes to the fact that I am incredibly lucky to be living in such a wonderful part of the world.

The dogs thought I smelt wonderful, slathered as I was in sheep gunk, and kept leaping up at me to have a sniff and a lick as I tried to get past them in the kitchen and run upstairs to take a shower. The dogs followed me excitedly, driven into a frenzy by the trail of Eau de Sheepbirth, watching me forlornly through the shower screen as I washed away this magnificent smorgasbord of sniffs and licks.

Once I was scrubbed up I made a cup of tea and then rang the vet, who came round and gave the ewe an antibiotic injection and checked that all was well with the lamb, who thankfully was fit and healthy and suckling like a Trojan on his mother's teat.

I gave this lamb the rather grand name of Raphael as since my stint as a midwife assisting at the birth of a living creature I was feeling slightly spiritual and otherworldly – until walking around the garden barefooted soaking up the rays of the late afternoon sun I stood in a dog turd and quickly reverted to type, my language anything but what you'd describe as saintly.

I've never sheared one of my flock as I wouldn't trust myself with a struggling sheep and a pair of electric clippers: I suspect only one of us would come out of it alive. Getting a sheep on its back isn't the easiest thing in the world for a neophyte like me to do. I had to pin Waupie down once to enable the vet to examine her hooves and it was akin to wrestling with Giant Haystacks. Not that I ever had the pleasure of entering the ring with Mr Haystacks but I should imagine being in a grapple with that good man was similar to attempting to pin a hefty Waupie down. Jonathon the farmer kindly does the shearing for me.

A question I'm frequently asked is 'Why do lambs lose their tails?' It's because a band is attached at the base of the tail, causing it to eventually fall off. It's called docking and is necessary because a tail would cause a build-up of faeces which would encourage flies and infection. Well, you did ask.

After writing this I took a walk down the field to see how my lot were getting on. The sun was out and it looked as if it was a warm late afternoon but the weather was deceptive as there was what's called 'a nip in the air' – an optimistic euphemism for 'bloody freezing'.

The sheep were still in their thick woollen coats and, unperturbed by my appearance, they remained lying under an oak tree like elderly concubines. I sat nearby and counted them as I always do, and slowly Ella rose to her hooves and came towards me to investigate, followed closely by her two young ones who love brown bread. They had a sniff, and seeing there was no food they lay down again, only this time fairly close to me.

Forget yoga, meditation and Valium, the way to relax is to sit with sheep and, just like them, think of nothing and enjoy the view. If the pay and conditions were better I wouldn't mind being a shepherd.

Cakes and Chaos

Once upon a time when I was young, fresh and naive – in other words a long, long time ago – I was on holiday with the family in North Wales. I was bursting to use the loo so I went into a public one, and written on the wall was a poem I've never forgotten. I like poetry, but I can only remember two: John Keats's 'Meg Merrilies' and, I'm ashamed to say, the ditty on the wall of this lav, which went like this:

> *It's no good standing on the seat,*
> *The crabs in here can jump ten feet,*
> *And if you think that is high,*
> *Then go next door,*
> *The buggers fly.*

Not quite Keats I know, and at the tender age of ten I assumed the crabs that the author of this ode was referring to were the same as the ones I caught in a bucket on New Brighton beach. I imagined that these crabs had somehow wandered from the sea into a sewage outlet and were lurking in the S-bend ready to leap at the first sign of an unsuspecting bare backside descending on to the seat. The flying ones I wasn't so sure about; maybe they were just better jumpers than the ones in my cubicle. Of course now that I'm much older and perhaps a little bit wiser I realize that the crabs in question were an entirely different species to the ones in the pools amongst the rocks around Fort Perch Rock.

There's a reason why I'm reminiscing about lavatorial graffiti concerning the habits of crabs and it's because I've just bought a dressed one.

I haven't eaten a dressed crab for years and as it looked tasty sitting there in the fishmonger's glass cabinet next to the prawns with a sprig of parsley stuck in its middle, I bought it.

Now as this is 'The Cookery Section' of the book, which I believe is obligatory in books relating to the countryside, I should be bragging about how I ate this crab accompanied by a glass of cold, crisp Riesling sitting in the sun on the patio, only I can't, because I didn't. I bought chips on my way home and sat in the car overlooking the sea eating them with the crab, which I discovered I've lost the taste for. I just don't like the texture, nor am I keen on the taste. There was nothing wrong with the crab, in fact the friend who demolished it later on said it was delicious, but crab and me are over.

I'm a fussy eater, I'll admit that, and yet for someone who wouldn't eat a boiled egg under torture I can quite happily knock back a dozen oysters – not the prettiest of shellfish you'll agree, but I love them.

When it comes to cooking I'd have to tick the box that said 'Good Plain Cook'. I'm pretty boring when it comes to menus and tend to make the same meals for convenience sake as I haven't got time to be faffing about searching for the obscure ingredients required by most recipes you find in the Sunday supplements never mind cooking the damn thing.

I once produced a bouillabaisse that took me two days to make and ten minutes for us to eat, and if I say so myself it was a surprisingly tasty if not lethal broth thanks to my liberal use of the absinthe bottle in the stock.

When I'm not being adventurous I'll normally dish up a spaghetti bolognese, mince and potatoes, cottage pie, corned beef hash with onion gravy, roast dinners and 'finny haddy' – undyed smoked haddock if you didn't know. Since I went filming in India I've developed a craving for genuine Indian food and I'll have a go at making curries, in particular coconut curry with prawns served with jasmine rice. It doesn't taste like the one I ate in a hotel in Agra – that dish was conjured up by a man who was a master of his craft; the best I can say about mine is that they're passable. I like the smell and the look of the various spices but the odour does seem to permeate the house for a while afterwards.

Fancy bouillabaisses apart, soups are really easy to make and much tastier and cheaper than most soups you can get in packets, tins and cartons in the supermarket; plus if you're worried about such additives as salt and sugar and artificial flavourings that are in some ready-made soups then by making your own *you* decide what goes into your stockpot. I love making soup, and usually have a pan on the go if I'm at home for a few days.

You seriously can't beat a big bowl of healthy homemade soup with a chunk of crusty bread to dunk in it. I get that glow of self-satisfaction that comes from knowing I've created something that is not only edible and extremely tasty but is also doing me good at the same time. Full of self-righteousness I'll eat an apple after a bowl of soup and then go out for a long run. That last bit was a lie – the run, not the apple.

I could quite happily live on soup – well, that and cheese on toast and corned beef. But as these pages are supposed to be about me being a dab hand in the kitchen, turning out all manner of goodies from the oven like a latter-day Fanny Cradock, I'd better come up with the goods.

Here's a couple of soup recipes that are tried and true and you can make in your own kitchenette – if you can be bothered that is.

Broccoli and Stilton Soup

I hate broccoli as much as I hate strong-smelling cheeses yet strangely enough I can really get stuck into a bowl of this. The combination of the Stilton and broccoli makes for one of the best double acts since Mavis and Derek. You'll need:

2 large onions
Butter
A nice big head of the dreaded broccoli (or a bit more, depending on your taste)
30g flour
A litre and a half of veg stock (Now then, you can make your own veg stock if you like – see page 306 – or simply use a couple of stock cubes that are low in salt: Marigold Swiss veg bouillon is good)
250–300g Stilton
A good squirt of lemon juice
Sherry (optional, depending if you've got any sherry in or not – and the same goes for cream or crème fraiche)
Chopped parsley, chives, or whatever herb you fancy

Peel and chop your onion into small pieces and soften in a nice dollop of butter in a large pan. Don't let the onions burn, keep 'em moving until they're sweating like a whore at confession.

Now for the broccoli. Give it a wash under the tap – and I don't mean with a flannel and some Lifebuoy soap. Just give it a good rinse in some cold water and then break up the florets with your hand. Chop the stalk up along with any long stems as I've been informed that these parts of the vegetable actually contain more nutrients than the actual florets.

Add the broccoli and stalks to the onions and give it a good stir. Do this on a low light – no need for a bonfire so keep it down and enjoy a moment's peace as you poke the ingredients with your wooden spoon, stirring until the veg has softened.

Next, add the flour and stir for a couple of minutes, still on the low light, until the flour is cooked.

Slowly add the stock to the pan with one hand – careful now, don't spill it or scald yourself – as you stir the concoction with the other. Don't just chuck it all in. This has to be done gradually if you want your soup to turn out successfully.

Turn the heat up now, and bring briefly to the boil, then cover and let it simmer gently – and I mean gently – for about thirty minutes on a very low flame, ring, complicated electronic hob or open turf fire in the bogs of Ballincurry.

Remove the pan from the heat and add your cheese, which has been chopped or crumbled, then get on with something else as you allow it to cool because you're going to put this little lot into the blender, and we know what happens when we put hot liquids into our blenders, don't we? That's right, the lid flies off and scalding-hot soup decorates both you and the kitchen, as I've found out in the past.

Blend the soup a bit at a time if using a glass jug blender, but if you're using the hand-held variety then I assume you just stick it in the pan and turn it on. I'm afraid I can't help you there as I haven't got one, but whichever way you choose to blend, afterwards put the soup into a clean pan and reheat.

If it's too thick for your liking then add some water, milk or stock until it's just the way you like it, and taste to see if it requires any seasoning. I always add lots of freshly ground white pepper because I love it but I tend to go easy on the salt, but once again it's up to you. Do it how you like it.

You can add a squeeze or two of fresh lemon juice to 'lift' the flavours, which I recommend you do, plus a drop of sherry if you want to liven it up, resisting the urge to take a quick swig from the bottle as not only is it common but if a passing neighbour sees you through the kitchen window then you'll be branded an alcoholic.

Swirl on some double cream or crème fraiche, and then add croutons, which are a doddle to make. Simply cut a slice of white bread (crusts removed) into little squares, rub a baking tray with a clove of garlic, throw the bread cubes on the tray, drizzle with oil, and put into a hot oven for five minutes or until crisp and golden. (Use more bread depending on how many people are going to eat.)

Finally, add a little chopped parsley or chives from the herb garden you're growing. Lovely.

Tomato and Dill Soup

I'm mad on dill, it's one of my favourite herbs, and although it looks a bit like fennel it has a totally different taste. An infusion made from dill seeds is a good way to shift indigestion, and gripe water, an excellent cure for colic in children, is made from dill. But there are already a few pages on herbs somewhere in this book and since this section is about cooking I'll press on. This is what you'll need:

10 lovely big ripe tomatoes
2 large onions
4 stalks of washed celery, chopped into chunks
A chunk of butter for frying (use as much or as little as
    you want depending on how you feel about butter,
    just don't use olive oil or one of those processed
    butter substitutes)
700ml of veg or chicken stock (make your own, or use
    low-salt stock cubes)
Lots of chopped dill, about ten tablespoons
Black pepper
Juice of half a lemon
A slug of white wine
Chopped parsley

First off, peel your toms by putting them in a bowl and pouring boiling water over them. Leave for a couple of minutes, drain, then cover them in cold water. The skins should come off quite easily. You can deseed them if you like, although for this soup I'm happy to leave them in.

Chop the tomatoes and set aside while you sauté the chopped onions and celery in a pan with the butter until soft.

Add the toms and the stock and bring to the boil. You'll notice what looks like scum forming around the edges of the pan: scoop this up with a slotted spoon and dispose of it.

Add a couple of spoons of the dill and some black pepper, then pop the lid on and let it simmer gently for half an hour.

Blend in batches, but remember to leave some of the soup unblended – about a teacupful.

Add the remaining dill, the lemon juice and white wine. Taste to see if it requires more seasoning.

Add the unblended soup, reheat and simmer for fifteen minutes. If the soup is too thick then thin it out with more stock or water. Add another splash of booze if you like although don't go mad as you wouldn't want your guests getting nicked for driving under the influence as they make their way home.

Pour into bowls, sprinkle with a little chopped parsley and serve.

This soup is just as tasty served cold. If you are going to dish it out hot then I find that it tastes better if it's not served with steam rising off it. Just warm it up gently.

Veg Stock

✦ ✦ ✦ ✦ ✦ ✦ ✦ ✦ ✦ ✦ ✦ ✦ ✦ ✦

Couldn't be easier.

4 carrots, scrubbed and chopped up

2 onions, washed and chopped in half (leave the skins on)
4 sticks of celery, washed and chopped
2 parsnips, scrubbed and chopped up
A teaspoon of black peppercorns
A bouquet garni
A good squeeze of lemon juice

Make your own bouquet garni as those little bags of dust you get in the shops are a waste of time. They sell kitchen herbs growing in pots these days in most supermarkets and if you look after them they'll last for ages. Take a bunch of parsley complete with stalks, a bay leaf, some sprigs of thyme and a sprig of marjoram and tie them around the leaves of a celery stalk with clean string.

Put all the veg in a pot with the bouquet garni, cover with a pint of water (maybe a bit more), bring to the boil and then simmer, scooping off any scum that forms on the top with a slotted spoon. Simmer on a very low heat for just over an hour and a half, giving it the odd stir, and then strain through a fine sieve. And there you have it, fresh veg stock as a base for your soup. The veg you've used for the stock you can throw on your compost heap or feed to the pigs.

I like the subtle tang of lemon in a soup as I think it lifts it, in particular the lighter soups, so add a good squeeze to your stock.

I really enjoy baking, and that's nothing to do with the current craze for these ubiquitous shows which I'm now led to believe 'have the nation baking', which isn't a bad thing at all: it's not that difficult if you stick to a recipe and do as you're told. I've always been interested in making cakes and desserts, and while I'd hate to dent egos, my influence was not down to the bakers and chefs on the telly but those family members who were skilled artisans when it came to making pastry and cakes.

My Uncle Hal was a master baker and confectioner for the Cunard Shipping Line producing all sorts of magnificent delights to tempt the sweet teeth of the transatlantic passengers on board those magnificent vessels. It was him who taught me how to make a perfect rose out of leaves of marzipan that had been dyed various shades of red ranging from blush to scarlet. Unfortunately I'm not called upon to churn out marzipan roses as part of my daily routine so it's a skill that's now been rendered redundant.

My mother made the most magnificent apple pies, as did my Aunty Chris, who baked a variety of cakes and pies every Sunday morning after everyone had gone to Mass and she had the kitchen all to herself.

I frequently skipped Mass, pretending to my parents that I'd gone to church straight after my Sunday morning round flogging papers and fags to the patients of St Catherine's Hospital. In reality I'd sagged off and gone up to visit Aunty Chris to shatter her peace.

'What the bloody hell do you want?' she'd exclaim, greeting me in her usual cheery manner as I stepped into the kitchen. 'You're not telling me you've been to Mass?'

'I have.' I'd lie. 'I went to ten o'clock as soon as I finished me papers.'

'Well you got up here quick then, it's only just gone ten past eleven,' she'd reply, removing the fag from her lip and resting it on the side of the kitchen table. 'What did you come by, a bloody rocket?'

'No, Mass finished at a quarter to and I legged it down the hill and by the time I'd got to Singleton Avenue there was a bus coming along Borough Road,' I lied again. 'He drove hell for leather. Got here in no time,' I added for good measure.

'Didn't know Stirling Moss was driving a Corporation bus these days,' she sniffed, studying me through hooded eyes as she rubbed some butter into a bowl of flour. 'Who was on the altar?'

'Father Doyle.'

'Did you go for Communion?'

'No.'

'Why not?'

'Cos I haven't been to confession for ages.'

'Too bloody scared to that's why,' she replied, taking her hand out of the bowl and carefully removing her fag from the side of the table to take a drag, the flour from the back of her hand getting up her nose and making her cough, causing a light dusting of ash to land in the mixture below.

'You've flicked ash in your bowl,' I said, hoping to get her off the subject of ten o'clock Mass.

She peered into the bowl and cursed under her breath. 'That's you that,' she said, fag in mouth, catching most of the ash on the tip of a teaspoon and tipping it in the flip-top bin. 'Bit of ash never hurt no one so don't you be saying anything or I just might sing like a canary and announce that you burst in here like a starving hooligan when you should be at Mass.'

Aunty Chris didn't go to church. It had been years since she'd sat in a pew and she described those who spent the best part of their lives attending daily Mass as 'altar rail eaters'. Still, she encouraged everyone else to go on a

Sunday, me in particular, always reminding me to 'say one for her'.

The family often visited my Aunty Anne and Chrissie's house on a Sunday afternoon and Aunty Chris would keep them fed with a steady stream of sandwiches, cakes and fruit pies, grumbling later that they were like a 'pack of bloody locusts, eating us out of house and home' when in reality she was proud as a turkey cock that her cooking was appreciated, her apple pie in particular, for ash or no ash, her pastry was unsurpassable.

After she died I took a few of her paperbacks home with me as something to remember her by. She was an avid reader and a big fan of crime and detective novels, one of her favourite authors being Agatha Christie. I found this recipe written on the back of a brown envelope between the pages of *Mrs McGinty's Dead*, which I hope doesn't put you off. It's easy to make and tastes gorgeous and I've even added a few touches of my own.

Aunty Chris's Apple Pie

Before we start, let me tell you something that will make life easy. We're going to be making pastry, and for that you need a cool kitchen and cold hands, so open all the windows and sit in the fridge for half an hour – and just in case you're thick enough to believe me, I was joking about the fridge bit. Just make sure that when it comes to making pastry the word du jour is 'cool'. Pastry-making tends to sort the men from the boys so if you manage to crack it and turn out a pastry that's crisp on the outside and soft as butter within then you've got it made.

For the pastry you'll need:

250g good plain flour
50g golden icing sugar
A pinch of salt
100g butter or margarine (Stork is good)
75g lard
1 large egg, whisked with a drop of milk
Fag ash (optional)

In a bowl, mix the sifted flour and sugar and a pinch of salt with your fingers and then rub in the butter, which should be cold and cut into cubes, along with the lard, which should be in a similar condition.

I don't do this as I've never managed to achieve the 'breadcrumb' effect that the cookery books say will happen. I use a food processor, which is not only quicker but does the job beautifully. Don't whizz it for too long though: as soon as it's turned to crumbs, stop the machine.

Return the mixture to the bowl and slowly add the beaten egg and milk, stirring it with a knife until it starts to turn from crumbs into something a little more solid.

You don't want a sloppy mess so you might not need all the egg and milk mix. Use common sense, and when it has all come together, shape it into a ball. Don't manhandle it, you're not a ball boy at Wimbledon; less is more when it comes to pastry, so just shape it quickly, wrap in clingfilm and put it in the fridge for twenty minutes.

Now for the apples.

Peel, core and slice into segments (not too thin now) a mix of five large Bramley and Granny Smith apples. Soak them in a little apple and lemon juice, with a good dash of an apple brandy such as a Calvados. Don't drown them in the mixture, a few tablespoons is sufficient. If you don't fancy going down the alcoholic route then simply pop the slices in a pan with a couple of tablespoons of water or apple juice and gently heat them up.

Keep an eye on this as you don't want the apples to catch and burn. Give them the odd stir. You want the apple slices firm – don't let them collapse into mush.

Remove the pan from the heat, add sugar to the apples and stir. How much or how little you use depends entirely on how sharp the apples are and how sweet you want it to be. I use about 100–110 grams of caster sugar, sometimes less.

Mix in a bit of ground cinnamon, a pinch of ground cardamom and some freshly grated nutmeg to give it a proper old-fashioned taste.

Now back to the pastry.

Split your ball of pastry in half and roll out on a lightly floured surface. A milk bottle (if you can find such a thing) that's been chilling in the fridge works for me, as does a floured rolling pin. Roll out to about a quarter of an inch thickness and then, by carefully folding the pastry over your rolling pin, lay it in a greased pie tin or dish. Make sure that you press it down (gently now) to both the base and the sides making sure that there's enough overhang for you to fold over the rim.

Trim off any excess with a knife and prick the base of the pastry all over with a fork.

Have you heard of baking blind? It doesn't mean that at this point you cover your eyes with a scarf or sleep-mask and stagger around the kitchen, it's simply pre-baking so you don't end up with a soggy base, or 'soggy bottom' as they say on that television programme (nudge, nudge, wink, wink, ooh-er missus).

Preheat the oven and a baking sheet to gas mark 5 (190°C) and bake for fifteen minutes. Keep an eye on it to make sure that it's not burning; it should be a light golden brown.

You can use baking beans or pulses to cover the pastry base if you want to but I've never really found the need and think it's a bit unnecessary.

When the base is ready, fill it with the apples and roll out the rest of the pastry to make a lid, leaving enough pastry hanging over the edge to form a seal. It's a good idea to brush the pastry rim with a little beaten egg and milk first before popping the lid on as it helps to stick them together.

Press the edge all round with a fork and trim off any excess with a knife.

With the leftover pastry you can have a bit of fun cutting out shapes to adorn your masterpiece: leaves, flowers, hearts, skulls, whatever takes your fancy. Just stick them on with the beaten egg-and-milk mixture using what's left of it to brush over the entire pie before adding the finishing touch of a good sprinkle of sugar. Make a couple of small slits in the top of the pie and bake for twenty to twenty-five minutes at gas mark 5 (190°C) until golden brown.

Give it another sprinkle of sugar while the pie is still hot and serve with either whipped cream to which a drop of apple brandy has been added, or a good ready-made vanilla custard from the supermarket.

Dutch Apple Pie

The Dutch, it is claimed by some, are not renowned for their cuisine, although I have to disagree as their apple pies are serious rivals to my Aunty Chris's.

There are many good restaurants and cafés in Amsterdam these days but they mainly serve up dishes from all over the world, and as much as I like Thai and Indian food I'm more inclined to look for traditional Dutch cuisine, which is not as easy to find.

Every café and bar has *bitterballen*, little round balls which I can best describe as meat- and gravy-filled croquettes which go down very well with a long glass of cold beer. Then there's the ubiquitous *stroopwafel*, a round biscuit comprising two thin layers of baked batter with something gooey that tastes of toffee inside. Proper *stroopwafels* freshly baked really take some beating and it's not hard to sit and eat your way through half a dozen before being dragged away screaming from the table for your own good.

The Dutch love mashed food, which they call *stamppot*. It's basically a simple meal of mashed spuds mixed with whatever ingredient you fancy. The kale *stamppot* is my favourite as it's more or less the same as the Irish dish of colcannon only with less butter and served with slices of a smoked sausage called *rookworst*. I've had *stamppot* made with a combination of small chunks of cheese and apple which was unusual but delicious, as was the *stamppot* made with mashed carrots and chunks of braised beef – although I was informed very solemnly in the way that only the Dutch can that this dish is technically a *hutspot* and not *stamppot*. So now you know.

It's all pretty similar to the mashed spud meals I eat back home. I daresay corned beef hash could be classed as a *stamppot*, although I haven't yet come across any onion gravy or Daddies sauce in a Dutch caff.

Stamppot is quick, easy and cheap to make. It's also ideal for those who haven't got a tooth in their head as there's hardly any chewing involved. You simply peel, slice and boil some spuds and then drain and mash with butter and salt and pepper. Add to the mashed spuds whatever cooked veg you like, mash them together, and dish it up with meat or fish, or simply eat it on its own. It's real comfort food, to be eaten on a miserable winter's night or when you've only got a couple of spuds and a bit of veg in the larder and you can't be bothered going out shopping.

But the jewel in any Amsterdam café's crown has got to be the Dutch Apple Pie. Reputations have been made on the quality of a café's apple pie, guaranteeing queues at the door and money in the bank.

I had this pie at a friend's house and managed to extract the recipe from the chef by tying him to the banisters and belting him repeatedly with a wet mop. You must understand that I do not condone torture, but desperate times call for desperate measures and I wasn't leaving that house without that recipe as the pie was the business.

This recipe has been handed down from person to person so its origins are unknown but I've been assured that it's the traditional one. Here's what you'll need:

300g good plain flour
125g golden caster sugar
A pinch of salt
225g butter, cut into cubes (this has to be cold and not at room temperature)
The yolk of a large egg
50g raisins
50g sultanas
100ml apple juice
1kg baking apples or a mix of bakers and dessert apples
A heaped tablespoon of custard powder
2 tablespoons of sugar
Half a teaspoon of freshly grated nutmeg (again, use more if you like the taste)
A heaped teaspoon of cinnamon, or more if desired
Warm apricot jam for the glaze

It's cold hands time again, folks, as we are about to make pastry.

Mix the sifted flour, caster sugar, salt and butter in a large bowl or a mixer using the cutting blade. The butter has to be cut into teeny pieces and mixed into the flour, and when you think it's sufficiently rubbed in then add the egg yolk, mix again briefly, and knead together with hands that should be colder than a corpse's. Roll into a ball, put it into a freezer bag and into the fridge.

You're going to need an eight-inch cake tin, one of those with a loose bottom (I really should be writing scripts for *Bake Off*), and once you've greased the sides and bottom well (here we go, I'm getting filthy now), line the base and sides with baking parchment.

Take three quarters of the pastry and line the base and sides of the cake tin with it, pressing it well in until it's even. Put the remaining pastry back in the fridge along with the cake tin as you prepare your moist, juicy filling (it's getting out of hand now).

In a pan, add the raisins and sultanas to the apple juice and bring to the boil, then simmer until the liquid has reduced slightly. Add the apples, peeled and sliced into decent chunks, along with the custard powder, two tablespoons of sugar and the nutmeg and cinnamon. Toss these (don't even go there) together making sure the apple slices get an even coating, then spread them on top of the pastry base.

Roll the remaining pastry out, making sure it's not too thin, and cut into strips about half an inch wide. Lay these across the apple mix in a lattice pattern and brush with a little egg yolk or milk.

Bake in a preheated oven at gas mark 4 (180°C) for approximately forty to fifty minutes until it's golden brown in colour. Leave it in the tin for fifteen minutes to cool. Remove from the tin and glaze the top with some apricot jam that you've warmed up in a pan.

Devour along with great artery-hardening dollops of whipped cream or a good vanilla ice cream.

I once visited the Imperial War Museum. I don't know why as I'm not really into old planes and tanks, but nevertheless it was interesting, a good way to spend an afternoon.

At the time there was an exhibition on about London during the war and they'd recreated what it was like to be inside an Anderson shelter during a heavy air raid. As there was no one inside I thought I'd try out the 'experience' for myself, but no sooner had I sat down on the bench than a large party of highly excited schoolchildren invaded, followed by the sound of the corrugated iron door closing behind them.

It was very realistic, with deafening bombs going off and soil coming through the cracks in the ceiling as the shelter shook with each boom. The kids were leaping about and screaming to high heaven, and the intermittent flashes of light that represented explosions had the effect of strobe lighting making the flailing tangle of legs and arms look like a scene straight out of an old Keystone Cops silent movie.

I emerged from this air raid shelter experience like the person in that painting *The Scream*. Hitler's bombers couldn't have done any more damage to my nerves than this party of schoolkids had, and I moved on quickly in search of the café as during the raid I'd been given a dig in the head, either accidental or deliberate, and I couldn't trust myself not to rip the little monsters' heads off.

I like museum caffs as much as I like their shops, and mooching around the latter I bought a book on wartime recipes. It was certainly inventive I'll give it that, but even so the majority of the recipes didn't sound very appetizing, except for one, which I made out of curiosity. And lo and behold it was delicious.

Lord Woolton's Pie

Lord Woolton was the Minister of Food during World War Two. Rationing was in force and many types of food were either scarce or non-existent. Meat in particular was in very short supply so the chef at the Savoy Hotel created this vegetable pie which Lord Woolton championed and made popular amongst desperate housewives looking to find a way to turn the limited food on offer into a decent, nutritious meal.

Here's the recipe then, with a few liberty-taking changes by myself. You will need:

A couple of large potatoes, peeled and cut into small-ish chunks
2 large carrots, peeled and chopped
Half a swede, or use the lot if you like swede, peeled and chopped into smallish pieces
A couple of diced spring onions

A large parsnip, chopped into pieces
An onion, chopped up
A veg stock cube dissolved in hot water
A spoonful of oats
A squirt of tomato purée
Fresh parsley and thyme
Salt and pepper

Put all the chopped veg into a pan and cover with the stock. Don't drown them, use enough to just cover them. Add the oats, tom purée and the herbs, and bring to the boil. Simmer gently until they are just tender – not mushy as they need to hold their shape. Drain them and transfer to a pie dish. (I've got an old blue and white enamel one that once belonged to a long-dead member of the family that's turned out more pies down the years than Mrs Lovett.) Season with salt and pepper.

You'll need to make a pastry lid, so take the following:

4oz lard (if you can't face the thought of lard, use
   marge instead)
8oz of wholemeal flour

Rub your marge or lard into the flour and add some water – not a lot, just enough to form a dough. Roll it out on a floured surface and place over the dish.

Trim the excess pastry from around the edge and cut out some leaf shapes.

Brush the pie with a drop of milk and stick the leaf shapes artfully on top. Make three slits in the middle.

Put in the oven at gas mark 4 (180°C) for thirty minutes. Have a look at it after twenty minutes to make sure it's not burning.

Serve with mashed spuds, steamed cabbage and gravy made from a beef stock cube and a dash of Worcestershire sauce, and thickened with Bisto.

It's a really healthy meal if you disregard the gravy. But I'm sorry, you can't eat Lord Woolton's Pie without smothering it in a thick velvety gravy – and, if your food ration permits it, a drop of Daddies sauce on the side.

When I left school and went to work for the DHSS in Liverpool one of my first purchases out of my wages was a book by Marguerite Patten entitled *Cooking for Two*. I've always liked cookery books as they make great bedtime reading, even if they do make me hungry and prompt me to get up and make cheese on toast at one a.m.

I made a dessert called Queen of Puddings for my poor mother and father, which by the time I'd served it up had curdled into a mess of cold, stringy scrambled eggs. My parents made a brave attempt at eating it but after one tiny mouthful they declared that they were both 'too full up to eat any more, but it was delicious'. Marguerite Patten was banished to a shelf after that and it wasn't until years later, when I'd emigrated down south, that I opened it again and managed this time to knock up some fairly decent meals – although the Queen of Puddings remained exiled.

I really took up baking cakes on a grand scale after moving to the country and getting myself an Aga which, after a brief period of trial and error involving shelf moving,

I suddenly got the hang of, discovering the secret that Aga owners have known for years: that they make the best cakes.

Agas are expensive to buy and aren't cheap to run, but that and my bed, which also cost an arm and a leg, were the best investments I ever made. My mother used to say 'never scrimp when it comes to buying a bed or a pair of shoes, for when you're not in one you're in the other', and she was right, although she didn't mention anything about Agas.

According to a survey I read somewhere (who are the people who participate in these surveys?), owning an Aga makes me middle class – though I've yet to lean against mine sipping a glass of Sancerre while listening to *The Archers*. I discussed the benefits of the Aga with Delia Smith when she appeared on my chat show and the good lady made it perfectly clear that she didn't hold them in the same high regard as I did. Now I'm not one to disagree with St Delia on any matter culinary, but on this occasion I had to gird my loins and bravely defend the Aga. I mean, what else can you cook on and dry your socks and underpants at the same time on the hotplate?

You don't need an Aga to churn these recipes out, a gas or electric oven will suffice, but I doubt very much that they'll taste anywhere as good as cakes baked in an Aga.

Making a cake should be a pleasurable experience, not something done in a rush or seen as a mundane chore – unless of course you work in a factory and are churning the bloody things out day after day, night after night, then I can fully understand how it might turn you doolally.

I get cake-making fits. I'll suddenly declare in the middle of something I'm watching on the telly that I'm going to turn out a lemon drizzle or a nutmeg loaf and head for the kitchen to see if I've got all the ingredients required to create a bit of magic and enjoy myself.

Because I am by nature a sloppy, dirty worker I've learned from experience to start with a clear, clean work surface with all the ingredients and tools I'm going to need close to hand. And by tools I mean bowls and spoons, not hammers and chisels – unless, that is, you really are just too plain thick to follow a recipe and you turn out something harder than hell's doorstep in which case the chisel and hammer will come in handy.

You don't really need fancy mixers and beaters to bake, although they do save a lot of time and hard work. I bought a KitchenAid mixer years ago from a shop in Lytham St Annes when I was working in Blackpool for the summer season. It cost me two hundred quid which seemed like an absolute fortune at the time but I couldn't resist its gleaming chrome bowl and smooth lines so all sensibility left me, as it's wont to do when you fall in love, and back to London it went where it lived in all its chrome splendour unused, it's beautiful bowl filled with taxi receipts, loose change, broken pens and a dog lead.

I would advise getting yourself a decent pair of weighing scales though as this is a necessity if you are to become a competent cake-maker. I've got an inexpensive digital one that is extremely reliable and compact and doesn't take up any space.

It wasn't till the KitchenAid transferred to Kent that she made her debut and helped me produce a reasonably edible, if not tough due to over-mixing, Victoria sponge. Indeed, if I'm honest this Victoria sponge was not the sort of feather-light confectionery to grace a parlour; in fact it was so 'ard a waterfront bar would've been it's more likely natural home.

Since those early days that KitchenAid has proved it was worth every penny of that two hundred quid. It's in constant use and nearly twenty-five years later is still going strong.

I find the best time to make a cake is when you might have the luxury of a few hours or so to yourself. Lay your stall out with everything you're going to need, turn your radio or music on, switch your phone to silent, make yourself a cup of tea or crack open a bottle, and enjoy yourself.

Aunty Sadie's Rhubarb Tart

+ + + + + + + + + + + + + +

When I was a kid I used to love going to visit my dad's sister, my Aunty Sadie, in Eastham. She lived with her husband Mick who could usually be found in the front room sat in an armchair smoking his pipe and reading the paper with his cap on.

I once shared a meal of cheese, pickle, raw red onion and homemade bread with him that was one of those memorable feasts that stay in the memory and can be recalled at any time. I remember feeling very grown up at the time, being brave enough to eat an onion raw. It's still one of my all-time favourites, a simple meal of good English cheese and raw onion and perhaps an apple, accompanied by a chunk of fresh bread slathered liberally with best butter and washed down with a mug of tea. Every time I have it now, which is fairly frequently as it's handy as a quick lunch, Uncle Mick springs to mind.

I thought Uncle Mick and Aunty Sadie lived in a very posh house because they had a dining room with French windows leading out on to a garden in which they grew some spuds, mint and rhubarb. Aunty Sadie always threw her used tea leaves on the rhubarb as she reckoned it made them grow, and I reckon she was right as she always seemed to have a plentiful supply to hand.

After Uncle Mick, trying to read his paper in the front room, had tired of my endless questions he'd shoo me away with a wave of his pipe, telling me to go and see what was going on in the kitchen and leave him in peace.

Aunty Sadie in her apron would stand at the kitchen sink and listen good-naturedly as I sat on a stool by the cupboard pouring out a steady stream of consciousness as she went about her business.

Her *spécialité de la maison* was the most incredible dessert of rhubarb cooked in the oven on a pastry base until the rhubarb caramelized. Oh my God, it was the best dessert I'd ever tasted, so what with that and the introduction to the joy of cheese and raw onion, meal times at Aunty Sadie's were always a pleasure.

When Aunty Sadie passed away she took the secret of her rhubarb recipe with her and I resigned myself to the fact that the rhubarb dessert was a joy from my childhood that was to sadly remain a distant memory.

Years later I was in a restaurant in Saint-Malo, Brittany, where I ate another memorable meal of oysters from Cancale served with a bread not dissimilar to the soda bread that my aunt and cousin in Ireland used to make, followed by a plate of scallops cooked simply and perfectly in just a little garlic and wine. The dessert turned out to be Aunty Sadie's rhubarb cake accompanied by an earthenware jug filled to the brim with Calvados-flavoured whipped double cream.

I couldn't believe it. Aunty Sadie's rhubarb dessert, here in a little French restaurant in Saint-Malo. Those prehistoric migrants must've taken the recipe with them to Ireland. It was one of the best meals I've ever had, and when I got back to my flat in London I made a determined effort to replicate Aunty Sadie's masterpiece.

I pored over recipe books from the Tate Library on South Lambeth Road to see if I could discover the alchemy that turned rhubarb and pastry into gold until eventually I came up with a combination that might just prove to be the key to Aunty Sadie's secret.

After getting all the necessaries and clearing the top of my tiny worktop to make space I casually threw the ingredients together and flung them in the oven. Result? Disaster, as apart from being cremated you'd've needed a chainsaw to cut it in half.

Defeated and annoyed with myself I chucked it out of the window into the yard below. Down it fell, like some enormous steaming meteor, demolishing a wall on the landing and killing two pigeons that were unfortunate enough to be sat on it at the time fighting over a crust of Mother's Pride. Of course, I'm making that bit up. There were no pigeons, nor was there any wall, but it made a hefty noise on impact all the same.

And behold there was another lengthy passage of time: fast-forward twenty years ... I was lamenting my longing for and subsequent failure to discover Aunty Sadie's recipe on my Radio 2 show one Sunday afternoon when a listener who was originally from Roscommon but who now lived in London answered my prayers by sending me a handwritten recipe for a dish called 'Roscommon Tart'.

'Well blow me over and call me Typhoid Mary,' I shouted, deafening the listeners as I read out the ingredients.

This was it. It had to be. All the evidence was there, particularly as the recipe hailed from Roscommon, the same county as my Irish family. I've since discovered this traditional recipe in quite a few Irish recipe books and they're all very much the same, but here's the recipe I was given as it's near perfect to Aunty Sadie's.

Try it. It's capable of curling both hair and toes with sheer happiness.

Aunty Sadie's Roscommon Tart

I use a cast-iron frying pan that no longer has its wooden handle after a careless accident on a campfire in the garden one night. But basically what you need is a ten-inch (or so) round cake tin that won't leak and has a good heavy bottom.

Now, these are the ingredients you'll need:

2lb rhubarb
2 inches of grated fresh ginger
8oz sugar, depending on taste
A little lemon juice
11oz self-raising flour (if using wholewheat flour then
  you'll need to use more milk)
1 teaspoon of baking powder
Half a teaspoon of freshly grated nutmeg
2oz butter
1oz golden caster sugar
A pinch of salt
A large egg
175ml full-fat milk
Some demerara sugar

Wipe the rhubarb with a clean damp cloth,
trim it and chop into small chunks no bigger
than an inch, then put them in the pan along with
the ginger and sprinkle over the 8oz sugar, adding
a few good squeezes of lemon juice if you prefer
it to have a slight edge as I do. Leave for thirty
minutes, then turn your oven on to gas mark 8
(230°C).

Sieve the flour and baking powder into a bowl,
add the freshly grated nutmeg, then cut the butter
into cubes and rub them in with clean fingers until
it eventually looks like dried breadcrumbs. Stir in
the 1oz caster sugar and pinch of salt and give that
a bit of a rub. Of course you can always do this in a
processor if you have one.

Whisk the egg into the milk, which you've hopefully put into a measuring jug. Making a hole in your flour mixture, pour it in gradually. Mix to a soft dough using the back of a knife but don't spend ages messing about with it. Pastry dough, like a secretary trapped in a lift with her lecherous boss, dislikes being fondled so as soon as it's ready get it out and on to a well-floured work surface and roll into a round about an inch thick to fit neatly inside your tin.

Carefully slide this on top of your rhubarb and tuck it in so it's nice and secure around it. Brush with a little beaten egg and sprinkle liberally with some sugar – granulated will do – then bake in the hot oven for fifteen minutes before lowering the heat to gas mark 3 (160°C) for another thirty-five minutes.

Remove from the oven and leave it alone for a little bit. Place an oven-proof plate larger than the pan over it and turn it upside down so the cake drops out of the pan and sits safely on the plate. Watch yourself here as there are hot juices bursting to escape, so go carefully.

Now sprinkle the rhubarb with a helping of demerara sugar. Slide the plate under a hot grill for a few minutes until the sugar starts to bubble and caramelize; better still, get one of those chef's blowtorches that run off lighter gas, the ones they use for crème brûlée, as they're great fun. I pretend I'm Goldfinger with his laser beam slicing James Bond in half with mine, but then I've baffled doctors as to how my mind works. You can do what you like with yours as long as you don't threaten anyone with it, injure yourself or burn the house down. I daresay my Aunty Chrissie would've used it to light her fag but I suggest you stick to using yours for cooking and keep it well away from any prying little fingers.

Serve this cake with some whipped double cream and then, not giving that diet a second thought, 'wire in' and enjoy.

Lemon Drizzle Cake

I knock one of these out almost every week as everybody likes it and they're easy to make. I've no idea where this recipe came from but I've been using it for years and it's never failed me yet so I am indebted to whoever originally thought it up, although I have changed it slightly.

You will need:

175g unsalted butter, softened
175g golden caster sugar
A large lemon
3 large eggs
100g self-raising flour
75g ground almonds
A drop or so of milk
Some demerara sugar to sprinkle on the finished cake

You'll need a loaf tin that you've lined with greaseproof paper or baking parchment or whatever it's known as these days. Line the sides as well as the bottom but grease the tin first with a bit of butter.

Right then, wash your hands and gather your ingredients and equipment around you, as you don't want to be looking for something halfway through the process.

In a large bowl or mixer beat the butter, caster sugar and zest of the lemon until fluffy. Beating by hand requires getting into a steady rhythm, and beating hard with a wooden spoon. I used to do it that way before the Lytham mixer but I'd end up with my mixing arm the size of Popeye's and the other arm, which didn't do much except hold the bowl, like Olive Oyl's.

Add the eggs one at a time, sprinkling in a little bit of flour with each egg until it's mixed in beautifully.

Add a pinch of salt, then fold in the sifted flour and almonds – be gentle and don't overdo it. Add a drop of milk as you want it so the mixture drops off the back of the spoon. Don't drown it for heaven's sake.

Pour into the prepared loaf tin and bake in a preheated oven at gas mark 4 (180°C), or in the baking oven on the lowest shelf if using an Aga, for around fifty minutes. Take a look after forty-five minutes and put a skewer in it. If it comes out clean then it's done; if not, put it back in for another five minutes.

When it's baked, leave to cool slightly and then tip the cake out of the tin and put it on a wire rack to cool. Sprinkle with demerara sugar and squeeze the lemon juice over the cake. Make some holes in the top of the cake with a skewer for the juice to seep into. If you want it really lemony then use the juice from two lemons, scraping a bit of zest on top of the cake with the sugar.

If the cake is still warm the sugar will dissolve into it when the lemon juice hits, so it's up to you how much sugar you use as long as you don't go overboard.

I've no idea how many days this cake lasts as mine are usually gone in an instant but I'm sure you'd get a couple of days out of it if you keep it in an airtight container.

This is an extremely moist cake and goes down well with a glass of Madeira. It's not bad with tea or coffee either.

In the seventies I used to work in a nightclub in Copenhagen called Madame Arthur's. It's been demolished now and replaced by a dull office block, which is a shame as the original building was old with lots of character. There was a barmaid called Lisa who worked at the club who I was very friendly with. She had a flat over the club that was at the end of the hall next to the two grim little rooms the acts stayed in, and more often than not that's where you'd find me.

Lisa liked a good time, and as we were night people our day began when the sun went down. When Madame Arthur's closed for the night we'd hit the various bars and cafés that stayed open till all hours, returning home as the sun came up. Now, although Lisa didn't seem to eat much in the way of a square meal, she always ate a substantial breakfast, which in our case was consumed at around four p.m.

Lisa had lived in Berlin for a while working as a barmaid in a club and it was one of her many German gentleman friends (she couldn't remember which one) who taught her how to make Arme Ritter, or Poor Knights.

I can see her now, mooching around the kitchen in a ratty old dressing gown with last night's mascara streaked underneath her bloodshot eyes and her red hair standing on end. She'd chatter away as she prepared this dish, her stream of consciousness interspersed with her raucous laugh and hacking cough.

Lisa made the world a better place to live in but sadly she's no longer with us as she died many years ago, but I always think of her when I make this dish as a snack and laugh as I remember the trouble we used to get into.

Lisa's Gentleman Friend's Arme Ritter, or Poor Knights

3 large eggs
8 fl. oz of milk
150ml double cream
1 teaspoon of vanilla extract
A pinch of salt
5 or 6 slices of white bread (this is a good way of using up bread that's going stale)
A good dollop of butter
Sprinkling of sugar, grated nutmeg and a pinch of cinnamon

Mix the eggs, milk, cream, vanilla extract and salt with a whisk and then dip the pieces of bread in it. Leave them to soak for about five minutes and then carefully lower them, using a fish slice, into a frying pan in which you've melted the butter. Cook slowly on both sides of the bread until done.

Sprinkle with sugar and cinnamon and grate a bit of nutmeg over it.

So there you have it, a few recipes for you to try out if you want. They're nothing out of the ordinary nor are they particularly healthy, with perhaps the exception of Lord Woolton's Pie. I've got a book full of recipes that I've collected over the years ranging from a simple casserole to an elaborate recipe for Christmas cake, and since moving to Kent and having a decent-sized kitchen that we all more or less live in, baking has become second nature. Friends moan about expanding waistlines and accuse me of being a feeder but it doesn't stop them wolfing down the cakes I make. Perhaps if they shift the blame on to me it eases their conscience, leaving them free to gorge guilt-free.

CONCLUSION

There was a bat in the front room last night. I was just going to bed when I heard Moira let out an almighty ear-piercing shriek. Thinking she was being murdered or, worse, she'd seen a rat, I rushed downstairs to see what the carry-on was about.

'A bat!' she gasped, clutching her throat and screaming again, only louder this time as it swooped dangerously close to her.

Running down the hall, she left me to it.

I went into the front room and, closing the door behind me, wondered how you catch a bat.

I'm quite used to bats as a colony of pipistrelles had set up home in the tiles underneath my bedroom window and every now and then one or two of them would fly in through the open window and have a flap about before settling on the curtains. This made it easy to pick them off and point them in the direction of the open window.

I let one cling to the arm of my sweater one night. It didn't seem a bit bothered and it allowed me to get a good look at its pug-like face. It was as light as a feather but a bit whiffy so before it took off around the room again I picked it up and out of the window it went.

This front-room bat seemed to be a lot bigger than the ones who visited my bedroom and as it flew about frantically I had a feeling that it wasn't going to settle anywhere any time soon and I had no idea how I was going to catch this bat without injuring it. Throw a towel over it perhaps? Shoo it out with a rolled-up copy of the local newspaper? Leave it alone, go to bed and deal with it in the morning?

Suddenly I had a brainwave. Normally my brainwaves are highly convoluted affairs but this one seemed relatively simple. Open the front-room window, turn all the lights out and stand outside with a torch hoping that, to quote television mediums, it would 'go towards the light'.

The bat was slow on the uptake. Moira and I stood outside in a light drizzle, each of us holding a torch up to the window, for over an hour until eventually Bela Lugosi (that's what we'd christened him) got the message and thankfully left the building.

The next morning it was my turn to scream for as I was feeding the chickens a rat ran out from underneath the hen house right over my foot. I was out of that chicken coop faster than an impala with a cheetah on its tail.

I returned to the house with my flesh creeping and every hair on my body standing on end. As I sat in the kitchen swigging tea I could still feel the imprint of the rat's nasty, scrabbling little claws as it ran across my instep and I made a mental note never to wear flip-flops again when feeding the chucks.

Once I'd regained my composure I braced myself and cautiously ventured back into the coop only this time carrying a large branch to fight any rats off with and a pair of stout wellies on my feet for protection.

Once inside the coop I didn't stray very far – in fact I stayed close to the gate in case I had to beat a hasty retreat – but if I stood on tiptoe and squinted I could see that there were a number of rat holes around the perimeter fence, which could only mean one thing: an infestation of rats that have more than likely been attracted by the chicken feed.

To catch a rat you have to be cunning. There's no point setting a trap and hoping they'll fall into it that very night for rats are wily buggers and will avoid anything alien that smells of humans so I always wear gloves when handling the trap.

There're two rat-traps in the barn, both humane. Basically they're a pair of long cages and at the end of the cage you plant a blob of peanut butter on the mechanism that brings the cage door down behind the rat, thereby trapping it. The rat can then be taken by car and dumped somewhere far afield by Sean. As much as they repel me I've vowed not to use poison or to kill them. Placing them along the fence with no bait in them I intend to leave the traps for a week for the rats to become accustomed to them.

On the plus side it's a nice day and the orchard is laden with apples, pears and plums. I've noticed that there's a number of lovely big Bramleys that would look better in a pie than on the tree.

This year I'm going in for bottling. I've already ordered the jars and I'm determined that none of the fruit goes to waste. The fig tree is doing extremely well and there's a few that are ripe for the picking which I'm going to eat later, split open and slathered in honey.

The two solitary peach trees have excelled themselves this year as the branches are hanging with fruit whereas normally I'm lucky if I get one. They're not quite ripe yet. A couple more days should do it before I can sink my teeth into a few – that's if the wasps don't get them first.

This year I'm ready for those pesky wasps. There's a contraption called a Waspinator that you can buy that resembles to all intents and purposes a wasps' nest. You hang this from your fruit trees and miraculously the wasps, believing that a colony has already set up home there, move on, leaving the fruit alone. I suppose you could make your own out of chicken wire covered with brown paper or papier-mâché and paint it a greyish brown with a swirl pattern; or you could try hanging brown paper bags from the trees. The trouble with paper bags is that they tend to vanish in a high wind and as soon as it rains they just hang from the branches, limp and sodden, fooling nobody, least of all a wasp.

Maybe they could show the kiddies how to make a faux wasps' nest on *Blue Peter*, get entire schools churning them out for us poor peasants in the country with fruit trees that are under attack from wasps.

Three ducklings are swimming about on the pond that I haven't seen before. The mother is quacking noisily in answer to this trio's frantic cheeps – they've strayed too far from her. She must have hatched them early this morning and I wonder if there had been a lot more and these three little ones are the survivors. Ducklings are easy pickings for carrion crows and magpies not to mention my arch enemy, the rat. Foxes are also quite partial to duckling, so with so many predators it's no wonder so few survive. Hopefully these three will make it.

Those folk in the Met Office had promised us a blazing summer and now, just like our Prime Minister, they've made a U-turn, declaring that we can expect torrential rain the like of which hasn't been seen since Noah built the ark. Maybe I should ask Sean to build an ark. According to the media we might need one.

Right now it's a mackerel sky with not a storm cloud in sight so I'd best enjoy it while I can. I've got some time off at the moment. One of the dangers of living in the countryside, particularly when the weather is glorious like it is today, is that it makes me reticent to travel further afield. I've done a lot of travelling in my time both for work and pleasure but these days I don't care if I ever go abroad again. I hate airports and the hassle involved getting in and out of them, even though I understand the need for such stringent security checks in these mean times. They're still a right royal pain in the arse. At airports like Schiphol the security routine they put you through borders on assault.

No, I'm more than happy to stay put, unless someone suggests a train trip – and I don't mean the Virgin Express to Liverpool, I'm talking about the Orient Express or the Blue Train or the Eastern and Oriental Express or any of those other beautiful luxury trains.

Vera and myself once travelled from Moscow to the Arctic Circle and back again by steam train. We were two weeks on board and there's no way I could simply dismiss that memorable trip as a mere holiday, it was an adventure – but that's another story.

As I said at the beginning of this book, I've lived here now for almost two decades and I've seen saplings that I planted grow into trees, and tiny lambs that I've hand-reared turn into geriatrics. Don't worry, I'm not about to reflect on age and how the pages of time have turned so rapidly: I've only just recently become aware that they have as I've trawled through the memory banks to write this book.

At one time I believed I was invincible, but now I'm older I'm aware of my own mortality and I often wonder how long I've got left on the planet. A bit of a morbid subject to dwell on I know, but once you reach a certain age you do occasionally ponder matters of life as you watch autumn turn the leaves brown and your friends and animals die off when you believed that they'd always be there.

There's a magnolia tree that is nearly as tall as the roof of the house which I planted on the day I moved in, mistakenly believing that it was only a small plant. Of course I realize now that it wasn't a 'small plant' as it towers above me, but when it blossoms in the early spring it's a ridiculously beautiful sight, even though its blooms are short-lived and within weeks the lawn is littered with pink and white petals.

When that tree is in bud and is bursting to explode into flower I know spring has arrived, and when they appear I enjoy its blooms for as long as they last. It's little things like this that make me aware that, just like the magnolia flower, we're all transient, and we must enjoy life for as long as the adventure lasts.

Bugger me, I've turned into Peter Pan.

I always intended to plant some rhododendrons until I learned that both the flowers and leaves are poisonous if eaten by animals. The rhododendron is also known as 'lambkill', and for very good reasons, so what with sheep, cows, goats and dogs roaming about I thought better of planting a row of rhododendron bushes along the drive and shoved a few bulbs in instead.

There's an old wives' tale concerning the honey made from the flowers of the rhododendron. It's known as Mad Honey and is purported to induce fits and hallucinations in humans. It's a load of rubbish of course as a single jar of honey would have to contain an enormous amount of the poisonous grayanotoxin for it to have the slightest effect.

Ragweed, azalea, foxgloves and even daffodil bulbs are also highly toxic if eaten by goats. I was fit to kill when I heard that a bunch of warped individuals had broken into Walton Hall's children's petting zoo and deliberately fed their pygmy goats rhododendron leaves, killing a number of them in the process. What is wrong with people? Society is sick. If it were me then the perpetrators would be shown no mercy. I'd skin 'em alive – metaphorically of course.

There's a man at the door selling 'frozen party food' which turns out to be little swirls of mashed potato with a prawn

and a sprig of parsley on top and some mini fish and chips
that come with cones of fake newspaper for you to put
them in once you've cooked them. I bought a box
containing twelve of the mini fish and chips as well as some
salmon en croute which will no doubt sit in the back of the
already cramped freezer until they're discovered years later
by an archaeologist.

I've done nothing all day but mooch about. I should be
dealing with post or one of the million other things that
really need sorting out but, as the song says, 'I'm busy doing
nothing'. It's taken me some time, years even, to learn how
to relax without feeling guilty. The whole point of moving
to and living in the countryside is to spend more time
outdoors than banged up indoors and on days like this I'm
not letting myself sit in front of a computer. After all, didn't
our mothers tell us that being outside on a nice day is good
for us? Especially if you've fields and woods to play in.

The landscape changes with the seasons and the air
is infinitely sweeter than the toxic fumes of the city's
congested streets, but for how long?

Looking back, I consider myself lucky to have
experienced working on the once extensive cabaret club
and pub circuit in the north of England. I remember clubs
in Yorkshire that would have two acts on the bill plus a
live band and a compère. Work was plentiful, and if you
were prepared to travel then you could work seven nights
a week, frequently playing a pub and a club in the same
night and in different towns miles apart, driving across the
Pennines in full regalia at one o'clock in the morning.

By the early eighties the pits, factories and mills had
closed down, taking these clubs and pubs with them. The
pubs that were once packed to the rafters with punters

singing along to 'We're having a gang bang' as the bar staff bashed tambourines, and where the acts got changed in toilets, are either boarded up or demolished. The big cabaret clubs where you could sit and eat scampi in a basket and watch Diana Dors or Dame Shirley Bassey have been turned into car parks, and entire communities have vanished. It was akin to the death of Variety and the subsequent closure of the music hall, so I'm glad that I was able to be there for the last knockings.

I hope that I never witness a similar decline in rural areas. As I mentioned earlier in this book, these proposed housing estates that are increasingly growing in number are encroaching on the land, and despite local council and government assurances that all is well it most certainly isn't. Wildlife will undoubtedly suffer and the once unspoilt landscapes will be littered with rows of Lego-like houses. Remember Joni Mitchell's warning: 'they've paved paradise'.

Well this won't get the baby fed, nor will it catch me a rat, so I'm off to put some peanut butter in the traps and then I'm taking the dogs for a walk, and tonight, as I've got a houseful at the weekend, I'm going to knock up a couple of Dutch Apple Pies. If the baking mood doesn't desert me I might push the boat out and make a Snot Pie (gooseberry tart) too.

Anyway, my *final* verdict on country living is that I can highly recommend it, only please stay where you are as there's enough of us down here as it is. However, should you ignore my warning, as well as the curse that goes with it, bear in mind this: if you're going to buy an old house as I have then be prepared for the expense of its upkeep.

Good luck, and thanks for reading.

ACKNOWLEDGEMENTS

I'd like to thank Andre Portasio, Beryl Chyat,
Joan Marshrons, Moira Stewart, and Doug Young
at Penguin Random House.

I'd also like to thank all the animals who've
enriched my life (with the exception of rats and slugs),
as well as those friends, relatives and persons unknown
whose recipes I've used.

PICTURE ACKNOWLEDGEMENTS

PICTURES IN TEXT:

Jacket photography and photos on
pages 46-7, 84, 111, 115, 151 by Nicky Johnston.

All other photos author's own,
except pages 41, 123 by Andre Portasio; pages 76, 82
by Beryl Chyat and pages 127, 133, 148 by Moira Stewart.

Herb illustrations on pages 202, 203, 205, 206, 208,
209, 210, 211, 213, 214 by Anna Repp.

PICTURE SECTION:

page 2, top right taken by Andre Portasio
page 1, top; page 2, top left, bottom left and bottom
right; page 3, top; page 4, top left and top right; page 5,
top; page 6, top; page 7, top left and top right; page 8, top
left and bottom all taken by Nicky Johnston.
All other photos taken by the author.